# THE TRANSLATOR'S DOUBTS VLADIMIR NABOKOV

## AND THE AMBIGUITY OF TRANSLATION

ACADEMIC
STUDIES
PRESS

# THE TRANSLATOR'S DOUBTS VLADIMIR NABOKOV

## AND THE AMBIGUITY OF TRANSLATION

JULIA
TRUBIKHINA

BOSTON
2015

Library of Congress Cataloging-in-Publication Data:
A bibliographic record for this title is available from the Library
   of Congress.

ISBN 978-1-61811-260-6 (hardback)
ISBN 978-1-61811-261-3 (electronic)


Book design by Ivan Grave


Published by Academic Studies Press in 2015
28 Montfern Avenue
Brighton, MA 02135, USA
press@academicstudiespress.com
www.academicstudiespress.com

*For my grandmother,*

**Valeria Kunina,**

*who—by her life worthy of a Soviet "Scarlett O'Hara" rather than any scholarly word she actually wrote—taught me a thing or two about what matters in art: perseverance, allegiance to ironic rationality, intolerance to cruelty, and the higher sense of loyalty that, if we are to believe Ezra Pound, "is hard to explain."*

# Table of Contents

# Acknowledgments

This book grew out of my doctoral dissertation. It would not have been possible without my friend and dissertation adviser, Richard Sieburth. Due to Richard and in the spirit of Walter Benjamin's understanding of the Translator's task, I was able to maintain this project with stoicism as a "chiasmus of hope and catastrophe." He had a wonderful vision of the whole while the project was in its disjointed parts. His enormous erudition and insightful suggestions were invaluable to me.

I am grateful to my colleague and friend Elizabeth Beaujour, who knew the project at its dissertation stage and at various points read and commented on its different parts. I feel enormous gratitude to the colleagues and friends who, along with Elizabeth, long ago were part of my dissertation committee: Eliot Borenstein and Mikhail Iampolski, thank you!

I am tremendously fortunate to work alongside terrific colleagues in the Russian Division of Hunter College, CUNY, and benefit every day from their knowledge, sense of companionship, and our shared love for Russian literature and culture.

I am grateful to my daughter Anya for being my anchor and unrelenting judge in all matters extraliterary. I want to thank my mother, Natalia Kunina, for enabling me to make my own "translation" in space and culture, to come to graduate school at New York University and, ultimately, to undertake this project. In her usual quiet way, she gave me the most valuable thing one can get from a parent—a strong sense of self.

Finally, everlasting thanks to my husband, Dennis Slavin, for being—in translation terms—both loyal and faithful, and for his selfless help and support throughout my work on this book.

# INTRODUCTION[1]

On Translating *Eugene Onegin*

## I.

What's translation? On a platter
A poet's pale and glaring head,
A parrot's screech, a monkey's chatter,
And profanation of the dead.
The parasites you were so hard on
Are pardoned if I have your pardon,
O, Pushkin, for my stratagem:
I traveled down your secret stem,
And reached the root, and fed upon it;
Then in a language newly learned,
I grew another stalk and turned
Your stanza, patterned on a sonnet,
Into my honest roadside prose—
All thorn, but cousin to your rose.

## II.

Reflected words can only shiver
Like elongated lights that twist
In the black mirror of a river
Between the city and the mist.
Elusive Pushkin! Persevering,
I still pick up Tatiana's earring,
Still travel with your sullen rake.
I find another man's mistake,
I analyze alliterations
That grace your feats and haunt the great
Fourth stanza of your Canto Eight.
This is my task—a poet's patience
And scholiastic passion blent:
Dove-droppings on your monument.

*Vladimir Nabokov* (1955)[2]

> "... It is not the highest praise of
> a translation, particularly in the age of
> its origin, to say that it reads as if it had
> originally been written in that language.
> Rather the significance of fidelity as
> ensured by literalness is that the work
> reflects the great longing for linguistic
> complementation. "
>
> Walter Benjamin[3]

This book singles out translation as a way of talking about literary history and theory, philosophy, and interpretation. Vladimir Nabokov is its case study. The advantage of making Nabokov a case study for an investigation of questions of translation is obvious. It is hard to separate Vladimir Nabokov from the act of translation, in all senses of the word—ranging from "moving across" geographical borders and cultural and linguistic boundaries to the transposing of the split between "here" and "there" and "then" and "now" (the essential elements of exile, components of every émigré experience) onto a metaphysical plane sometimes suggested by private maps of his personal Zemblas and Antiterras. Obviously, the issue of exile, so central to Nabokov's praxis and status, ties in closely with the problematics of translation, since, for one thing, overcoming the linguistic consequences of exile "caused him more torment than any of the other sufferings imposed upon him by emigration."[4] Walter Benjamin's requirement that a translator should not convert a foreign language into his own but should instead allow his own language to be powerfully affected, even penetrated by the foreign one, resonates profoundly with Nabokov's bilingual status. Nabokov's linguistic polyphony is both the "matter and form" of his oeuvre. To borrow George Steiner's definitions, *The Gift*, *Lolita*, and *Ada*, as well as Nabokov's self-translations, are "tales of erotic relations between speaker and speech," while Nabokov's recurrent motifs of "mirrors, incest, and constant meshing of languages" are dramatizations of "his abiding devotion to Russian."[5] Just as Nabokov's Russian prose seemed "strange" to his contemporaries despite the indisputable mastery and finesse of his Russian language, his English-language works since the 1940s struck readers as either brilliant and witty or, on the contrary, precious or "maddeningly opaque," but always written in a language "alien in details of lexical usage," whose "primary rhythms . . . go against the natural grain of English and American speech."[6] This "polysemic nature" of Nabokov's usage of language, however, helps keep "words and phrases in a charged, unstable mode of vitality."[7] In her treatment of Nabokov's bilingualism, Elizabeth Beaujour notes that it "has made him both a 'native user' and a 'foreigner.'"[8] Nabokov's bilingualism (in fact, polyglottism) is always a whole that is more than a sum of its components: translation between languages and cultural codes becomes a complex system of mediation of various linguistic and non-linguistic elements within a unified context. Investigating translation as a transformational rather than mimetic experience allows us to understand the strikingly original end result: in what emerges, both the "target language" and the "native" language undergo something new that dispenses with the quest for and the "anxiety" of influences.

In this sense, Nabokov constitutes a perfect object for comparativist study because his oeuvre offers us the unique opportunity to look at his major texts twice: as originals and as translations. *Laughter in the Dark* (*Camera obscura*), *Glory* (*Podvig*), *Mary* (*Mashenka*), *The Gift* (*Dar*), *Lolita*, *Despair* (*Otchaianie*), *Speak, Memory*, *Conclusive Evidence*, and *Other Shores* (*Drugie berega*), and other texts all function as their own doubles in two languages (translated by Nabokov or by Nabokov and his son, or by other translators with considerable contribution on Nabokov's part). The translations are also carefully supplied with Nabokov's prefaces, which, though much shorter, possess the same explanatory and revelatory features of his commentaries to *Eugene Onegin*. Thus one could easily envision a comprehensive monograph focused entirely on Nabokov's career as a translator, from his translations of others (Rupert Brooke, Walter de la Mare, William Butler Yeats, William Shakespeare, Pierre de Ronsard, Alfred de Musset, Charles Baudelaire, Arthur Rimbaud, Johann Wolfgang von Goethe, Lewis Carroll, Roland, Aleksandr Pushkin, Fyodor Tiutchev, Mikhail

Lermontov, etc.) to his self-translations into French and English and back into Russian.

However, the aim of my study is not to provide a survey or a single overarching narrative of Nabokov's career in translation, but a series of "papers" on its problematics. It could be entitled "Three Essays on Translation's *Raison d'être*." I have always thought that the composition of a study on Nabokov ideally should by itself create a tantalizing internal pattern (derived from a chess game, a waltz, or one of Nabokov's own novels, for example), tracing through its parts a version of Nabokov's intricate structural trajectories and becoming its own object in the process. I settled on a compromise: a three-part structure, forming a Nabokovian triad of sorts, in which the whole, I hope, might constitute a certain synthesis, albeit necessarily an open-ended one. Each chapter is a study of a particular kind of translation, with its own purpose and relationship to Nabokov's "original" work and philosophy. As de Man observes in his commentary on Walter Benjamin's "Task of the Translator": "The text is a poetics, a theory of poetic language."[9] Like Nabokov's works themselves, the three chapters of this book are examples of different critical genres—ranging from a philological study to a metaphysical investigation to an essay on literary and film theory. I have attempted to talk about the philosophy of translation, as well as Nabokov's own uncertainty about the process and its results, while attending closely to specific texts. As Andrew Benjamin notes in his introduction to his *Translation and the Nature of Philosophy*: "Translation is an act. It is also an enactment and if Derrida's lead is followed, what comes to be enacted is the practice as well as the possibility of philosophy."[10]

One might question why I have chosen from the huge body of Nabokov's works *these* texts specifically—his early translation of *Alice in Wonderland*; *Eugene Onegin*, the pinnacle of Nabokov's literalism; and his screenplay of *Lolita* in conjunction with two cinematic versions by Stanley Kubrick and Adrian Lyne. I believe that, on the one hand, these texts trace a certain chronology of Nabokov's career. On the other hand, and most importantly, these three specific examples allow us to consider all three types of translation, which Roman Jakobson defined as "interlingual," "intralingual," and "intersemiotic."[11] Considering these in turn makes it possible to see what changes and what stays remarkably constant in Nabokov's approach to translation. I examine what seem to be examples of interlingual translation (or what Jakobson calls "translation proper" from one language into the other) by considering texts that are profoundly different in their practical application of the principles of translation. These texts constitute the very beginning and the pinnacle of Nabokov's career in translation (Nabokov's Russian version of *Alice*, *Ania v strane chudes*, and *Eugene Onegin*, respectively). Next I consider intralingual translation (Jakobson's "rewording . . . of verbal signs by means of other signs of the same language")[12]—i.e. Nabokov's "re-formulation" of *Lolita* as a film adaptation. Finally, the two cinematic versions of *Lolita* constitute intersemiotic translations, or the "interpretation of verbal signs by means of signs of non-verbal sign systems."[13]

This approach is effective in uncovering a profound ambiguity in Nabokov's relationship to translation as a philosophical oscillation between the stability of meaning and the instability of meaning, the possibility of divination and deep metaphysical uncertainty. The cinematic *Lolitas* and Nabokov's film adaptation (a self-translation of sorts) to some extent remove the pressure of including in the equation the mammoth of Nabokov's self-translation into Russian—*Lolita* the novel. Theoretical investigations in the field of self-translation are a relatively recent endeavor (the term itself has been around only from the late 1970s), and so far have been considered within the framework of bilingualism and linguistics. It seems to me to be a hugely interesting and virtually inexhaustible object of investigation, more appropriate for a separate study that should not be structurally or philosophically constrained by the Jakobsonian triad, the framework I have chosen.

Nabokov as a case study for a book about the history and philosophy of translation presents many challenges. The central challenge involves the sheer volume of studies of Nabokov's art and world that have emerged in the last two decades: few modern authors spanning different cultures have a comparable ability to continue generating never-ending controversy and ongoing debate, which seemingly encompass a staggeringly diverse range of problems—from lepidoptery to metaphysics. The Nabokov centennial in 1999 witnessed a virtual explosion of interest in Nabokov and his work, both from academia and the world at large. As Jane Grayson wrote, introducing a two-volume post-centennial collection of essays dedicated to Nabokov's world: "The teasing complexity and rich allusiveness of Nabokov's art makes him a challenging subject for exegesis and commentary. He is a problem solver's delight, an annotator's dream. Small wonder then that he has attracted such interest in academic quarters in the past thirty or so years on both sides of the Atlantic. But he is also, with his supreme craftsmanship and style, his sharp eye and acute ear, very much a writer's writer, a 'novelist's novelist,' as Henry James memorably said of Turgenev."[14]

The centennial explosion of "Nabokoviana" in the West—contributions to symposia and conferences, academic monographs, and new multi-language editions of his works—was augmented by conferences and publications in Russia, where, after a long "separation," Nabokov was actively reclaimed as one of the most important Russian authors of the past century. Furthermore, as always happens with literary ancestors who have been long alienated and charged with "un-Russianness," he was reclaimed with passion. However, due to Russia's volatile political situation, growing religious intolerance, and homophobia, the most recent developments might be an indication that Nabokov's "fortune" in Russia, as it were, is changing once more: the cancellation of a theatrical production of *Lolita* at the Erarta museum in St. Petersburg in October 2012[15] and the beating of its director in January 2013,[16] as well as the attacks on Nabokov museums in Petersburg and Rozhdestveno in January and February 2013.[17] A vicious attack on Nabokov himself was made in February 2013 by the conservative *Literaturnaia gazeta*'s Valerii Rokotov, whose tone evoked the infamous literary denunciations of the long bygone era. He claimed that Nabokov in Russia has been "crowned by his liberal admirers" and is now being "dethroned," becoming, once again, a mere "émigré."[18] On the other hand, Russia did not hesitate to claim Nabokov as its national treasure and pride "for export" in the "Azbuka" (ABC) segment of "Dreams about Russia" at the opening ceremony for the 2014 Olympics in Sochi. Nabokov represented letter "N." While the theatrical-looking nationalistic "Cossacks" in today's Petersburg attacking theater directors to fight what they perceive as "Nabokov's pedophilia," as well as critics such as Rokotov, are outside the scope of this study, the contradiction that I see in the scholarly studies of Nabokov (is he primarily concerned with the perfection of form or with profound metaphysical complexities?) is pertinent to the goal of this book. If one is to raise Nabokov's "ghost" yet again, it should be for better reasons than those of pure literary devotion. Because translation studies that involve Nabokov have not fully reacted to the "seismic" shift that happened in Nabokov studies over the last two decades, in this study I attempt to "bridge the gap," as it were, between the scholarly fields.

A bird's-eye overview of the scholarship on Nabokov in the narrower framework of translation studies yields the following generalized picture. In the 1970s, straightforward investigations of the use of the Russian language in Nabokov's English novels and comparisons of his Russian and English prose dominated.[19] The 1980s and 1990s in turn contributed studies on the relationship between self-translation and autobiography,[20] and on bilingualism and exile,[21] as well as a number of studies on specific texts and aspects of translation.[22] The more recent publications on Nabokov and translation continue the investigation of bilingualism, self-translation, and exile[23] (the latter involving inevitable comparisons between Nabokov and Joseph Brodsky, who received the Nobel Prize in Literature in 1987, as well as parallels to other linguistic exiles, such as Milan Kundera), while also drawing on the more specific issues of hybridity, mimesis, and erasure.[24]

Since the early 1990s, Nabokov's presence on the Internet (both the English-language Internet and its Russian segment) has been actively shaping the reception of Nabokov's texts and the direction of Nabokov studies.[25] However, when one considers the sheer volume of academic publications in the exploding field of Nabokov studies in the West and in Russia, and attempts to evaluate the approximate direction in which the field as a whole is going, one is intrigued by a "tectonic" shift that has occurred in the last twenty years and that, so far, has not seemed to manifest itself or register in translation studies focusing on Nabokov's oeuvre. A concise formulation of the shift in question is evident in the exchange between D. Barton Johnson and Brian Boyd at the Cambridge conference dedicated to Nabokov's centennial in July 1999 (Vladimir Nabokov International Centennial Conference). The introduction to their discussion points out that "the subject of the beyond, and its place in Nabokov studies, is a recurring and keenly debated topic, as of course is the past and future of Nabokov studies in general."[26] The earlier dominant critical trend focused on Nabokov's style and structure at the expense of "focusing on the ethical and philosophical issues that were equally important to Nabokov's work."[27] An approach "sometimes known as the 'metaphysical' (as opposed to the earlier 'metaliterary'), hinted at as early as the 1930s by the Russian émigré critic Pyotr Bitsilli, and most finely elaborated by Vladimir Alexandrov in his *Nabokov's Otherworld* (1991), dominated the 1990s. It is the matrix for most current criticism. . . ."[28] Johnson is less than thrilled with this turn of affairs, and understandably so, since the full swing of the critical pendulum towards this new trend might easily turn Nabokov into a moralist and "a system builder," at the expense of the concrete details and sheer unadulterated delight of Nabokov's vicious and rigorous art. He praises Boyd for finding a "synthesis" that combines "technical mastery of Nabokov's texts with the first thorough consideration of Nabokov's philosophy."[29] The subtext, however, is clear: there is little hope that everybody could be as subtle as Boyd, who, in his own riposte to Johnson's concerns, affirms Nabokov's metaphysics as "a vitally important aspect of his work," but also points to Nabokov's ultimate lack of any "conclusive evidence" of what exactly lies beyond (if anything), while observing that Nabokov's ethics and epistemology operate very much "within the constraints of this world."[30]

In what Jane Grayson called the "Holy Wars" between the "earthlings" and the "otherworldly interpretations,"[31] I assume Boyd, in his discussion, has in mind Nabokov's metaphysical uncertainty (that is not some garden variety of theosophy or happy Neo-Platonism)—which seems to be a cautious and accurate understanding. It is abundantly clear that Nabokov himself both implicitly (in the body of his own creative work) and explicitly (in his English and Russian memoirs, in *Strong Opinions*, and elsewhere) suggested that the "two worlds" are not mutually exclusive. Claiming that a creative artist should "study carefully the works of his rivals, including the Almighty," he also pointed out that "the artist should *know* the given world. Imagination without knowledge leads no farther than the backyard of primitive art."[32] Defining the human condition in *Speak, Memory* as being trapped in the short second stage of the three-stage structure, that is in a "spherical prison" of time between two "abysses" of timelessness, he talked of possible escapes as translations in space in moments of higher consciousness (presumably, those of artistic epiphany), when time ceases to exist.

Another aspect of such escapes is that of the past and present forming patterns of repetitions. Nabokov envisioned his own life as a "colored spiral in a small ball of glass," which is a "spiritualized circle. In the spiral form, the circle, uncoiled, unwound, has ceased to be vicious; it has been set free," and "Hegel's triadic series ... expressed merely the essential spirality of all things in their relation to time."[33] This Hegelian spiral, with its coils repeating the previous ones but staying always open-ended, is realized by Nabokov as an artistic method. The metaphor he uses to describe this method is that of a magic carpet, folded "in such a way as to superimpose one part of the pattern upon the other,"[34] which echoes a famous metaphor for translation from Miguel de Cervantes's *Don Quixote*: a carpet or tapestry looked at from the wrong side of the weave.[35]

Since Nabokov's creativity is inextricably woven into the process of translation, I believe that both his "metaphysics" and "uncertainty" should also be central to an investigation of Nabokov's activity as a translator in the broad sense of this word, much as "sacred revelation" and "nihilistic rigor" were combined for Paul de Man in Walter Benjamin's understanding of translation and its purpose.[36] In this study, I attempt to talk about the philosophy of translation, as well as Nabokov's own metaphysical uncertainty, while attending closely to specific texts (to alleviate Johnson's concerns against generalized excursions into morality or ethics).

The first chapter is a philological piece. This "return to philology," to use de Man's term,[37] is justified, since the analysis of language and style "cannot fail to respond to structures of language which it is more or less [the] secret aim of literary teaching to keep hidden," if one thinks of literature primarily as a "substitute for the teaching of theology, ethics, psychology, or intellectual history."[38] This "philological" chapter deals not only with Nabokov's translation of Carroll's *Alice in Wonderland* (1922, published in 1923) but also, in a broader manner, with several little known earlier Russian translations of *Alice* published in 1879, 1908, 1908-1909, and 1923 (the latter, by A. D'Aktil, came out in the same year as Nabokov's *Ania*). "Ideologically" close to those early Russified translations, the text Nabokov produces is nevertheless not so much a translation per se, but a playground for his own nascent fiction. His originality and innovativeness can be understood only in relationship to his "secondary" position vis-à-vis those earlier translations, as it were. His "indebtedness" (which he, of course, never acknowledged) and originality are a paradox realized through the process of translation, which "deterritorializes" tradition. In a broader sense, "deterritorialization" relates to Deleuzian subversive and deconstructive readings of texts, in which the world becomes a closed language structure that needs an inviolable internal organizational principle. In a work of art, this principle is provided by the author-magician. Nabokov, a young exile at the time, displaces both the original and the Russian tradition into what de Man calls "a kind of permanent exile," but "not really an exile, for there is no homeland, nothing from which one can be exiled"; this non-exile is a "permanent disjunction which inhabits all languages as such, including and especially the language one calls one's own."[39] I consider several distinctive features of this deterritorialization of tradition that are developed in Nabokov's translation of *Alice* and later used in Nabokov's fiction. Looking closely at the tradition itself and the Russian versions of *Alice* that preceded his own helps make these "fault lines" visible.

The second chapter links his novel *Pale Fire*, whose central focus is the process of translation via the appropriation of the original, to Nabokov's "über-translation," the pinnacle of his literalism—the translation of Pushkin's *Eugene Onegin*. The problematics of this chapter hinge on the suggestion of the following paradox: what is usually considered to be a radical change in Nabokov's approach to literary translation is not really a change at all. Nabokov's peculiar metaphysics defines his literary translation all along, just as it defines his fiction throughout his literary career; the only change occurs in his practice—that is, in *the way* he chooses to implement his remarkably stable theoretical understanding of translation.

The first part of the second chapter focuses almost exclusively on Nabokov's metaphysical uncertainty in *Pale Fire* as a hesitation between different hermeneutic possibilities (metaphysics "filtered," as it were, through the Nietzschean repudiation of it), with the signification of death (the "beyond") as its central element. The very title of *Pale Fire* and the Shakespearean passage from which it originates are treated as an allegory of writing, translation, and commentary. This passage from *Timon of Athens* is presented as a scrambled version of a metaphysical ladder to the source of light (in the ironically Platonic sense of the word). From among the many metaphysical "pointers," I draw on Nabokov's butterfly as a formula, a graphic depiction of the infinity sign and, by extension, of the Nabokovian triad (the foretime, the aftertime, and the node in-between). Just as Eros in Plato's *Symposium* is a spirit and messenger between the worlds, the gift (*dar* or *talant*) is perhaps Nabokov's often-mentioned "secret" and the node at the center of the formula, a passage, a tunnel to this much debated "beyond." Because the metaphysical mysteries cannot be explained or articulated,[40] definitive interpretation is never an option, but their presence can be made known through re-creation of the "creation gesture," through inscribing them into the "texture" of a work of fiction (John Shade's "not text, but texture").

Taking a shortcut into the discussion of the nature of allegory by way of Elizabeth Bronfen's analysis of the signification of death in *Over Her Dead Body*, I argue in the second chapter that the allegorical mode (as a trope of metaphysical uncertainty—a "withdrawal from any semantically fixed encoding")[41] not only defines Nabokov's fiction, but should also be extended to his literary translation. The allegorical mode allows the translator to partake of the same "gesture" as the original by signifying difference, by focusing on other things (commentary, criticism). Nabokov's translation of *Onegin* is not "metaphorical" in the sense that it is not supposed to be "like" the original. It is allegorical (or, more specifically, metonymical) insofar as it allows the Commentary and Index to perform in English the function that Pushkin's text of the poem is supposed to perform in Russian—that is, it functions (in Goethe's terms) not instead of the original, but rather in its place.[42] The Commentary and Index in *Pale Fire* can be seen as a parody of this: the allegorical model is transformed into a metaphorical one through a distorted comical and tragic mirror. In fact, *Pale Fire* is a diagnosis of metaphoricity run amok: everything is substituted for everything else, the appropriation of the original is completed through an epidemic of metaphors. By looking closely at how the Index and Commentary to Nabokov's *Onegin* function, I find mechanisms of concealed design and patterns of signification strikingly similar to those of *Pale Fire*—the metaphorical tension within the metonymical (allegorical) model of the poem-commentary-index triad as a whole.

Finally, the process of translation becomes a trip "down [Pushkin's] secret stem," to use the words from Nabokov's poem—the meticulous search for Pushkin's European sources. Thus re-rooted back into its sources, the original becomes "secondary" in its own right. The remaining part of the second chapter deals specifically with *how* literalism is achieved and with the criteria for its assessment. I make use of Mikhail Gasparov's term from his essay on Valerii Briusov's literal translation of the *Aeneid*: the "length of context"—a unit of the original text for which there exists an equivalent unit of near absolute correspondence. For the purposes of translation, such a unit might be as short as a word, a verse, or a stanza, or as long as a whole work. Depending on the "length of context," translations can be made more literal or less. I argue that Nabokov's method for achieving literalism involves the shortening of the "length of context" to that of the line. On the one hand, this short "length of context" makes the lines of the translation intensely usable for quoting, turning the entire *Onegin* into a giant literal quotation. This makes sense, since Nabokov's *Onegin* was conceived as a translation suitable for teaching purposes and was claimed with pride to be just a "pony" or a "crib" for students. On the other hand, the allegorical (metonymical) model of translation, while retaining the iambic meter, brings the translation closer to prose and reclaims it as a novel. In this light, it is perhaps significant that Jakobson, drawing on similarity and contiguity disorders, maintains that, unlike poetry, "prose . . . is forwarded essentially by contiguity."[43] In conclusion, however, I suggest that Nabokov aims at more than he claims his translation to be—a utilitarian "crib" with a helpful apparatus. By transcending likeness (metaphoricity, mimicry—and for the fiercely anti-utilitarian Nabokov, mimicry was always the gift of art), he attempts to achieve a metaphysical goal of the internal affinity of the unlike, a complete metamorphosis.

The third chapter is concerned with intralingual and intersemiotic translation: Nabokov's work on the screenplay of *Lolita* for Kubrick in 1959 and the early 1960s, and its subsequent transmutation by means of a different sign system (film) in its two cinematic versions by Kubrick and Lyne. The first part of the chapter is concerned primarily with the dynamics between the novel and the screenplay. Drawing on archival materials (the Nabokov-Kubrick correspondence) from the Berg Collection of the New York Public Library, I view the Kubrick-Nabokov collaboration as a palimpsestic process of the two *auteurs'* struggle for control of the narrative. In the second part of the chapter, I probe the theoretical issue of metaphor, metonymy, and their tension in the symbolic workings of the novel, as well as the redeployment of the cinematic codes shaping the narrative structure of each film version of *Lolita* vis-à-vis the novel. I chose to look at Kubrick's and Lyne's *Lolita*s through the critical lens of metonymy and metaphor to consider the issue of fidelity and freedom, central to translation theory. Though film adaptation in a broad sense is a metaphoric procedure, I argue that the marked prevalence of metaphor or metonymy as the organizational principle of the cinematic narrative points beyond the personal style of a specific filmmaker. The discursive practices heavily leaning on metaphor result in the possibility of a final interpretation, while a cinematic narrative whose organizational principle is primarily metonymic would avoid any definite interpretation. In his novel,

Nabokov leaves unresolved the tension between metaphoric mechanisms and the metonymic narrative of *Lolita,* and so does Kubrick, whose "reinterpretation" stays essentially faithful to the metonymic nature of the text. Perhaps "loyal, not faithful" would describe Kubrick's strategy better. In contrast, Lyne's more textually faithful version betrays the novel on a more profound level—by transforming its essentially metonymic figuration into a metaphoric one, thus providing an unambiguous hermeneutic option.[44]

Nabokov's own attitude towards literary translation is explicitly stated, albeit in a parodic form of a sonnet-like structure (asking a question, expanding on it, and answering the question by using metaphor), in his poem "On Translating *Eugene Onegin,*" which I have placed at the beginning of this introduction. The poem, itself written in the so-called "*Onegin* stanza" ("patterned on a sonnet"), preceded by nine years the publication of his English translation of the famous novel in verse by Alexander Pushkin. It accurately conveys Nabokov's ideas as they evolved over his more than thirty years of activity as a literary translator, of which his *Onegin* translation was the result.

The question asked by Nabokov in the first line of the poem, "What is translation?" lies at the core of all debates around translation. As Edwin Gentzler put it: "People *practiced* translation, but they were never quite sure what they were practicing."[45]

Nabokov's response to this question is divided into two parts, as is the poem itself, and concerns both theory and practice. As far as theory of translation is concerned, expectations are set low— pessimistic would be a mild way to describe them. Though Nabokov was not very impressed with formalist and structuralist theories (he was openly hostile to Jakobson because he could not, as he put it, "stomach" Jakobson's "little trips" to totalitarian countries),[46] and would probably have objected to poststructuralist and deconstructionist theories of language, he shares their theoretical pessimism toward translation. Indeed, the prevalent metaphor he uses is of death and mutilation. The "pale and glaring" head of the poet on a "platter" evokes Salomé's macabre dance and the poet (the original) as the brutally slaughtered precursor (John the Baptist, the man who was, metaphysically speaking, "not the Light, but *was sent* to bear witness of that Light" [John 1:8]). In Nabokov's oeuvre, the image of a severed head has a long and, one is tempted to say, tortured history.[47] It suffices to recall the "dead head" moths swarming in Nabokov's novels, as well as Cincinnatus's execution in *Invitation to a Beheading*. One interpretation of this motif might be that of the "ancient mythologem of a 'severed head' as a metonymy of truth."[48] Images of mutilation also occur in Nabokov's disdainful attacks on his critics after the publication of *Onegin*, when, for instance, he called Robert Lowell a "mutilator of his betters—[Osip] Mandelstam, Rimbaud and others."[49] It is perhaps significant that in his remarks on Walter Benjamin, Paul de Man metaphorized translation in a way quite similar to Nabokov: "translations are harbingers of death."[50]

Nabokov also conceptualizes translation as "profanation of the dead," reiterating the motif of sacrilege. His own practice, however, admits a vampirism of sorts: a translator "feeding upon" a defenseless, mutilated, "dead" poet. This brings us to Charles Kinbote in *Pale Fire*, Kinbote the king of his (perhaps imaginary) kingdom, but certainly the tyrant of his Commentary and Index, described by the poet's wife as a "kin-bot," an "elephantine tick; a king-sized botfly; a macao worm; the monstrous parasite of a genius."[51] In Kinbote's Index, one encounters the definition of his alter-ego, Botkin, as a "maggot of [an] extinct fly" that has hastened the "phylogenetic end" of mammoths.[52] "Translation," such as Kinbote's, far from securing the "after-life" of the original, in Benjaminian terms, accelerates its death. On the other hand, the "worm" comes up several lines later in Nabokov's poem, as a "traveller" down the "secret stem" of the original.[53] The one who travels "down [the] secret stem" in Nabokov's poem is not just a vampiric parasite, but also the lost son in search of the origin, who "has kept [his] word" (to art? to his native language? to Pushkin?) and thus deserves pardon. As far as vampirism is concerned, there is also a certain vampirism in Ezra Pound's "re-energizing" theory of translation as a "model for the poetic art: blood brought to ghost."[54] However, there is a big difference. For Pound, translation opens up possibilities for creating a new compound out of old elements; for Nabokov it is a grudgingly admitted, inevitable evil.

The metaphor of a "parrot's screech, a monkey's chatter" in Nabokov's poem, used to evoke the mechanical imperfection of language that inevitably fails the translator in rendering the beauty and perfection of the original, is reiterated in Nabokov's articles theorizing translation. In "The Art of Translation," drawing on his translating of Pushkin's famous lyrical poem, Nabokov wrote: "Now if you take a dictionary and look up those four words you will obtain the following foolish, flat and familiar statement: 'I remember a wonderful moment.' What is to be done with this bird you have shot down only to find that it is not a bird of paradise, but an escaped parrot, still screeching its idiotic message as it flaps on the ground."[55] Monkeys and parrots are also evoked as a metaphor for "aping," "imitating," or, in other words, for mimesis. Nabokov's understanding of mimesis in art is fully developed in *The Gift*, a novel not incidentally infused with Pushkin's "voice." Nabokov scorns mimesis as a supposedly direct correspondence between art and reality (Nikolai Chernyshevskii's dissertation, the subject of the protagonist's devastating analysis, is entitled "On Aesthetic Relation of Art to Life"). He juxtaposes mimesis to the anti-positivist, anti-Darwinist model of mimicry ("the incredible artistic wit of mimetic disguise, which was not explainable by the struggle for existence" that seems to be created by some "waggish artist precisely for the intelligent eyes of man"—a "hypothesis that may lead far an evolutionist who observes apes feeding on butterflies").[56] This kind of mimetic re-interpretation, both in nature and in art, is not concerned with producing a replica, but an illusion, an artistic deception, which apart from similarity also contains difference. Both the subject and object of mimicry (the "original" and the "translation") can stand in each other's place, so it is no longer possible to understand who is imitating whom, and why.

Herein lies an unresolved tension, inherent also in Plato's outrage against mimetic representation: condemning the dissimulation of mimesis, Plato (or Socrates) is himself engaged in a mimetic game. Derrida of course discusses this as a paradox: the revelation of truth, *aletheia*, is both revelation and masking at the same time. While Nabokov tries to transcend mimicry and achieve complete metamorphosis in his art (and translation), the line in his poem about monkeys and parrots definitely refers to the first, scorned type of straightforward mimesis. "Chatter" as repetition, especially repetition of "received ideas," was often conceptualized by Nabokov as *poshlost* (the term introduced by Nabokov in his critical biography of Gogol for which he claims no English equivalent exists, but which roughly signifies mimicry of banality passing itself for art). The parrot in this line of Nabokov's poem also brings out the "ghost" of Gustave Flaubert. As Christopher Prendergast wrote in *The Order of Mimesis*, the "perroquet," deriving from "parroco," meaning a parish priest, is, "by perverse yet compelling logic," "but a step to one of Flaubert's most extraordinary narrative *coups*: the delirium of the 'simple' Félicité's dying moments in which she hallucinates the parrot Loulou as the Holy Ghost."[57] Julian Barnes, in *Flaubert's Parrot*, evokes the stuffed parrot that Flaubert owned and that sat on the side of his desk as he was writing *Un Coeur Simple*, and asks: "Is the writer much more than a sophisticated parrot?"[58] Thus the very notion of mimesis for Flaubert, as for Nabokov, is filled with tensions and ambiguities.[59] Repetition as the ironic "citational mode," as a strategy of both Flaubert and Nabokov, is "irreducibly enigmatic, deeply resistant to 'interpretation,'" and linked to "the project of disorienting the reader."[60] Quoting an alien source, by way of commentary, always marks the creation of Nabokov's own highly parodic "stratagem."

However imperfect, translation, in Nabokov's poem, grows as a new plant from the same root. This metaphor of organic growth fittingly refers back to the Romanticism out of which the Russian translation tradition developed; in other words, back to its roots. Briusov—a Russian Symbolist for whom Nabokov had little respect but who nonetheless, in his articles of 1916-1920, came close to a version of literalism while theorizing translation—used Percy Bysshe Shelley's Romantic metaphor of a violet thrown in a crucible in order to discover the principle of its scent and color. The plant, argued Briusov, can only grow anew from its own seed or it won't produce a flower.[61] However, while recognizing the imperfection of the plant he has grown vis-à-vis the original, Nabokov insists on their kinship ("all thorn, but cousin to your rose").[62] One can think here of "cousinage" as kinship without resemblance, which brings us back to the paradox inherent in Benjamin's discussion of translation as being *like* philosophy, criticism, and history, but at the same time *not like* them, not metaphorical, not imitative. De Man writes in his comments on Benjamin: "There is no resemblance between the translation and the original." Metaphor is not a metaphor: "all these activities (philosophy, history, criticism) resemble each other in the fact that they do not resemble that from which they derive."[63] They are "intralinguistic" in the sense that "they relate to what in the original belongs to language, and not to meaning as an extralinguistic correlate susceptible of paraphrase and imitation."[64] The adjective "honest" (in "honest roadside prose") again places translation within the discourse of truth, while "roadside prose" again evokes the reclaiming of *Onegin* as a novel. It also signifies metonymical contiguity ("by the side of the road," *par-odos* as parody), and brings in echoes of Nabokov's quintessential novel, *Lolita*, as a "road narrative."

Finally, the second part of Nabokov's poem refers to the practice of translation that, as he himself readily admitted, does not always meet the translator's own high standards.[65] Translation practice is essentially a compromise. As Briusov put it, "It is impossible to render a work of a poet from one language into the other, but it is equally impossible to give up this dream."[66] The "elongated lights" on the "black mirror" between "the city and the mist" recall Nabokov's metaphysical uncertainty and the way it relates to translation: his vision of human existence as a "brief crack of light" (a "crack" is always elongated) between the prenatal, uncannily familiar world without one's presence in it and the completely mysterious "beyond."[67] Essentially, what Nabokov evokes in the poem is a "glimpse" of divination, which is ultimately impossible to achieve. The original stays and will stay "elusive." The translator's chiasmic task, "a poet's patience and scholiastic passion blent" (a version of the paradoxically twisted Benjaminian "nihilistic rigor" and "sacred revelation") in pursuing the elusive original, requires the ultimate virtue of a translator: humility. The devil is in the details, and Nabokov pursues these details with "scholiastic passion." For many reasons, largely personal, he never acknowledged any achievements of the Soviet school, be they in translation or criticism—which in Nabokov's case are closely interrelated. Much of *Onegin*'s commentary therefore is dedicated to attacking and ridiculing other (especially Soviet) scholars—the trait that so upset Edmund Wilson. The reference in the poem to finding "another man's mistake" may be to Mikhail Gershenzon,[68] to Aleksandr Chizhevskii's mistake in the spelling of Jean-François Marmontel's name,[69] or to Nikolai Brodskii's mistake in the title of "Contes Morales."[70] Nabokov's attacks on Boris Pasternak's translations, which he characterized as "vulgar, inept, and full of howlers as any of the versions from Tolstoevski concocted by Victorian hacks,"[71] are well known.

Despite the pronounced humility vis-à-vis translation, the self-derogatory description of his own enormously ambitious work as "dove-droppings" on Pushkin's monument strikes one as forced modesty or, indeed, as parody. The monument, evoked in the last line of the poem, is an immediate reference to Pushkin's "Pamiatnik" ("Ia pamiatnik sebe vozdvig nerukotvornyi," which is usually known in English as *"Exegi Monumentum."*) It is Pushkin's reinterpretation of Gavrila Derzhavin's reinterpretation of Horace, which Nabokov translated at least twice (first in the early 1940s, for *The Three Russian Poets*, and then in his Commentary on *Eugene Onegin*).[72] It suffices to say that the most important change Nabokov made in his translation of Pushkin's poem was putting its first four solemn stanzas in quotation marks, thus pointing out the two contrasting voices in the poem—one pompous and serious, speaking of the poet's immortality, the other, in the last stanza, belonging to the author Pushkin, and subversively parodying this unrealistic expectation.[73]

Nabokov, in his Commentary to *Onegin*, claims that Pushkin "parodied Derzhavin [that is Derzhavin's 1796 imitation of Horace] stanza by stanza. . . . The first four have an ironic intonation, but under the mask of high mummery Pushkin smuggles in his private truth."[74] In her article "Nabokov's *Exegi Monumentum*: Immortality in Quotation Marks," Vera Proskurina argues convincingly that Nabokov derived his conclusions from the metaphysical theory of Pushkin's art developed by Gershenzon, the distinguished Russian Silver Age critic and writer. Nabokov, however, disguised the source in his Commentary through a mystification, attributing the opinion he agreed with to someone who would have been Gershenzon's opposite (Vladimir Burtsev, quite a "Chernyshevskian" figure, in terms of art criticism). The mysterious Koncheev, a poet and the protagonist's conversationalist in *The Gift*, engages in a similar ironic discussion about *Exegi Monumentum*, the nature of *slava* (glory/fame), and the ridiculousness of its expectations.[75] Gershenzon's analysis of "Pamiatnik," Proskurina argues, "challenged the whole history of Pushkin's posthumous mythology," with which Nabokov was engaged in his painstaking investigation of Pushkin's foreign sources in *Eugene Onegin*.[76] Even the "doves," which enter Nabokov's poem "On Translating *Eugene Onegin*," parodically by way of "traces" they leave behind, apparently come from Gershenzon, quoted by Nabokov in his Commentary to *Onegin*: Onegin, nauseated by the *poshlyi* (banal and trivial) quality of Lenski's romance, "whirls away Olga, like any lad pitching a pebble at a pair of cooing doves."[77] Nabokov disparages Gershenzon as "silly," but makes full use of his conclusions (another reason Nabokov's Commentary *is not* to be seen primarily as a straightforward critical apparatus!).

What interests us in the context of Nabokov's poem and his vision of translation is the "prism of parodic game"[78] through which he views both Pushkin's original and his own "two cents" — a contribution to both Pushkin's and his own very dubious "immortality." As de Man writes, commenting on Benjamin: "Translation belongs not to the life of the original, the original is already dead, but the translation belongs to the afterlife of the original, thus assuming and confirming the death of the original."[79] The two voices of Nabokov's translation of Pushkin's "Pamiatnik" (the quoted voice of metaphysical certainty and the mocking voice of the hidden author, parodying the metaphysical certainty), like the two parts of the poem "On Translating *Eugene Onegin*" (theory and practice), sum up Nabokov's profound ambivalence about translation. This ambivalence is manifested in the very oscillation between humility and violence within the space of a single poem. It is further seen in the recognition of the inherent failure of untranslatability in theory (the translation is an "exemplary failure")[80] coexisting with the ambitious insistence nonetheless on the kinship, however impaired, of translation to the original. Finally, this ambivalence is revealed in the reverse formula, the paradoxical combination of scholastic ardor and artistic perseverance—the translator's *Aufgabe* in practice.

## Notes

1   Parts of this introduction, along with parts of the conclusion, were previously published as: Julia Trubikhina, "Romantic Unreformed: Vladimir Nabokov's Literalness Within Russian and Western Translation Theories," *The ATA Chronicle* vol. xxix, 7 (July 2000): 43-49.

2   First printed in *The New Yorker* (8 Jan. 1955): 34; reprinted in Vladimir Nabokov, *Poems and Problems* (New York and Toronto: McGraw-Hill, 1970), 175.

3   Walter Benjamin, "The Task of the Translator," in *Illuminations*, ed. Hannah Arendt (New York: Schocken Books, 1978), 79.

4   Elizabeth Klosty Beaujour, "Vladimir Nabokov," in *Alien Tongues: Bilingual Russian Writers of the "First" Emigration* (Ithaca: Cornell University Press, 1989), 84.

5   George Steiner, "Extraterritorial," in *Extraterritorial: Papers on Literature and the Language Revolution* (New York: Atheneum, 1976), 8.

6   Ibid., 9.

7   Ibid., 10.

8   Elizabeth Beaujour, "Vladimir Nabokov," 105.

9   Paul De Man, "Conclusions: Walter Benjamin's 'The Task of the Translator,'" in *The Resistance to Theory* (Minneapolis: University of Minnesota Press, 1986), 80.

10  Andrew Benjamin, *Translation and the Nature of Philosophy: A New Theory of Words* (London and New York: Routledge, 1989), 1.

11  Roman Jakobson, "On Linguistic Aspects of Translation," in *Language in Literature*, ed. Krystyna Pomorska and Stephen Rudy (Cambridge, MA: Harvard University Press, 1987), 429.

12  Ibid.

13  Ibid.

14  Jane Grayson, Introduction to *Nabokov's World*, Jane Grayson, Arnold McMillin, and Priscilla Meyer, vol. 1 (New York: Palgrave, 2002), 3.

15  "Piterskie pravoslavnye pobedili Nabokova—'Lolitu' otmenili," *Newsru.com*, 12 October 2012, http://www.newsru.com/cinema/21oct2012/nololita.html.

16 "V Peterburge izbit organizator spektaklia 'Lolita,' na kotoryi opolchilis 'kazaki,'" *Newsru.com*, 15 January 2013, http://www.newsru.com/cinema/15jan2013/nololita.html.

17 "Muzei Nabokova v Peterburge atakuiut 'bortsy s pedofiliei,'" *Newsru.com*, 11 January 2013, http://www.newsru.com/cinema/11jan2013/mrakobesy.html.

18 Valerii Rokotov, "Ledianoi tron: literatura v iashchike," in *Literaturnaia gazeta*, no. 5 (6402) (2 June 2013), http://old.lgz.ru/article/20834. The full quotation from Rokotov in Russian is: "Nabokov skhodit so svoego trona. Koronovannyi liberalnymi obozhateliami, postavlennyi vysoko nad sovetskoi literaturoi, on tikho otplyvaet ot nashego berega vmeste so svoim osobennym sintaksisom. On snova stanovitsia emigrantom, i ego tvorchestvo snova vygliadit chem-to beskonechno chuzhim."

19 See Joseph Michael Nassar, "The Russian in Nabokov's English Novels" (doctoral dissertation, State University of New York at Binghamton, 1977), http://books.google.com/books/about/The_Russian_in_Nabokov_s_English_Novels.html?id=I1WonQEACAAJ. See also Jane Grayson, *Nabokov Translated: A Comparison of Nabokov's Russian and English Prose* (Oxford: Oxford University Press, 1977).

20 See, for example, Judson Rosengrant, "Nabokov's Autobiography: Problems of Translation," (doctoral dissertation, Stanford University, 1983); and Elizabeth Klosty Beaujour, "Translation and Self-Translation," in *The Garland Companion to Vladimir Nabokov,* ed. Vladimir Alexandrov (New York: Garland, 1995), 714-724.

21 See, for example, Beaujour, *Alien Tongues,* and "Bilingualism," in *The Garland Companion to Vladimir Nabokov,* 37-43. Other examples include: Christine Raquet-Bouvart, "Vladimir Nabokov: The Translator's Perplexity in a Maze of Languages," in *Cross-Words: Issues and Debates in Literary and Non-Literary Translating,* ed. Christine Pagnoulle and Ian Mason (University of Liège: L3-Liège language and literature, 1995), 121-138; David Bethea, "Brodsky's and Nabokov's Bilingualism(s): Translation, American Poetry and the Muttersprache," *Russian, Croatian and Serbian, Czech and Slovak, Polish Literature* [Amsterdam, Netherlands] 37 (15 February 1995-1 April 1995): 2-3, 157-84; Ann Deborah Levy-Berthérat, "Le dilemme du bilinguisme: Pnine ou la metamorphose inachevé," *Europe: Revue Litteraire Mensuelle* [Paris, France] 73 (March 1995): 791, 48-56; Liuba Tarvi, "Poetika i bilingvizm: Iz opyta sravnitelnogo analiza stikhov V. V. Nabokova," *Nabokovskii vestnik* (St. Petersburg: Dorn, 1999), 101-113.

22 See Julian W. Connolly, "Ania v strane chudes," in *The Garland Companion to Vladimir Nabokov,* 18-24; A. Dolinin, "Eugene Onegin," in ibid., 117-129; William Mills Todd III, "A Hero of Our Time," in ibid., 178-183; Elizabeth Klosty Beaujour, "Nikolka Persik," ibid., 556-560; Harvey Goldblatt,"The Song of Igor's Campaign," in ibid., 661-671; Galya Diment, "Three Russian Poets," in ibid., 709-713. Also see Elizabeth Welt Trahan," The Strange Case

of Vladimir Nabokov as a Translator," in *What Price Glory—in Translation?* (Whitestone, NY: Council on National Literatures., 1987), 27-37; Judson Rosengrant, "Nabokov, Onegin, and the Theory of Translation," *Slavic and East European Journal* 38, no. 1 (Spring 1994): 13-32; Alicia Borinsky, "Where Do you Come From? Posing and the Culture of Roots," in *Reading the Shape of the World,* ed. Henry Schwarz and Richard Dienst (Boulder, CO: Politics and Culture, 1996), 278-287; Jane Grayson, "The French Connection: Nabokov and Alfred de Musset; Ideas and Practices of Translation," *Slavonic and East European Review* 73, no. 4 (Oct. 1995): 613-658; *An English-Russian Dictionary of Nabokov's Lolita,* compiled by A. Nakhimovsky and S. Paperno (Ann Arbor: Ardis, 1982); Michael Eskin, "'Literal Translation': The Semiotic Significance of Nabokov's Conception of Poetic Translation," *Interdisciplinary Journal for Germanic Linguist and Semiotic Analysis* 2, no. 1 (Spring 1997): 1-32; Christine Raguet-Bouvart, "Les masques du traducteur chez Vladimir Nabokov," in *Masques et mascarades: Dans la literature nord-américaine,* ed. Christian Lorat et al. (Talence, France: Maison des Sciences de l'Homme d'Aquitaine, 1997), 115-127; N. M. Zhutovskaia, "Vladimir Nabokov—perevodchik 'Evgeniia Onegina,'" *Nabokovskii vestnik,* Vypusk 1 (St. Petersburg: Dorn, 1998), 109-117; Jennifer Coates, "Changing Horses: Nabokov and Translation," *The Practices of Literary Translation: Constraints and Creativity,* ed. Jean Boase-Beier and Michael Holman (Manchester: St. Jerome, 1998), 91-108; Pekka Tammi, *Russian Subtexts in Nabokov's Fiction: Four Essays* (Tampere, Finland: Tampere University Press, 1999).

23  See Laurence Guy, "*Feu Pâle,* ou l'indicible tourment du bilinguisme et de la traduction littéraire chez Nabokov," in *Double Vision: Studies in Literary Translation,* ed. Jane Taylor (Durham, England: University of Durham, 2002), 119-146. Also see Mary Besemeres, "Self-Translation in Vladimir Nabokov's *Pnin,*" *Russian Review* 59, no. 3 (July 2000): 390-407; Igor Klekh, "O pisateliakh—dvuiazychnom i beziazychnom," *Voprosy literatury* 1 (January-February 2001): 172-183; Beth Holmgren (ed.), "English as Sanctuary: Nabokov and Brodsky's Autobiographical Writings," *The Russian Memoir: History and Literature* (Evanston: Northwestern University Press, 2003), 167-185; Kamila Kinyon-Kuchar, "Models of Exile: Koestler, Nabokov, Kundera" (doctoral dissertation, University of Chicago, 2000); Hana Píchová, *The Art of Memory in Exile: Vladimir Nabokov and Milan Kundera* (Carbondale, IL: Southern Illinois University Press, 2002); Zinovy Zinik, "The Double Exile of Vladimir Nabokov," in *Nabokov's World,* vol. 1, 196-215; and Maria Louise Ascher, "The Exile as Autobiographer: Nabokov's Homecoming," in *Realism and Exile,* ed. Dominica Radulescu (Lexington: Lauham, 2002), 67-86.

24  See Rachel Trousdale, "Imaginary Worlds and Cultural Hybridity in Dinesen, Nabokov and Rushdie," DAI [*The Humanities and Social Sciences*] 63 (September 2002): 3A; Dieter Zimmer, "Mimicry in Nature and Art," in *Nabokov's World,*

vol. 1, 47-57; and Maurice Courtier, "Writing and Erasure, or Nabokov's Other Texts," in *Nabokov's World*, vol. 1, 173-185.

25  See Ekaterina Rogachevskaia, "Nabokov v Internete," in *Imperiia N: Nabokov i nasledniki*, ed. Yurii Leving and Yevgenii Soshkin (Moscow: Novoe literaturnoe obozrenie, 2006), 193-209.

26  Barton D. Johnson and Brian Boyd, "Prologue: The Otherworld," *Nabokov's World*, vol. 1, 19.

27  Ibid., 20.

28  Ibid., 21.

29  Ibid., 20.

30  Ibid., 24.

31  Grayson, Introduction, *Nabokov's World*, vol. 1, 12.

32  Vladimir Nabokov, *Strong Opinions* (New York: McGraw-Hill, 1973), 32.

33  Vladimir Nabokov, *Speak, Memory: An Autobiography Revisited* (New York: Putnam's, 1966), 275.

34  Ibid., 139. See also Vladimir Nabokov, *Drugie berega* (Moscow: Khudozhest-vennaia literatura, 1988), 442.

35  See Miguel de Cervantes, *The Ingenious Gentleman Don Quixote de la Mancha*, trans. Peter Motteux (New York: Random House, 1950), 869. Alexandrov correctly points out the earlier instance of the same metaphor in Nabokov's "Parizhskaia poema" (1943). See "The Paris Poem" in Nabokov, *Poems and Problems*, 122-123.

36  De Man, "Conclusions: Walter Benjamin's 'The Task of the Translator,'" 79.

37  De Man, "Return to Philology," in *The Resistance to Theory*, 21-26.

38  Ibid., 24.

39  De Man, "Conclusions: Walter Benjamin's 'The Task of the Transla-tor,'" 92.

40  It is interesting that when asked if he believed in God, Nabokov answered in an elusive manner that evokes both Socrates's famous formula and St. Augustine's musings on the nature of Time in Chapter XI of his *Confessions* ("When I am not asked, I know what Time is. When I am asked to explain, I know not"). Nabokov said: "I know more than I can express in words, and the little I can express would not have been expressed, had I not known more." Cited in W. W. Rowe, *Nabokov's Spectral Dimension* (Ann Arbor: Ardis, 1981), 107.

41  Elizabeth Bronfen, *Over her Dead Body: Death, Femininity and the Aesthetic* (New York: Routledge, 1992), 45, 229.

42  In Johann Wolfgang Goethe, *Westöstlicher Diwan* (München: Deutcher Tachenbuch Verlag, 1961), 244. Goethe describes the third and last period in the history of translation as one in which "we would want to make translation identical with the original in such a way that the new text does not exist instead of the original [*anstatt*], but in its place [*an der Stelle*]." Cited in Parvis Emad, "Thinking More Deeply into the Question of Translation," in *Reading*

*Heidegger: Commemorations*, ed. John Sallis (Bloomington and Indianapolis: Indiana University Press, 1993), 339.

43  Roman Jakobson, "Two Aspects of Language and Two Types of Aphasic Disturbances," in *Language in Literature*, 114.

44  Surprisingly little work has been done on Lyne's *Lolita*, though there have been a small number of articles dealing with this film, ranging from those that coincided with what Johnson called "a renewed wave of feminist outrage and public interest in child abuse" (Johnson and Boyd, "Prologue: The Otherworld," 19) to an insightful, balanced essay by Ellen Pifer. See Ellen Pifer, "Reinventing Nabokov: Lyne and Kubrick Parse *Lolita*," in *Nabokov at Cornell*, ed. Gavriel Shapiro (Ithaca: Cornell University Press, 2003), 68-77. See also Paola Loreto, "Kubrick's and Lyne's *Lolitas*, or: What Gets Lost in a Beautiful Betrayal," in *America Today: Highways and Labyrinths*, ed. Gigliola Nocera (Siracusa, Italy: 2003), 409-420. Among the more recent Russian-language articles, see Ekaterina Vasileva-Ostrovskaia, "Mifologiia Lolity: geroinia Nabokova v sovremennom iskusstve i massovoi kulture," *Imperiia N: Nabokov i naslledniki*, 162-180. I, however, chose to deal primarily with the multiple reviews at the time the film came out, since I found their immediacy most illuminating.

45  Edwin Gentzler, *Contemporary Translation Theories* (New York: Routledge, 1993), 43.

46  See Letter to Roman Jakobson, 14 April 1957, in *Vladimir Nabokov: Selected Letters 1940-1977*, ed. Dmitri Nabokov and Matthew Bruccoli (San Diego, New York, and London: Harcourt, Brace, Jovanovich, 1989), 216.

47  For the detailed analysis of this motif and its implications, see Svetlana Kozlova, "Gnoseologiia otrezannoi golovy i utopia istiny v 'Priglashenii na kazn,' 'Ultima Thule' i 'Bend Sinister' V. V. Nabokova," in *V. V. Nabokov: Pro et Contra: Materialy i issledovaniia o zhizni i tvorchestve V. V. Nabokova*, vol. 2 (St. Petersburg: Izdatelstvo Russkogo Khristianskogo Gumanitarnogo instituta, 2001), 782-809. In her article, Kozlova traces the motif of the "beheading" back to Plato, Nietzsche, and Dostoevsky and their preoccupation with the possibility of revelation of metaphysical truth. In *Human, All Too Human*, Friedrich Nietzsche, under the impression of his reading of Fyodor Dostoevsky's *Idiot*, follows Plato's *Timeaus* in discussing perception through Plato's utopia of the construction of human body (everything in the "objective" world is seen "through the head." So what would be left of the world if the head were to be cut off?) Nabokov was definitely an attentive reader of Plato. The juxtaposition of a being that has no becoming and a becoming with no being resonates with Nabokov's metaphysical vision. In *Invitation to a Beheading*, however, it is a cruelly inverted Plato: the ineffable truth, revealed to Cincinnatus when his head is severed, is that of the "real" world being a puppet show, an unreliable Platonic cave. (In Nietzschean terms, *nothing* is left after the head is cut off). I also would like to point out the direct influence

of Khodasevich, which, to the extent of my knowledge, has not been noted in this context. In his "Berlinskoe" ("A Berlin Poem," 1922), a poem on the irreality of life in exile, the poet suddenly recognizes with disgust—in the reflection in the windows of the passing tram—his own "severed, dead, night-time head" ("otrublennuiu, nezhivuiu, / nochnuiu golovu moiu").

48  Kozlova, "Gnoseologiia otrezannoi golovy," 808. Translation is mine.

49  See Letter to *Encounter*, 18 February 1966, in *Correspondence Between Vladimir Nabokov and Edmund Wilson, 1940-1971*, ed. Simon Karlinsky (New York: Harper & Row, 1979), 385.

50  Cited in Eve Tabor Bannet, "The Scene of Translation: After Jakobson, Benjamin, de Man, and Derrida," *New Literary History* 24, no. 3 (Summer 1993): 583.

51  Vladimir Nabokov, *Pale Fire* (New York: Vintage International, 1989), 247 (171-172).

52  Ibid., Index, 306.

53  As a distant echo, perhaps, the traveller who is "pardoned" comes into this poem by way of Nabokov's early infatuation with Walter de la Mare's poetry during his time at Cambridge as a student. The famous *Georgian Poetry* series (1912-1922) published de la Mare's poetry, which was later endlessly anthologized and admired by many, including such poets as T. S. Eliot, who characteristically entitled his essay on de la Mare "A Poet of Two Worlds." See D. Barton Johnson, "Vladimir Nabokov and Walter de la Mare's 'Otherworld,'" in *Nabokov's World*, vol. 1, 73.
In the then oft-quoted poem by de la Mare, "The Listeners," a mysterious lonely traveller knocks at the moonlit door and utters his famous line: "Is there anybody there?" As nobody answers, he says before riding away: "Tell them I came and no one answered / that I kept my word." Only phantoms quietly listen to the "voice from the world of men" (ibid., 74). A "solitary traveller" in search of self, pardon, and absolution, of the same provenance, I believe, appears also in Virginia Woolf's *Mrs. Dalloway*. One of the characters, Peter Walsh, perambulating in a state of suspension in time and space, falls asleep in the park on a bench next to a Moira- or Parcae-like "grey nurse knitting over a sleeping baby." "An atheist perhaps," but also a lost son, an exile, the "solitary traveller" is overcome by "extraordinary exaltation" beyond the here and now and taken along the journey to "search for a rider destroyed," for his own past and origin (Virginia Woolf, *Mrs. Dalloway* [New York: Harcourt & Company, 1981], 56-58). Peter Walsh wakes up from his dream with the words "the death of the soul" (ibid.,58).

54  Hugh Kenner, *The Pound Era* (Berkeley: University of California Press, 1971), 150.

55  Vladimir Nabokov, "The Art of Translation," in *Literature and Liberalism: An Anthology of Sixty Years of the "New Republic,"* ed. Edward Zwick (Washington: The New Republic Book Comp., Inc.), 268.

56  Vladimir Nabokov, *The Gift* (New York: Vintage International, 1991), 110.

57  Christopher Prendergast, *The Order of Mimesis: Balzac, Stendhal, Nerval, Flaubert* (Cambridge: Cambridge University Press, 1986), 180.

58  Cited in ibid., 180.

59  I would like to thank Richard Sieburth, who drew my attention to the fact that in *Salammbô*, the parrot is the insignia of the Carthaginian military interpreters, who are slaughtered in a scene signifying the "death of translation."

60  Prendergast, *The Order of Mimesis*, 181.

61  Valerii Briusov, "Fialki v tigle," *Izbrannye sochineniia v dvukh tomakh*, vol. 2 (Moscow: Goslitizdat, 1955), 188ff (186ff).

62  *Cousinage, dangereux voisinage*, as it is widely known (in part thanks to *Ada*, though Van and Ada are not, technically speaking, cousins). *Ada* also creates a subtle echo that brings together the motif of the insect and that of a "cousin" (*cousin* being a French word for "mosquito." Van "spends the night fighting the celebrated mosquito, or its *cousin*. . . ." See Vladimir Nabokov, *Ada* (New York: Vintage International, 1990), 179.

63  De Man, "Conclusions: Walter Benjamin's 'The Task of the Translator,'" 83, 84.

64  Ibid., 84.

65  Nabokov, "The Art of Translation," 270.

66  Briusov, "Fialki v tigle," 188.

67  I previously mentioned the reflected light and its metaphysical implications in relation to *Pale Fire*. If I were to make a guess here (and it is impossible to prove), the city on the black river would be St. Petersburg, conjuring transparent irreality and death, evoked, for example, in Mandelstam's poetry: "We will die in transparent Petropolis, where Proserpine rules us. " One confirmation of this interpretation might be the description of "the crystalline course of [the protagonist's] clairvoyance" in *The Gift* (Nabokov, *The Gift*, 23). Fedor, as a child, has an episode of the aforementioned translations in space without time during an illness—an out-of-body experience, in which he "follows" his mother around the city while a "distant stripe of radiantly pale sky stretches between long vesperal clouds" (ibid., 22).

68  Vladimir Nabokov, *Eugene Onegin: A Novel in Verse by Alexander Pushkin*, trans. from Russian, with a commentary, by Vladimir Nabokov, vol. 2, Pantheon Books, Bollingen Ser. LXXII (1964; New York: Bollingen Foundation, 1975), 513.

69  Ibid., 517.

70  Ibid.

71  See Letter to *Saturday Review*, 19 June 1959 (not mailed), *Vladimir Nabokov: Selected Letters*, 292.

72  For the many details of Nabokov's "re-writing" of this particular "original," one may refer to Vera Proskurina's article, "Nabokov's *Exegi Monumentum*: Immortality in Quotation Marks." See Vera Proskurina, "Nabokov's *Exegi Monumentum*: Immortality in Quotation Marks" ("Nabokov, Pushkin and Mikhail Gershenzon," in *Nabokov's World*, vol. 2, 27-39).

73  Cf. Vladislav Khodasevich's poem "Pamiatnik" ("*Exegi monumentum,*"1928), in which he writes: "I am the beginning, I am the end./ I carried out so little!/ Yet I am a reliable link:/ this happiness to me is granted./ In Russia, new but great,/ they will install my two-faced idol/ at the crossing of two roads,/ where there is time, wind, and sand." Translation is mine.

74  Nabokov, *Eugene Onegin*, vol. 2, 310.

75  Nabokov, *The Gift*, 352-353.

76  Proskurina, "Nabokov's *Exegi Monumentum,*" 29.

77  Nabokov, *Eugene Onegin*, 513.

78  Proskurina, "Nabokov's *Exegi Monumentum,*" 31.

79  De Man, "Conclusions: Walter Benjamin's 'The Task of the Translator,'" 85.

80  Ibid., 80.

# Chapter 1

## NABOKOV'S BEGINNINGS:
## "ANIA" IN WONDERLAND
## OR
## "DOES ASPARAGUS GROW IN A PILE OF MANURE?"

In the summer of 1922, Gamaiun, a Russian publishing company in Berlin, commissioned the twenty-three-year-old Nabokov to translate *Alice in Wonderland* into Russian. As Nabokov's biographer Brian Boyd aptly noted, Nabokov apparently "found the translation easy work after *Colas Breugnon*," his first serious work of translation.[1] Though Nabokov later claimed he had translated Romain Rolland and Lewis Carroll simultaneously, Boyd, based on the evidence of Nabokov's letters from Cambridge, dates the Carroll translation to the summer of 1922. The translation, with Sergei Zalshupin's illustrations, was published in 1923 as *Ania v strane chudes* ("Ania in Wonderland") under Nabokov's pen name of his European years, Sirin.[2] For ideological reasons, Nabokov's translation never functioned in the Soviet Union on equal footing with the other available translations and was brought to public attention in Russia for the first time in 1992, when it was published in Moscow by the Raduga Publishers.[3]

In her 1970 article "Voice and Violin: On the Translation of Lewis Carroll's Eccentric Tales," Nina Demurova mentions Sirin's translation and even discloses that it is Nabokov's pseudonym; her awareness of his translation's existence came, as she herself admits, from reading Warren Weaver's *Alice in Many Tongues: The Translations of "Alice in Wonderland."*[4] However, she failed to locate a copy of Nabokov's translation at that time, and noted that the book was not available in the Soviet Union.[5] It was reasonably well-known in the West, however, and was even praised by Weaver as the best rendition of *Alice* in any language.

This early translation is interesting also insofar as, along with the *Colas Breugnon* translation, it launched Nabokov's literary career. However, much of what Nabokov said about the work of another literary prodigy, Mikhail Lermontov, can be turned against his own work in this case: "the depressing flaws" of the *Alice* translation ("the banalities we perceive are often shocking, the shortcomings not seldom comic")[6] are understandable, as we are dealing with an "incredibly gifted ... but definitely inexperienced young man."[7] Nabokov's language *does* already possess the allure and touch of the strict verbal logic of his later writings, but it is at times stiff and almost non-native (especially noticeable in his translation of onomatopoeic words and use of regionalisms). Still, the *Alice* translation is fascinating because we are allowed to see a point of departure of sorts—a translation that goes against all of Nabokov's later, much publicized principles of literalism. Alice becomes the Russified Ania, and she apparently comes to Wonderland directly from the world of a Moscow or Petersburg nursery. Trying to remember Isaac Watts's trivial rhymes about a hard-working bee, Alice/Ania comes up with a distorted and twisted Pushkin poem; she imagines sending letters to her feet with an address that features "Parketnaia guberniia" (Parquet Province); the Mouse, left behind after Napoleon's retreat from Moscow, tells the audience not of William the Conqueror and the Archbishop of Canterbury but of the Olgovichi and the Kievan Prince Vladimir Monomakh (the exasperated audience demands that the Mouse "speak Russian"); the interaction of the Rabbit's servants can be traced directly to Nabokov's readings of Nikolai Gogol, Vladimir Dal's *Explanatory Dictionary of the Live Great Russian Language*, and the archetypical "peasants' talk" of Russian nineteenth-century literature ("ne ndravitsia mne ona, Vashe Blagorodie, ne ndravitsia").

Several translations of *Alice* preceded Nabokov's: the first anonymous Russian version *Sonia v tsarstve diva* (*Sonia in the Kingdom of Wonder*) in 1879; a version by Matilda Davydovna Granstrem (M. D. Granstrem, wife of a well-known publisher Eduard Granstrem), *Prikliucheniia Ani v mire chudes* (*The Adventures of Ania in Wonderworld*) in 1908; one by Aleksandra Nikolaevna Rozhdestvenskaia, *Prikliucheniia Alisy v strane chudes* (*The Adventures of Alice in Wonderland*) serialized in the children's journal *Zadushevnoe slovo* (*The Heartfelt Word*) between 1908 and 1909[8] and later published as a book; and one by Allegro (the pseudonym of Poliksena Sergeevna Solovieva, sister of the famous philosopher Vladimir Soloviev), serialized in the children's journal *Tropinka* (*The Path*), issues 2-19 (1909), and later published in book form by Tropinka Publishing in the series called The Golden Library, with an introduction by Zinaida Vengerova in 1910.[9] In addition, a version by A. D'Aktil (the pseudonym of Anatolii Frenkel) came out in 1923, the year that Nabokov's translation was published.[10]

Of all these versions, Allegro's *Alisa v strane chudes* has been mentioned most often in connection with Nabokov's *Ania*. The coincidences in the choice of Russian poems parodied by Allegro/ Solovieva and Sirin/Nabokov prompted Simon Karlinsky to suggest that Nabokov had been acquainted with Allegro's translation— an indebtedness he never acknowledged.[11] Nabokov maintained that he had never seen any Russian translation of *Alice* before he completed his version.[12] In 1963 (when Nabokov's name was unmentionable in Soviet editions), Efim Etkind, a leading Russian scholar on translation, accused Allegro's version of inconsistency: "We find ourselves . . . in an absurd anglicized Russia . . . where there is no historicity, no interest in national coloring, no respect for the psychological makeup of Englishmen."[13] To be fair to Allegro (Demurova justly judged her to be "a talented and cultured translator"), the "inconsistency" of her translation lies mainly in the fact that an otherwise consistently English girl is intimately acquainted with Pushkin's long narrative poem *Poltava* and other classic Russian verse.[14]

Young Sirin/Nabokov's version has been pronounced as superior to all of these early versions, as well as to subsequent ones.[15] Julian W. Connolly observes: "Perhaps Nabokov was aware of the inherent implausibility of a young English girl knowing by heart some lines of Pushkin. Faced with this contradiction, he moved a decisive step beyond Solovieva: he made Alice a young *Russian* girl named Ania, and he worked a wholesale transformation of characters and contexts, substituting Russian names and backgrounds for English ones."[16] However, Nabokov's "decisive step" was a step back to a well-established tradition, and to at least two previously published Russified *Alices*: the anonymous *Sonia v tsarstve diva* of 1879, and Granstrem's *Prikliucheniia Ani v mire chudes* of 1908. It is not so important whether Nabokov was acquainted with those translations. Their poor quality and total lack of linguistic luster cannot compete with Nabokov's linguistic proficiency and self-assured allure. What is important is the understanding of the nature of translation by the translators themselves: in Nabokov's case it is as ambivalent as ever. One can argue that, being ideologically close to the first Russified translations of *Alice*, Nabokov's *Ania* is not so much a translation per se[17] as a playground for his own nascent prose and should therefore be considered along the lines of his soon-to-appear Russian novels.[18]

In a few years, young Sirin/Nabokov would, in his own fiction, make use of his playful exercise in transposing a foreign text, which is based on proliferating literary devices. I would call Nabokov's tactic Deleuzian, since it was a strategy based on "deterritorialization" of existing cultural and discursive practices. Of course, the Deleuzian concept of "deterritorialization" derived from the Lacanian usage, but it came to be understood as the liberation of desire from its locus of investment and the reinvestment of it elsewhere. In a broader sense, this multifaceted term relates to any of the Deleuzian subversive and deconstructive readings of texts. In *What Is Philosophy?* Deleuze comes to define thinking itself as a form of absolute deterritorialization.[19] Concepts, the main products and instruments of philosophy, are taken along the path of being endlessly transformed into something else. Characteristically, Deleuze's analysis of Carroll's *Alice*, linking Carroll with the Stoics' preoccupation with the difference between cause and effect, is predicated on the concept of surface as a base along which fragments of discourse are arranged; he sums up Alice's adventures as "the conquest or discovery of surfaces."[20] The organization of language becomes a question of "discovering surface entities and their games of meaning and of non-sense, of expressing these games in portmanteau words, and of resisting the vertigo of the bodies' depths and their alimentary, poisonous mixtures."[21] A Deleuze scholar, Jean-Clet Martin, talking of the philosophical concept of surface versus depth in Deleuze, observed: "We can see it in Lewis Carroll where nothing stays in place, where things as much as words scatter in all directions. Alice's problem is how to produce a rhythm, a *gestus* which can adapt to this line in the mirror peopled by cards without thickness."[22] One can also look at Carroll in more general terms as a Romantic author perceiving the world with a great deal of skepticism and Romantic irony. Such a world is chaotic and can be confronted and structured only by "producing a *gestus*," by arranging it as a game, be it a logic game, a game of cards or chess, or labyrinths, or those word games, "mischmasch" or doublets, or anagrams, or the alphabet codes that Carroll invented for his little friends. In other words, the world becomes a closed language structure operating according to a strict, inviolable internal logic. *Homo ludens*, the author-magician, carefully arranges the world, in which there is nothing beyond its surface, beyond language itself. Carroll's own words here are more than appropriate: "plain superficiality is the character of a speech."[23]

It is along these lines that one could consider Nabokov's "deterritorialization" of tradition in his early novels. This "deterritorialization" passed unnoticed by the readers and reviewers of young Nabokov's first novel, *Mashenka* (*Mary*), published in 1926 in Berlin by an émigré book company, Slovo, because of its still seemingly ingenuous and traditional framework. Yulii Aikhenvald, an émigré critic and writer, at the first reading of *Mary* in Berlin, exclaimed: "A new Turgenev has appeared."[24] *Mary* was also said to be "reminiscent of Pushkin's and Lermontov's prose."[25] The readers who perceived Sirin as a writer in line with the classical Russian tradition needed a shift to a shockingly new subjectmatter to notice the subversive literary devices he was using. Therefore, it was his second novel, *Korol, dama, valet* of 1928 (*King, Queen, Knave*), that took its readers by surprise; it puzzled and befuddled them. Gleb Struve, for example, called it something "different from anything else in Russian literature both at that time and before."[26]

There are several distinctive ways in which deterritorialization of tradition stems from Nabokov's translation of *Alice* into all of his later writings: a pseudo-autobiographical discourse with its complex coding of data and numbers; the fantastic; the structural organization of text according to a game principle; and, finally, the arrangement of events along the plane of pure language devices in which materialized metaphors become a vehicle of the plot.

However, it is necessary to place Nabokov's translation in the context of the tradition and those versions that preceded his to make the "fault lines" visible. There certainly have been several excellent readings of Nabokov's *Ania* against the version of Allegro,[27] although Karlinsky's theory that Nabokov's version is influenced by Allegro's is disputable. The context for my consideration of Nabokov's *Ania*, however, will be not only Allegro's version, as in previous analyses, or Rozhdestvenskaia's version, but the two early

Russified versions that have not yet been closely analyzed. The obvious similarity in strategy (Russification) might illuminate the cardinal difference in the end result. I will limit my discussion of Allegro's and Rozhdestvenskaia's versions to a brief comparative overview.

## "Which dreamed it?": Allegro, Rozhdestvenskaia, Nabokov

Neither Allegro's nor Rozhdestvenskaia's *Alice* is, technically speaking, a Russification. Both of these versions represent a departure from the two Russified versions that had appeared earlier and will be discussed below. Rozhdestvenskaia's serialized translation *Prikliucheniia Alisy v strane chudes*, of 1908-1909, was later published as a book (hard cover, no date). Demurova noted: "It was customary to bring out a book very soon after serialization in a magazine."[28] *Knizhnaia Letopis* (*The Book Chronicle*) of 1912 indicates that Rozhdestvenskaia's translation was published as a book in 1911 by M. O. Volf Publishing. The anonymous Foreword maintains that, despite the enormous difficulty of conveying all the humor and originality of Alice's adventures, the translator tried "to reproduce all of the subtleties of the English original as faithfully as possible."[29] To give young readers a complete impression of the book, writes the author of the Foreword, the translator tried to escape emendations of or alterations to the verse parodies.[30] The literal translation of parodies makes the effect of parody disappear, since it is impossible to understand how they depart from the "original" poems, which were not known in Russian culture. Characteristically, "How Doth a Little Crocodile" is not treated as a parody at all; Alice *intends* to recite a poem about the little crocodile, so her tears and despair about getting it all wrong are incomprehensible.[31] Rozhdestvenskaia is a poor poet: the first introductory poem ("All in the golden afternoon ..."), rendered in monotonous amphibrachic lines, rhymes "oni — gresti" and "v zharu—ne mogu," which are non-rhymes in both the nineteenth- and twentieth-century Russian poetic tradition. Some poems, like the Mouse's tail/tale-poem, fail to fulfill even their literal function (the tail does not look like a tail and the text itself is incoherent and puzzling).[32] In general, the translation is literal and non-inventive—a murderous combination for a text based almost entirely on play, punning, and logic games with the reader. A curious digression from literalness is the use of Russian units of measurement (*vershki*, *arshiny*, and *sazheni*) and currency (rubles). As a result, Rozhdestvenskaia gets confused about the multiple transformations of Alice's height and their "translation" into the Russian units of measurement. Thus Alice, who has become "*four vershki* tall,"[33] is afraid of drowning in a "tear pond" that is said to be "*three vershki* deep."[34] It is worth noting that, unlike Allegro's version with John Tenniel's illustrations, Rozhdestvenskaia's translation uses the *art nouveau* illustrations by Charles Robinson, which at some points serve an explanatory function.

The supposition of Nabokov's awareness of the existence of Allegro's version arose, as mentioned earlier, from his choice of the parodied Russian poems. However, of the seven poems parodied in the text, in only three cases did Nabokov and Allegro choose the same Russian "source-poem": Aleksandr Pushkin's "God's Little Bird" from *The Gypsies* (for Watts's "Against Idleness and Mischief" from *Divine Songs Attempted in Easy Language for the Use of Children*, 1715; Carroll's "How Doth a Little Crocodile"); a well-known Russian rhyme, "Chizhik-Pyzhik," which belongs to the genre conventionally defined as "city folklore" (for Jane Taylor's "Twinkle, Twinkle, Little Star"; Carroll's "Little Bat"); and Pushkin's "The Song of Prophetic Oleg" (for Watts's "The Sluggard"; Carroll's "'Tis the voice of the Lobster"). The other parodied texts in Allegro and Nabokov do not coincide. While Nabokov proceeds with the next verse of "The Song of Prophetic Oleg,"[35] Allegro parodies Lermontov's poem "Alone I Come Out onto the Road."[36] In the episode with the blue caterpillar, Allegro parodies Pushkin's *Poltava*, retaining its iambic tetrameter in a narrative poem on the birth of the king of all mushrooms, "Borovik."[37] Allegro's parody is not nearly as funny as Carroll's "Father William" and vaguely calls to mind a Russian folktale, "The War of the Mushrooms," which was much illustrated by the Russian *art nouveau* artists of that time, some of whom contributed to *Tropinka*. Nabokov, on the other hand, chooses Lermontov's "Borodino" as a crib for his "Father William" (in Lermontov's poem a young man is talking to his uncle about the decisive battle against the French)—a parody done with much gusto but also, perhaps, with too much of a gleefully disgusting physicality that goes against the grain of the much more physically reserved Carroll.[38] Nabokov also chooses to parody Lermontov's "The Cossack Lullaby" for "Speak roughly to your little boy," the song the Duchess sings to her sneezing baby.[39]

It has not been pointed out, however, that one of the "source-texts" that Nabokov shares with Allegro, Pushkin's "God's Little Bird," had been first parodied by the anonymous translator as early as 1879[40] and has been a pervasive source for parody for many subsequent Russian translators of *Alice*.

While Connolly finds Nabokov's choice of Lermontov's "Borodino" "an unusual target" for parody and that of Pushkin's "The Song of Prophetic Oleg" "unexpected but wryly apt,"[41] there is indeed little unusual or unexpected in this choice: only Pushkin's *Eugene Onegin* might have been parodied more frequently than these staples of the Russian classroom curriculum. Except for the coincidence of the three "source-texts" parodied in Allegro's and Nabokov's versions (one of which had been parodied at least twice before either translation was published), I find little other textual evidence that could support a claim of conscious or unconscious plagiarism on Nabokov's part. Other claims of similarity between the two versions are simply erroneous. Demurova's statement that the Mouse in Allegro's version reads aloud a passage about Vladimir Monomakh from a Russian history textbook, thus indicating a connection to Nabokov's version, is incorrect.[42] On the contrary, the passage in Allegro is not Russified and is a fairly literal rendering of Carroll's original.[43] On the other hand, Nabokov does quote a passage on Monomakh. So this "proof" of Nabokov's dependence on Allegro's version evaporates.

Stronger evidence of Nabokov's awareness of Allegro's version would be a coincidence in the rendering of Carroll's literary devices, such as puns and wordplay, of which there is virtually none. Indeed, one may wonder if Allegro was aware of the slightly earlier version by Rozhdestvenskaia, since the two have much more in common in this respect than those of Allegro and Nabokov. Thus, for example, the pun on tail/tale in the Mouse's story is rather ingenuously rendered by Allegro as one based on the same principle of homophony: the Mouse asks not to be called "khvastunia" (a boast, a showoff), which Alice interprets as "kh*vos*tunia" — an invented word with a transparent meaning of a "long-tailed one."[44] Rozhdestvenskaia's slightly earlier version uses the same pun but does not change the spelling, so Alice keeps thinking of the mouse as "khvastunia," leaving it to the reader to guess that the two words are intended as homophones.[45] Rozhdestvenskaia's pun is therefore flawed and one may assume that Allegro improved on it. At another instance (where Nabokov does not reproduce Carroll's pun at all), Alice demonstrates her knowledge to the Duchess by saying that it takes the earth twenty-four hours to turn "on its axis." The Duchess responds: "Talking of axes . . . chop off her head!"[46] Both Rozhdestvenskaia and Allegro reproduce the "axis/axes" pun identically, playing on the same unfinished sentence, which is not found in Carroll's text: "it was discovered by a certain scientist and from that same time . . ." — "S tekh-to por"/"topor" (from that same time/an axe).[47] Both Allegro and Rozhdestvenskaia translate "caterpillar" as "cherviak" ("worm"). Allegro's departure from Rozhdestvenskaia's strategy consists in making the translated text culturally functional, as Vengerova's article on Allegro's translation, "Who Wrote 'Alice,'" explains: "For the readers of *Tropinka* the translation has been made so that not a single joke was lost and so that Russian children could understand from the examples of Russian verse the amusing way little Alice remembered in her dream what she had studied in real life."[48] One has to conclude, however, that there is not sufficient evidence to identify either of these two versions as an influence on Nabokov's *Ania*. In fact, as I will show below, in his translation Nabokov pursues different goals and uses different means to achieve them.

# Moral and Educational Trends in Children's Literature: Granstrem's Translation

Granstrem's translation of *Alice* is representative of a well-established tradition in children's literature—that of moral edification through informative and factual knowledge. Considering this tradition, both within its own context and vis-à-vis Nabokov, helps further illuminate a very different strategy in Nabokov's *Ania*. The genre of children's literature in the nineteenth century can be characterized by what Ronald Reichertz called "a battle between several major kinds of literature: religious, rational/moral, and informational on one side and imaginative on the other."[49] Showing how Carroll's *Alice* emerged in the context of this struggle, Reichertz points out that Alice, as she tries to make sense of the trials of Wonderland, unmistakably resorts to knowledge drawn from educational and moralistic children's literature. Thus, struggling with the haunting question "Who are *you?*," Alice tries to "reassert her sense of self" by reciting Watts's "Against Idleness and Mischief" and repeating her lesson in geography and the multiplication tables.[50]

The publishing of children's books in Russia, which began with the activity of Nikolai Novikov in the mid-eighteenth century, evolved into a complex and multi-dimensional phenomenon in the nineteenth century. Iurii Lotman observed that the children's world in the nineteenth century was an inalienable part of the women's world, and as women's readership grew, so did children's: children read what women read.[51] The influence of women's readings (mostly novels), as well as the new, idealized status of women established by the Romantics, accounts for the spirit of the Decembrists' generation—people whose very upbringing prepared them for the life of idealistic heroics and stoicism. *Don Quixote* and *Robinson Crusoe* were translated from their French versions. *Children's Plutarch (Instruction on Child Rearing)*[52] made the ideal of a Roman republic irresistible for adolescents. For example, the young Muraviev brothers, Aleksandr and Nikita, future Decembrists, dreamed of the island of Sakhalin, where, as new Robinsons, they would start the whole history of mankind anew, without slavery, money, or social oppression—an ideal republic of Choka.[53] On the other hand, the ambivalence of the controls exercised by women in society— which posited them as the embodiment of the social ideal, but one that was promulgated only through private moral influence— accounted for carrying over the ideals of piety, domesticity, and submissiveness to child rearing. The channel for diffusion of this domestic ideology was, as Diana Greene argues, "the translation into Russian of English, French, and German conduct books."[54] Such translations as Josephine Lebassu's *Blagovospitannoe ditia, ili kak dolzhno sebia vesti (s frantsuzskogo)* (*A Well-Bred Child, or How a Child Ought to Behave* [Translated from French]), 1847; "Sovety malenkim detiam" ("Advice to Little Children"), an 1844 translation from the French children's magazine *Le Bon Genie*; and Maria Edgeworth's *Prakticheskoe vospitanie* (*Practical Eduction*) were published and reviewed in leading Russian journals.[55]

Rational/moral didacticism was the prevalent discourse of the prominent *Zadushevnoe slovo*, a children's magazine founded by Sofia Makarova in 1877 (two illustrated versions for children ages 5-9 and 9-14). It reiterated themes and a genre of stories from the French "Bibliothèque Rose," described by Nabokov in relation to his own childhood as "an awful combination of preciosity and vulgarity."[56] "All those *Les Malheurs de Sophie, Les Petites Filles Modèles, Les Vacances*,"[57] written by Comptesse de Ségur, née Sophie Rostopchine, a "Frenchified," idealized version of sentimental childhood, and the subsequent original Russian stories by Lidia Charskaia, very popular at the turn of the century, also terrify Martin, the protagonist of Nabokov's Russian novel *Podvig* (*Glory*, 1932), and lead him to a profoundly misogynistic conclusion about books written by women.[58]

The enduring popularity of this kind of children's literature is attested to by the entries in the children's section of the systematic catalogue of 1853-1905 of the M. O. Volf St. Petersburg and Moscow Publishing Association ("tovarishchestvo M. O. Volf") and that of the "newest books of *belles lettres* and all branches of knowledge" of 1913.[59] Along with the "new foreign literature"—Louisa May Alcott, Frances Hodgson Burnett (Mikhail Nikolskii's 1901 translation of *The Little Lord Fauntleroy*), and *Uncle Tom's Cabin* (in Matvei

Peskovskii's adaptation)—the 1905 catalogue lists the 1903 Russian version of Mme de Ségur's *Filles Modèles* ("Twenty eight stories in conversations for small children") and L. Charskaia's *Princess Dzhavakha.*[60]

Children's literature also reinforced gender stereotypes: "While all children were expected to be submissive to (that is, controlled by) adults, boys and girls were subject to different kinds of control. . . . Little boys only had to submit to physical control; they were not to fidget. Little girls, who, it was assumed, would not fidget, were expected to be psychologically and emotionally submissive as well. . . ."[61] Greene's interesting comparative analysis of two Russian children's journals of the mid-nineteenth century— *Zvezdochka* (*Little Star*) 1842-1849 for girls and *Biblioteka dlia vospitaniia* (*Library for Education*) 1843-1846 for boys—shows that piety, purity, and domesticity appeared to be exclusively female concerns,[62] while emphasis on factual information, including history and mythology, characterized the boys' magazine. The informational strand in children's literature was best represented by the proliferation of children's encyclopedias. The first Russian encyclopedias for children appeared in the 1760s and were translated from French or German. By 1800, at least eighteen titles were published.[63] Many encyclopedias were based on the catechetic question-answer principle; some, like the multi-volume *Spectacles of Nature and Arts* (the translation of the Viennese *Scaupaltz der Natur und der Künste*), were beautifully illustrated and republished several times. The first original Russian encyclopedic edition for children, first published at the end of the eighteenth century, saw eleven re-editions, the last of them appearing in 1837.[64] The enduring presence of informational literature for children (like Peter Parley's tales and magazine in England) is evident also in Russian children's magazines, even at the beginning of the twentieth century. For example, the issues of *Tropinka* in which Allegro's *Alice* was serialized contain assorted short informational entries, "Vesti otovsiudu" ("News from everywhere"), that range from the discovery of the North Pole by Robert Peary to descriptions of elements of natural history, such as the northern lights (aurora borealis).[65]

These moralistic and informational trends in children's literature may account for the features of the 1908 translation of *Alice* by Granstrem, *Prikliucheniia Ani v mire chudes*. The word "translation" in this case deserves quotation marks, for this version, in all innocence, does not claim to do more than fulfill—however unsuccessfully—its function as an adaptation for Russian children. The edition itself indicates that it was "composed" or "compiled" rather than "translated" by Granstrem. In and of itself, the result is quite a paradox: Carroll's tale, which distorts and parodies the pervasiveness of informational and moralistic children's literature, is boomeranged back into a version of that same dominant discourse. Perversely understanding the original along the lines of edifying didacticism, the translation purports to explain and round the edges of this strange and eccentric tale and to use it to teach a few lessons under a thin veil of a plot. It is a Russified version (Granstrem was the first to introduce "Ania" as the Russian "Alice"), but its Russification is strictly utilitarian: it is Russian textbook material that relies on memorization for entertainment. Thus, examining a magic bottle, the good girl Ania muses on all the bad things that can happen to children "when they don't obey their mama and papa."[66] The plot develops as a series of vignettes, providing Ania with an opportunity to recite Ivan Krylov's fables, which had been, to use Karlinsky's words, "endlessly anthologized and traditionally memorized by the Russians practically since their infancy."[67] She recites them all without a single mistake and concludes with satisfaction: "Yes, I haven't forgotten this one!"[68] The Mouse's story turns into a recitation of hexameters—an excerpt from *The War of Mice and Frogs*, Vasilii Zhukovskii's version of the Greek *Batrachomiomachia*.[69] Immediately before meeting a *pink* caterpillar (the only explanation for this remarkable change in color might be that the story is written for young girls: pink was considered more of a "girls' color" in Russia because of the pink ribbon of the order of St. Catherine, awarded at birth to all female newborns of the Imperial family since the late eighteenth century), Ania sings a song. The singing comes completely unprovoked and unmotivated: the song is the same "God's Little Bird" from Pushkin's long poem *The Gypsies*—the pervasive text for all Russified versions of *Alice*, including Nabokov's. However, in Granstrem's translation, it is not material for parody: it is sung correctly and completely and even the musical notation is provided.[70] All scenes not directly serving the straightforward educational purpose as well as all puns are simply omitted. The last chapter is tellingly entitled "Ania Outsmarts Everybody."

There are many absurdities in this translation: the Caterpillar accuses Ania of making a mistake as she recites yet another fable, while indeed there is none;[71] the text of the letter read in the court scene as a piece of evidence is as cryptic as a piece of post-modern poetry: "hungry . . . one two three . . . they (women) are here . . . don't swim . . . nobody knew";[72] the child-turned-pig "pants as a locomotive,"[73] etc. While Carroll's text is able to "take material that is diametrically in opposition to fantasy, generically alien material, and give it a home in his fantasies,"[74] the Granstrem translation undertakes the opposite operation: it takes a fantasy and purports to accommodate it within an uncomfortably alien discourse. The resulting lack of sense is a compliment to the stubborn resistance of the original. The only things that Nabokov seems to share with this version are the Russified name of the heroine—Ania—and the fact of Russification itself. Instructing or morally edifying little girls was the last thing on his mind. In fact, Carroll and the young Nabokov stand in solidarity against the very *raison d'etre* of Granstrem's *Ania*, which foreshadows the militant anti-utilitarianism of Nabokov's future fiction.

## Imaginative Children's Literature and Folklore: The First Russian *Alice*

To understand Russification as a translation strategy that Nabokov shared with other translators described here, one must—to quote Nabokov's "On Translating *Eugene Onegin*"—"travel down [its] secret stem" to its Romantic roots. In the context of the developing genre of Russian children's literature, which still heavily relied on translations from European languages, national imaginative literature was naturally relegated to and dependent on folkloric tradition. In other words, it made use of what was available. Indeed, the nineteenth century, both in Europe and in Russia, was marked by the development of folklore studies and by a growing interest in this field that went far beyond the narrow circle of scholars. Romantic ideas developed by Friedrich Wilhelm Joseph Schelling and the young Georg Wilhelm Friedrich Hegel, their philosophy of the *Volksgeist* as an instrument and vehicle of history, Johann Gottfried Herder's *Stimmen der Völker in Liedern* (*The Voices of Peoples in Songs*, 1779), Achim von Arnim and Clemens Brentano's *Des Knaben Wunderhorn* (*The Boy's Magic Horn*, 1805), and the Grimm brothers' tales (1812-1815) and writings influenced the emerging "mythological" trend of folklore studies. Its renowned representatives, Adalbert Kuhn, Max Müller, and Wilhelm Mannhardt, and their French, Belgian, and Italian counterparts greatly affected Russian nineteenth-century scholarship, which itself had been preceded, as in Europe, by a period of intellectuals collecting folk poetry and of Romantics using it to their own literary ends (Pushkin, Zhukovskii, early Gogol). The early 1830s were marked by the intense interest of Russian writers and journalists in *narodnost*, a concept close to the German *Volksgeist*. Pushkin's tales started appearing in 1831; likewise, Gogol's short stories that are rooted in folklore, *Evenings on a Farm Near Dikanka*, were published in 1831. In the 1830s-40s, Vladimir Dal collected Russian proverbs and tales. His materials—including his multi-volume *Explanatory Dictionary of the Live Great Russian Language*, Nabokov's favorite reference source—were published only after the death of Nicholas I in the late 1850s. The early nineteenth-century collectors of Russian folk songs and epics (*byliny*), Pyotr and Ivan Kireevskii, the poet Nikolai Iazykov, and others, were spurred by the philosophical and political debate between the Slavophiles and Westernizers, and especially by the publication of Pyotr Chaadaev's "Philosophical Letters," which, among other things, denied Russia any substantial or edifying historical and cultural heritage. It is obvious that this early stage of division over Russian national identity corresponded to the nationalistic trend in European and especially German Romantic philosophy. The Kireevskii brothers, for example, traveled to Germany in the 1820s, attended lectures by German philosophers, and knew some of them personally. The Slavophile collectors of folklore were not scholars proper, but rather used their findings to further their own political and philosophical stances. The coming of age of folkloric studies led to the formation of the Russian mythological school by Aleksandr Afanasiev (whose collection of Russian tales, based on the principles of Grimm brothers and published in 1855-1863, is widely acclaimed and known in the West), Orest Miller, and Aleksandr Potebnia. The spread and influence of positivism in European philosophy, the pervasive interest in orientalism and, as a consequence, the change of trends in European folklore scholarship (the emergence of Theodor Benfey's "historical-comparativist" theory, concerned with tracing the borrowing or migration of themes and "wandering plots") made Russia follow suit. The publication of "The Genesis of the Russian *Byliny*" in 1868, an article by Vladimir Stasov, a well-known music and art critic, had the effect of a bomb. Discrediting the mythological school and claiming that *byliny*, the Russian national form of epic tales, were not original but borrowed and had an oriental origin, he caused a narrow scholarly debate to spill over into a passionate political and literary polemic, which eventually involved a wider reading public. A new school emerged in the works of Aleksandr Veselovskii and became the leading trend in Russian folklore studies at the end of the nineteenth century.

This background might provide a context for an understanding of Russification as a natural course taken by nineteenth-century translators. It would be fair to conclude that any late nineteenth-century Russian translator of some education (which the knowledge of a foreign language, especially English, certainly suggests), facing the challenge of a fairy tale of a foreign origin, would be affected by those passionate wars about and around the genesis, origin, and value of folklore as national heritage. However, unless a translator were also a scholar, he or she most likely would be affected indirectly; in other words, the ideology of a translation would be filtered through the existing and established literary tradition. The self-righteously moralistic alterations to the source-text would be foregrounded by the nineteenth-century Romantic vision of translation, by those "Liudmilas" and "Olgas" of Zhukovskii and

Pavel Katenin's literary age.[75] The inertia of sensibility in translation (often setting translation apart from other literary activities unless it is specifically chosen as a venue for the new) purports to "bring a version of the SL [source language] text into the TL [target language] culture as *a living entity*,"[76] reiterating the Romantic mode long after it went out of fashion in the original literary production. Susan Bassnett-McGuire evokes a similar paradoxical situation in the context of English language translation of the first half of the twentieth century: the continuation of Victorian principles and "the anti-theoretical developments in literary criticism" vis-à-vis the rise of Czech Structuralism, the New Critics, and the strikingly new developments in English language literature,[77] which made it difficult to believe that these developments took place during the same time. This short survey of the meshing effects of the folk and Romantic strands in translation of imaginative literature brings us to the very first attempt at domesticating and Russifying *Alice*.

In 1879, fourteen years after *Alice* was published in England by Macmillan, the first Russian translation appeared. It was entitled *Sonia v tsarstve diva* and did not indicate the name of either Carroll or his translator. Weaver was the first Western scholar to mention the existence of this translation, though not without a curious mistake of mistranslation—a verbal twist that would undoubtedly amuse Nabokov, if not Carroll himself. Weaver, a mathematician and one of the first to develop the idea of machine translation, was also an enthusiastic collector of first and rare editions of Carroll's classic. He relentlessly hunted for a copy of the 1879 Russian edition at auctions in the United States, where it eventually emerged at Sotheby's, but he failed to locate it: "At Sotheby's on March 3, 1958, there was sold to Maggs (and subsequently to J. Gannon, Incorporated, of New York City) a Russian *Alice* dated 1879, having Tenniel illustrations and carrying a title printed in the auction catalogue as *Son v Tsarsteve Deva*. It has unfortunately not proved possible to examine this book, nor have I been able to get any information as to its present location or owner."[78]

After speculating about obvious misspellings and the complexities of the Russian genitive case, Weaver, who knew no

Russian and had to rely on his not very reliable Russian assistants, arrived at the conclusion that the correct title should be *Son v tsarstve devy*, that is "A Dream in the Kingdom of a Maiden." There is a certain verbal logic in this mistranslation, since both *deva* (maiden, virgin) and *divo* (marvel, wonder) are archaic and belong to the same lexical plane.[79] Since 1970, the title has been identified, though the translator remains anonymous. The title page says only: "Moscow. The Printing House of A. Mamontov & Co. 3 Montevskii Lane. 1879." Carroll went on his Russian tour in 1867 and could have met his Russian translator then. However, his *Journal of a Tour in Russia in 1867* makes no note of such an encounter.[80] Weaver mentions in passing Charles Dodgson's (Lewis Carroll's) letter of March 31, 1871 to Macmillan about a "Miss Timiriasef," who had wished to translate *Alice* into Russian, and cautiously suggests that she could have been the translator.[81]

The poor quality of the first translation and the compression of twelve chapters into ten (they retained their titles but the numbers are omitted) are well in line with the tradition of the nineteenth-century *Biblioteka dlia chteniia* (*Library for Reading*), which published abridged and altered versions of foreign novels. For instance, a severely abbreviated version of *The Pickwick Papers* was published and identified as an early seventeenth-century novel![82] The *Library for Reading* was organized by Osip Senkovskii (aka Baron Brambeus), "a major employer of the translator underclass," which "comprised mostly women, who were mercilessly exploited."[83] The translators mostly remained anonymous and usually their only concern was to meet the deadlines and preserve the plots.[84] The state of Russian translation between the 1870s and 1890s, after Senkovskii's death in 1858, is characterized by Kornei Chukovskii, an important Soviet translator and theoretician, as "God-awful" in terms of preserving the style and individuality of the original.[85] It is all too plausible that the first translator of *Alice* was a member of this army of anonymous, underpaid women. Some peculiarities of style and choice of words may contribute to this hypothesis (e.g. specific "lady" words, such as the regular usage of *bezdna* [abyss] in the sense of "much, many").[86] There is also a hypothesis that *Alice* was translated by the publisher, Anatolii Mamontov, himself.

However deficient this first translation might be in terms of its literary merits, it has never been properly analyzed as a text. The first and apparently only attempt was made in a book by Fan Parker, which, in keeping with its furiously accusatory tone, seems to be aimed solely at settling scores with two of *Alice*'s Soviet translators—Demurova and Boris Zakhoder (the latter's name is misspelled by Parker).[87] To her credit, Parker does seem to be the first Western scholar to have noted, albeit in passing, that Nabokov's was not the first Russification of Carroll.[88] When discussing *Sonia*, Parker mentions some of the characters' names the anonymous translator uses and comments on "the good command of [the translator's] English and Russian" as well as the "ingenuity" of the puns and the "charming rhymes,"[89] which is, to put it mildly, an overstatement. She also quotes some of the names incorrectly (e.g. Persian Cat, instead of Siberian Cat), possibly conflating the first anonymous version and that of D'Aktil'. Meanwhile, *Sonia*, being the first Russian version of *Alice*, deserves a closer inspection.

The inherent problems of the first Russified *Alice* (which Nabokov so masterfully avoided), start with the authorial tone. The tone set from the first passages is that of *skaz*, an oral folk narrative. *Skaz* in *Sonia* is mediated through the nineteenth-century literary tradition, most notably the narrative style of Krylov's fables.[90] This discourse requires the prevalence of the present tense with occasional unmotivated shifts to the past tense, as well as the abundance of sentences lacking a verb. The examples are numerous. The very first paragraph starts out as follows: "Den zharkii, dushno" ("A hot day, [it is] stuffy").[91] The fall of Sonia into the rabbit hole is described in the following fashion: "Vse nizhe i nizhe spuskaetsia Sonia. 'Kogda zhe etomu budet konets?'" ("Sonia is coming down lower and lower. 'When will there be an end to this?'")[92] The folktale devices also involve idiomatic units based on repetition of paired or tripled verbs, such as "bezhit-speshit" ("runs and hurries");[93] "smotrit, ne naliubuetsia" ("looks and admires/cannot have enough");[94] "stoit, vsia triasetsia" ("stands and trembles all over");[95] "rastet da rastet" ("grows and grows");[96] "postoiala, podozhdala" ("stood and waited for a while");[97] "dumala, dumala, nakonets pridumala"

("thought and thought, and finally thought [something] out").[98]
Other examples of stylistic folktale devices include:

- *zachin*, a traditional beginning akin to the English "once upon a time": "dolgo li net lezhala Sonia" (e.g. "whether for a long time or not Sonia lay on the ground");[99]
- the extensive use of conventional Russian folktale idioms: "sled prostyl" (literally, "the track became cold," i.e. "disappeared");[100] "budto ee i ne byvalo" ("[disappeared] as if it never existed");[101] "ni zhiva, ni mertva" ("neither alive nor dead," in the sense of "half-dead with [fear]");[102]
- colloquialisms, or so called *prostorechie*: "da nikak ia stala umenshatsia?" (in the sense of "looks like I'm becoming smaller");[103] "skolko bish?" (in the meaning of "how much?");[104] "edak" (meaning "so, this way");[105] "ne privykat stat" (in the sense of "[somebody] being accustomed to");[106]
- rhetorical questions typical for a folk narrative: "kak byt?" (as an expression of puzzlement: "what's to be done next?").[107]

The national coloring of a text—expressed in the national specificity of its imagery and situations combined with idiomatic language—usually complicates translation. This is especially true of translation of folklore. The translator of folklore must choose either to preserve the specificity and end up sounding exotic, or to drop the particular national specificity and replace it with one of the specific discourses of the target language. However, *Sonia* is a reversal of this situation: the national folkloric discourse of the target language is picked to convey the content revolving around the specificity of the author's individual style rather than any national specificity. The entire setup of *Sonia* is a Russified environment, so one cannot reproach the translator for inconsistency in this respect. Sonia's girlfriends become Masha and Ania[108]—the first "Ania" of all the Russified versions! The cat Dinah is Katia,[109] which is confusing since it is also the name of Sonia's older sister.[110] Length and height are measured in *sazheni* and *vershki* (Russian units of measurement) instead of feet and inches; the Dodo becomes a conventional folktale crane; the March Hare is also a more traditional "zaiats kosoi."[111] The Rabbit's servants have conventional names of Russian *muzhiks*, Petka and Vaska (they are Petka and Iashka in Nabokov's translation). However, unlike in Nabokov's *Ania*, these secondary characters fulfill not only the Russified functions but also the folktale ones. Thus Pat becomes "Petka-petukh," the traditional Petia-the-rooster of Russian folktales; Bill-the-lizard becomes a roach; the guinea pigs are transformed into regular pigs. Naturally vodka, not whiskey, is the drink that works magic on Bill/Vaska to revive him after his flight through the chimney. The cook stirs *shchi*, the Russian cabbage soup, in a *korchaga*—a word whose regional specificity requires consulting Dal's *Explanatory Dictionary of the Live Great Russian Language*.[112] The Cheshire Cat changes its gender to female and becomes a "female Siberian cat" that, naturally, bares her fangs instead of smiling. Siberian cats apparently do not smile, which entails the literal disappearance of the whole smile issue in the text.

However, the real tension in *Sonia* is the sharp dissonance between the non-folkloric nature of the translated text and the choice for the narrator's folkloric discourse, as well as between the narrator's and the characters' discourse. The translator seems quite baffled by the "strangeness" of the text, hence the impossibility of setting the right tone. The words "latitude" and "longitude" are out of place in a folktale, as is "for external use only"—the label Sonia reads on a small bottle.[113] Other instances include croquet (which requires a footnote: "a game with balls akin to lawn billiards")[114] and the trial scene. Omission of the entire "Alice's Evidence" chapter and the radical cutting of the trial scene testify both to the translator's inability to cope with an original text that resists being fit into the Procrustean bed of a folk narrative, and to his or her growing awareness of the original's ultimate incompatibility with such a narrative. The legal formalities of the British courtroom do not stand the trial of being introduced into a Russian folktale.

Stylistic irregularities in translation may betray the presence of more than one translator, or they may testify to the effect of a single translator's puzzlement or indecisiveness about what to make of the text. In *Sonia*, there are occasional intrusions of other discourses into the speech of the characters: for instance, the sudden and unmotivated intrusion of a Russian Orthodox liturgical formula into the promise of the Frog-Footman to "sit here, . . . till tomorrow — . . . or next day, maybe . . ."[115]

Some characters also become problematic, most pointedly the Hatter and the Mock-Turtle — quite unusual characters for a Russian folktale, to say the least. The Hatter apparently puzzled the translator, whose knowledge of idiomatic English was not sufficient to discern the motif of madness. Since no ready folktale character was available, he was transformed into "Vral-Iliushka" (Iliushka-the-Liar), whose remarks vaguely suggest that he is a coachman, or at least works in some capacity with horses rather than hats.[116] However, the accompanying Tenniel illustration (with a "50 kopecks" sign on the Hatter's hat, an edifying piece of uninvited information about the prices in 1879) and Iliushka's subsequent testimony in the scrambled trial scene clearly show that he is a hatter.

The Queen is called "Chervonnaia kralia" (the colloquial "kralia," as opposed to "koroleva" or "dama," lowers the social status of the speaker); the Duchess's name is changed to "Pikovaia kniaginia," the "Princess of Spades." The choice of suit might have been prompted by Tenniel's illustrations, while the unnatural "kniaginia" instead of "dama" ("Queen of Spades") once again reveals the translator's discomfort about the disparity between his or her folkloric narrative and that which the Pushkinesque literary tradition might connote.

Vissarion Belinskii, a famous nineteenth-century critic, once reproached Mikhail Pogodin for the fact that the characters in Pogodin's translation of Goethe's *Götz von Berlichingen* all "speak like bearded shop owners and coachmen."[117] This complaint could very well be applied to *Sonia*. While the narrator speaks like a Russian folk storyteller, Sonia herself speaks like a maid or, at best, a provincial young girl from a merchant estate. For example, Sonia, speaking of her cat, Katia, exclaims: "Uzh takaia eta Katiusha laskovaia, takaia milashka! . . . Uzh takaia eta Katiusha u nas dragotsennyi zverok!" ("So cuddly this Katiusha is, such a sweetie! . . . Such a precious little kitty-cat!")[118] And referring to the owner of a little dog that masterfully catches mice, Sonia calls him "our starosta" — the elected head in the Russian peasants' commune, the word that later came to mean an elected leader of students at a school.[119] It is interesting that the Rabbit mistakes Sonia not for a maid but for a cook, "Matrena Ivanovna."[120] While Sonia changes her social status, the Rabbit also changes nationality and for no particular reason becomes Polish, a head of protocol (*tseremonimeister*), and goes by the name of "Krolikovski."[121]

Nabokov, conversely, made sure that in his Russified translation only servants spoke the Gogolian mix of pseudo-folk language, while Ania always spoke like a *baryshnia*—a Russian miss from an educated, if not aristocratic, family. In *Sonia*, the bizarre shifting between rude and frivolous speech completely changes Sonia's/ Alice's personality: instead of a character whose common sense, sound judgment, and invariable politeness carry her safely through the trials of absurdity and false logic of the magic world, we have in Sonia a character who hardly comes across as a role model.

In the famous episode when Alice is crammed inside the Rabbit's house, she hears the Rabbit talking to Pat: "'Pat! Pat! Where are you?' And then a voice she had never heard before, 'Sure then I'm here! Digging for apples, yer honnor!'"[122] As Reichertz points out, the response "combines a French/English pun (*pomme/ pomme de terre*) with transposed nature and a tricky servant wit that affronts social order."[123] Sonia hears a "strange rooster-like voice: 'Here I am, in a pile of manure, digging for asparagus for your honor.'"[124] "Asparagus in a pile of manure" is a neat image to sum up the problems of the first anonymous translation: a painful transplantation of foreign fancy onto native soil. Frustrated with the failure of his servant to free his house from Sonia's presence, the Rabbit, after a long pause utters thoughtfully: "Podzhech razve dom?" ("Or shall we set fire to the house, maybe?"),[125] intoning with that unmistakably Russian indolence with which one sets fire to a house, broods vaguely about metaphysics, and makes revolutions.

# Nabokov's *Ania v Strane Chudes*

Sometimes, however, a native pile of manure can grow, if not asparagus, then unexpected blossoms. Nabokov's *Ania* is a translation insofar as it was commissioned as such. At this stage, Nabokov's ideas on translation are not theoretically articulated, though he partakes of the best of the nineteenth-century Romantic tradition. He shares with Zhukovskii an understanding of the translator as co-creator. Maurice Friedberg retells an anecdote about how Zhukovskii was asked by a German correspondent to send some of his own work for translation into German. Zhukovskii sent him a list of the poems he had translated and appended a note: "While reading them, make believe that they are all translations from Zhukovskii's Russian originals, or vice versa."[126] Nabokov feels the right to alter Carroll's text neither out of desire to "smooth" the idiosyncrasies of the English text—a desire, after all, more neo-classical or sentimentalist than Romantic—nor because of a less than perfect command of the language—as in the two previous Russified versions—but because he wishes to replace Carroll's idiosyncrasies with his own. His *otsebiatina*—the emendations of the original text—are not arbitrary, and are not dictated by propriety, good taste, or a laudable desire to instruct Russian children (as, for example, in Granstrem's version of *Alice*). In other words, Nabokov's version is anything but innocent and—here I would argue against Demurova's conclusions—is not written for children.[127] Zinaida Shakhovskaia, in *In Search of Nabokov*, rather observantly wrote about the young writer in his European years:

> In those times it seemed that the entire world, all men, all streets, all buildings, and all clouds interested him to the extreme. He looked at everybody and everything he met with the gusto of a *gourmét* before a delicious dish; he fed not on himself but on his surroundings. Noticing everything and everybody, he was ready to pin them down like the butterflies of his collections: not only the clichéd, philistine [*poshloe*], and ugly, but also the beautiful; though there was already the sense that the absurd gave him more pleasure.[128]

Like all translators of *Alice* before him, Nabokov faced multiple challenges that such a complex text entailed. While studying versions of *Alice* in numerous languages, Weaver classified some of the major problems of its translation: parodies whose sources were familiar to the contemporaries of Reverend Dodgson; puns; nonsense play and the use of new words constructed according to the nonsense principle; jokes of logic; and, finally, specific shifts in meaning, usually quite original and unexpected.[129] Demurova, elaborating on the specific difficulties that any translator of Carroll faces, and in an attempt to justify her own alterations to Carroll's text, adds to the above the problems of authorial speech versus the speech of the characters; Carroll's realization of metaphors understood literally; and the transposition of proper names.[130]

But for Nabokov, Carroll's text is, in a sense, ideal: it presents structural and compositional difficulties akin to those of a complex puzzle, a crossword, or a chess problem—that is, the very problems of writing immanent in Nabokov's fiction. Since Carroll's humor is verbal and logical, not situational, any translator of Carroll is bound to choose between, as Demurova put it, *"what* is said and *how* it is said"[131]—in other words, between literalism and device. The inherent link of Carroll's work with Nabokov's becomes apparent when one remembers Khodasevich's perspicacious remark in 1937 about Nabokov as "for the most part an artist of form, of the writer's device, and not only in that well-known and universally recognized sense in which the formal aspect of his writing is distinguished by exceptional diversity, complexity, brilliance, and novelty."[132] According to Khodasevich, Nabokov astonishes and catches everyone's eye "because Sirin not only does not mask, does not hide his devices ... but, on the contrary, because Sirin himself places them in full view like a magician who, having amazed his audience, reveals on the very spot the laboratory of his miracles. This, it seems to me, is the key to all of Sirin. His works are populated not only with the characters, but with an infinite number of devices which, like elves or gnomes, scurry back and forth among the characters and perform an enormous amount of work."[133]

Most of the technical problems are quite ingeniously solved by Nabokov. His transposition of proper names is very inventive: the Rabbit becomes the "nobleman krolik Trusikov"[134] (either from the Russian verb *trusit* with an accent on the second syllable, "to trot along"; or from the verb *trusit* with an accent on the first syllable, "to be fearful," "to have jitters"—a characteristic ascribed to hares in Russian folklore). The echo of this *krolik* can be heard in the name of Dr. Krolik from Nabokov's *Ada*. The lizard Bill is "Iashka-Iashcheritsa" ("Iashka-the-Lizard"), an added effect of sound repetition absent in Carroll, as was noted by both Karlinsky and Connolly;[135] the Dormouse is called "Sonia" (both "sleepy head" and the generic name for a rodent); the Cheshire Cat becomes "Maslenichnyi kot,"[136] the Shrovetide Cat, the name derived from the Shrovetide week (*maslenitsa*), a festival parallel to *Mardi Gras*. This association allows an interesting shift of logic to explain the cat's perpetual grinning: a Russian proverb, "ne vse kotu maslenitsa" ("it's not always the Shrovetide season for the cat," meaning roughly "only so much for the indulgence"). The Duchess quotes the proverb and adds: "But it's always Shrovetide for my cat: this is why he is grinning."[137] The least successful name transposition might be the Gryphon, who becomes simply "Grif,"[138] a vulture, stripped of his heraldic and mythological connotations. Coincidently, he is "Grif" in Allegro's, Rozhdestvenskaia's, and Granstrem's versions, while in *Sonia* he remains the Gryphon.

For some shifts in meaning, Nabokov utilizes a device that he later so exuberantly put to use in his fiction: a misunderstanding based on a misheard word that may sound vaguely like a homophone.[139] When the Mouse tells her tale, interpreted by Carroll's Alice as a convoluted story in the shape of a "tail," Nabokov makes his Mouse say that the tale is "prost" ("simple"), while Ania mistakes it for "khvost" ("a tail").[140] Similarly, when the Rabbit informs Alice that the Duchess has been sentenced to be executed, Carroll's Alice asks "What for?," which the Rabbit misinterprets as "What a pity!" Nabokov's Ania asks "Za kakuiu shalost?" ("For what kind of mischief?"), and the Rabbit thinks she said "Kakaia zhalost!" ("What a pity!").[141] These exchanges remind one of the famous dialogue in *Lolita* between Clare Quilty and Humbert Humbert that turns on deliberate misinterpretation: "'Where the devil did you get her?' 'I beg your pardon?' 'I said: the weather is getting better. . . .'"[142]

Nabokov's congeniality with Carroll is especially apparent in their shared delight in etymology, the creation of portmanteau words, games, puzzles, and anagrams. Nabokov's translation delights in invented etymology, as evidenced by the list of grotesque disciplines that the Mock-Turtle had to study: "Reeling and Writhing," "Ambition, Distraction, Uglification, and Derision"[143] ("chesat i pitat," "sluzhenie, vymetanie, umorzhenie i pilenie").[144] Nabokov misses the opportunity to play on "French, music and washing—extra,"[145] subjects derived from a conventional formula on boarding school bills. He replaces "French, music and washing—extra" with "behavior,"[146] which, as a separate subject that the Mock-Turtle could not afford, is of course funny; nevertheless, it was a habitual category in Russian school report cards, and was graded as all other subjects. The name of the Mock-Turtle (mock-turtle soup being an alien notion for Russia) presented enormous difficulty for all preceding translations: the Mock-Turtle, for example, is turned into a female in *Sonia*, and *she* is more a calf than a turtle, telling about the time she actually was a calf taught by a turtle at the bottom of the sea—a translator's fancy run amok.[147] In Allegro's version, the Mock-Turtle's gender is very confusing: called "cherepakha iz teliachei golovki" ("a turtle made of a calf's head") and referred to as female, she is nonetheless addressed by Alice as "sir."[148] Nabokov also makes the Mock-Turtle a female (which is inconsistent with her clear role as a male partner in the Lobster Quadrille), and invents for her a perfectly "Carrollian" portmanteau name, "Chepupakha"— half "cherepakha" (turtle), half "chepukha" (nonsense).[149]

In addition to the impressive example it presents of the young translator's verbal virtuosity, *Ania* previews the paths along which Nabokov would take his own fiction in just a few years. Those paths, the fault lines of the tradition delineated at the beginning of this chapter, feature a complex play on coded autobiographical/pseudo-autobiographical information and on the fantastic element, which undermines the "objective" reality of the narrative; strategic games with the reader; and, finally, the centrality of language itself and its devices.

Nora Bukhs, in her insightful analysis of the structure of Nabokov's early novels, points out the pseudo-autobiographical setup in *Mary* and *Glory*, noting that the image of the protagonist is created "as a projection not of Nabokov's personality per se, but as a certain conventional, compound personage of an Author" that "incorporates fragments of the biographies of Nabokov, Pushkin, a poet par excellence in Nabokov's understanding, and those of literary characters from Pushkin and Shakespeare."[150] In the introduction to the English translation of *Mashenka* (*Mary*), Nabokov calls his first novel "a headier extract of personal reality ... than [that] in the autobiographer's scrupulously faithful account" of his *Speak, Memory*.[151] Any attentive reader of Nabokov knows that dates and numbers in his texts are never accidental; they are a complex code, the deciphering of which lays bare a solution to a puzzle, sometimes revealing and sometimes intentionally misleading. Nabokov always tries to preserve this coded information in translation. For example, in the translation of *Mary* (done in collaboration with Michael Glenny), Nabokov introduces calendar changes, "the switch of seasonal dates in Ganin's Julian Calendar to those of the Gregorian style in general use," which he carefully orchestrates and points out in the preface to the English edition.[152] The seven days during which the action of *Mary* develops, as Bukhs observes, refer the reader to a closed cycle of creation—in this case, the creation of the world of the past.[153] According to her, the symbolism of the novel's seventeen chapters is that of the Roman number XVII, which—when transformed into letters and anagrammatically shifted—can form the word *vixi* in Latin, "I lived."[154] She reads the structure of the novel as an allusion to Pushkin's *Eugene Onegin*: starting with an epigraph (omitted in the English edition) from stanza 47 of its first chapter and ending with an allusion to stanza 50 (on Pushkin's imagined origin and the origin of his ancestor, Abram Gannibal—Africa).[155] This is the protagonist's possible destination, his way out from "his dream-life in exile."[156] Similarly, the biography of another of Nabokov's pseudo-biographical protagonists, Martin Edelweiss, "a distant cousin of mine," as Nabokov calls him in the preface to the English edition,[157] is a reference to Pushkin's biography and to *Eugene Onegin*'s chronology.[158]

It was in his translation of Carroll, however, that Nabokov first discovered delight in the seemingly innocent manipulation of numbers, whose synchronization provokes multiple echoes, allusions, and a structural order in the flux of complex narratives. In Carroll's trial scene, the witnesses—the Hatter, the March Hare, and the Dormouse—give three different dates for the beginning of their endless tea-party: the fourteenth, the fifteenth, and the sixteenth of March.[159] The jury then "wrote down all three dates on their slates, and then added them up, and reduced the answer to shillings and pence."[160] Nabokov's Hatter gives a mad date of "chetyrnadtsatoe martobria" (the fourteenth of Martober—proof that Gogol was very much on Nabokov's mind: the date refers to "Martober 86 between day and night" in Gogol's "Diary of a Madman").[161] The Hare, rather than contradicting, confirms the date, and the Dormouse maintains it was the sixteenth.[162] As a result, the jury comes up with the exact number of forty-four kopeks. The rationale for the change becomes clear in the subsequent quoting of the non-existent "Rule Forty-two" by the King in the next (and last) chapter of Carroll's *Alice*, according to which "all persons more than a mile high [should] leave the court."[163] In Nabokov's *Ania*, the rule becomes "Law Forty-four."[164]

The translation of *Alice* might have started and shaped Nabokov's tendency to bestow "on the characters of my novels some treasured item of my past," as he defined it in *Speak, Memory*.[165] The nostalgic theme of reliving one's childhood—fascination with their respective childhoods is a theme Nabokov shared with Carroll—accounts for the specific tangibility and concreteness of objects, transported from memory into Nabokov's texts and generously distributed among his characters. In his *Ania*, as Demurova observed in "Alice on the Other Shores,"[166] the treacle drawn by the three sisters in the Dormouse's story is replaced by the syrup of Nabokov's childhood—"patochnyi sirop" (treacle syrup) in the Russian version of Nabokov's memoir *Drugie berega*, and "Golden Syrup imported from London [that] would entwist with its glowing coils the revolving spoon" in *Speak, Memory*.[167]

In her essay "Lewis Carroll" (1939), Virginia Woolf wrote that childhood remained whole in Carroll, like a hard crystal in the jelly of life: "For some reason, we know not what, his childhood was sharply severed. It lodged in him whole and entire. He could not disperse it."[168] Nabokov's Russian past, "severed" in its entirety, turned into "intangible property, unreal estate";[169] it inhabited his fiction and the *Alice* translation alike. Many years later, Nabokov described *Alice* in an interview as "a specific book by a definite author with its own quaintness, is own quirks, its own quiddity. If read carefully, it will be seen to imply, by humorous juxtaposition, the presence of a quite solid, and rather sentimental, world, behind the semi-detached dream."[170]

Nabokov's translation of *Alice* is essentially paraphrastic (the term that he himself later used as an insult), in the Romantic sense of this word. Romantic irony, which underscores text as an artifice and reflects on its conventional nature, accounts for its essential aspatiality. Russification notwithstanding, Ania's wonderland is not Russian, not only because of its quaint and non-folkloric characters, nor because queens, duchesses, and judges in wigs are not typical Russian realia. Nor is this world English, for that matter. Its Gogolian mode combines the frivolous lucidity of "nonutilitarian and deceptive craftsmanship,"[171]—device for delight's sake—with a structure that has, as it does later in Nabokov's novels, ambiguous relations to what is "real." Drawing on Nabokov's metaphysics, Vladimir Alexandrov points out as a uniquely Nabokovian feature "the tantalizing possibility that there is only one correct way in which details can be connected, and one unique, global meaning that emerges from them. This follows from the fact that Nabokov elevates the creation of extraordinarily cunning puzzles to a fundamental esthetic principle, and draws explicit parallels between this literary tactic, the phenomenon of mimicry in nature, and the composition of chess problems."[172] Nabokov later defined Gogol's style as "the sensation of something ludicrous and at the same time stellar, lurking constantly around the corner," the difference between its comic and cosmic side depending "on one sibilant."[173] The non-space of Nabokov's Russian *Alice* derives from its atemporality (ahistoricity might be a better term), as a synthesis in a Hegelian triad, still tracing the "initial arc" of a Russian childhood (to paraphrase Nabokov's dialectical musings).

When as a young boy Nabokov discovered Hegel, he came to the very specific understanding of Hegel's triads as an expression of the "spirality" of things in relation to time and, as a consequence, to the understanding of memory and imagination as a negation of time. Nabokov wrote in *Speak, Memory*:

> The spiral is a spiritualized circle. In the spiral form, the circle, uncoiled, unwound, has ceased to be vicious; it has been set free. I thought this up when I was a schoolboy, and I also discovered that Hegel's triadic series (so popular in old Russia) expressed merely the essential spirality of all things in their relation to time. Twirl follows twirl, and every synthesis is the thesis of the next series. If we consider the simplest spiral, three stages may be distinguished in it, corresponding to those of the triad: we can call "thetic" the small curve or arc that initiates the convolution centrally; "antithetic" the larger arc that faces the first in the process of continuing it; and "synthetic" the still ampler arc that continues the second while following the first along the outer side. And so on.[174]

Time, defined by Hegel in *Philosophy of Nature* as the self-negating of space itself,[175] is not a form of intuition, as in Immanuel Kant, but an abstract, ideal being, "becoming directly intuited."[176] Place, however, is a spatial point enduring through time.[177] The Hegelian principle of sublation (negation of negation) underlies the dialectic found everywhere in Nabokov's fiction. In *Speak, Memory*, he describes his own life in these terms: the thetic arc of his Russian childhood, the antithesis of his European exile, and—negating the negation—the stage of synthesis, his life in his "adopted country," and, consequently, a new thesis.[178] This disbelief in time is more straightforwardly (but without references to Hegel) expressed in the Russian version of Nabokov's memoir, *Drugie berega* (*The Other Shores* in English, 1954, the revised version of *Conclusive Evidence*, 1951):

> I confess I don't believe in the flying of Time—the light, liquid, Persian time! I learned to fold this magic carpet in such a fashion that one pattern would concur with the other. . . . And the utmost delectation for me—outside the diabolic time but very much inside the divine space—is a landscape selected at random, it

does not matter where, be it tundra or steppe, or even among the remains of some old pine grove by the railway between Albany and Schenectady, dead in this present context (where one of my favorite godchildren is flying, my blue *samuelis*)—in other words, any corner of this earth where I can be among butterflies and the plants they feed on. This is the ecstasy, and behind this ecstasy there is something that resists definition. It is something like an instantaneous void into which everything I love in this world is emptied out to fill it in. Something like an instantaneous flutter of tenderness and gratitude, addressed, as American letters of reference say, "to whom it may concern"—I don't know to whom or to what, be it the human fate's counterpoint of genius or benevolent spirits, spoiling their earthly pet.[179]

Extended from the realm of fate to that of art, the sublation principle defines Nabokov's antipathy to a thetic solution. A passage in *Speak, Memory*, absent in the Russian memoir, describes Nabokov's completion of a chess problem that formally concluded the antithesis of his European exile: an elegant problem designed for the delectation of a sophisticated connoisseur. The unsophisticated solver would go for an illusory reality of a "fairly simple, 'thetic' solution," while the sophisticated one would pass through the "'antithetic' inferno . . . as somebody on a wild goose chase might go from Albany to New York by way of Vancouver, Eurasia, and the Azores." The experience compensates for the "misery of deceit, and, after that, his arrival at the simple key move would provide him with a synthesis of poignant artistic delight."[180]

Whether the actual chess problem was real or fictional (the surgical precision of the details makes one suspicious), this passage, almost at the conclusion of the memoir, reads as an artistic manifesto. Nabokov's penchant to impart distinctive traits of his own artistic personality even to his villains, thus probing the nature of evil by infinitely stretching its borders, reveals the same Hegelian pattern of tongue-in-cheek humor. Thus Rex (Gorn), the evil caricaturist of *Laughter in the Dark* (1938; revised, 1960), "a very fine artist indeed," is characterized by "the Hegelian syllogism of humor": "Thesis: Uncle made himself up as a burglar (a laugh for the children); antithesis: it was a burglar (a laugh for the reader); synthesis: it still was Uncle (fooling the reader)."[181]

Disbelief in time was carefully suppressed in Nabokov's translations after *Alice* (especially when he arrived at literalness) but loomed large in his fiction: his interference into his own texts (thus, according to Alexandrov, redefining nature and artifice "into synonyms for each other");[182] his bestowing his characters with immortality once their personal metaphysical intuitions failed them; the characters' engagement in quite Hegelian "creative destruction" in philosophy (e.g. Krug in *Bend Sinister*); and, finally, in *Ada*, addressing the topic head-on.[183]

The game of nonsense as a principle of *Alice*, according to Elizabeth Sewell, realizes and suspends the two opposite tendencies of chaos and order, bringing them into an endless interplay and leading both of the *Alice* books to their seemingly arbitrary endings.[184] Beginning with his translation of *Alice*, games become the dominating structural principle in Nabokov's novels. The title of *King, Queen, Knave* suggests a game of cards and refers back to *Alice* and its "characters without thickness" ("those three court cards, all hearts," as Nabokov slyly states in his preface).[185] Bukhs convincingly argues that *King, Queen, Knave* is constructed according to a waltz principle. The rules of the dance are the rules of the game, in which all characters are players.[186] In *The Defense* (*Zashchita Luzhina*, 1930), Nabokov's third Russian novel, the game is chess. It is important that the element of dream versus reality becomes a leitmotif of Nabokov's fiction, whose characters seek to escape (Ganin, Martin Edelweiss), to find a window or a brilliant move (Luzhin), a hole, an opening in the closed structure of the narrative, which would allow them some sovereignty from the conceit of the author-magician. Alice's adventures, as Gilles Deleuze argued, are "but *one* big adventure: her rising to the surface, her disavowal of the false depths, and her discovery that everything happens on the borderline."[187] We know that Alice breaks out by waking up, but the uncertainty of "which dreamed it" is pervasive in *Through the Looking Glass*: the sequence of the Red King dreaming of Alice within Alice's own dream opens up a vertigo of mirrored reflections. The possible derivation of the finale of *Priglashenie na kazn* (1935; *Invitation to a Beheading*, 1959) from the scene of Alice's awakening from her dream has been noted by scholars more than once.[188]

The endless suspense of the struggle between chaos and order in nonsense, which involves the process of selection and organization of the material into detailed yet abstract systems "on the borderline" of language, has a certain kinship to the principle of fantastic literature. Tzvetan Todorov, defining the concept of the fantastic in relation to the real and the imaginary, notes that "the fantastic occupies the duration of . . . uncertainty . . . that hesitation experienced by a person who knows only the laws of nature, confronting an apparently supernatural event."[189] Uncertainty, the hesitation between the author-magician's scheme and the characters' independence, between dream and reality, accounts for the additional fantastic level of Nabokov's early novels. Thus, the characters and drama of *King, Queen, Knave* might be, in fact, the mere sleight of hand of a mad old landlord, who fancied himself a magician named Pharsin in the English version and, characteristically, Menetekelperes in the Russian version—a preview of McFate and a reference to the writing on the wall at the feast of king Belshazzar in the Old Testament ("Mene, Mene, Tekel, Upharsin"—hence the English name "Pharsin").[190] Luzhin evaporates in the chasm of a chessboard in the finale of *The Defense*. Martin Edelweiss, in *Glory*, crossing the border into Zoorland, virtually disappears on a path into a dark forest in a picture on the nursery wall. Connolly observes that "fairy-tale elements occur frequently in Nabokov's work" (one of the examples he cites is the inversion of a folktale plot in *King, Queen, Knave*—the transformation in Frantz's eyes of Martha, Frantz's lover, into a toad, as his infatuation with her dwindles).[191] Nabokov, when teaching world literature, often referred to all great novels as fairy tales.

Finally, translating Carroll's wordplay, punning, and portmanteau words was good practice—the stretching and flexing of literary muscles—for the appropriation of these devices in his own technique. The Duchess calls her crying baby a pig, and the metaphor is realized in his transformation into a real pig.[192] Similarly, Carroll's characters "realize" their names: thus the Knave of Hearts realizes his name ("knave" as "villain" or "rascal").[193] The literal realization of a metaphor, Carroll's favorite device, becomes a plot point in Nabokov's *Mashenka* (absent in the English translation, *Mary*): Podtyagin, an old Russian émigré poet, going through the torturous process of getting a visa to leave Berlin, triumphantly claims that "delo v shliape" (literally, "the thing is in the hat" or "it's in the bag now," as it was translated in *Mary*).[194] On the way to the French embassy, he grabs for his hat as it is blown off by the wind, losing his precious passport and, consequently, his life.[195] Zoorland/ Russia in *Glory* is a scary fairy tale "where plump children are tortured in the dark,"[196] and its toponyms are the literal realizations of metaphors: "Rezhitsa" and "Pytalovo" in Russian, they are carefully rendered in English as "Carnagore" and "Torturovka."[197] Portmanteau words become a recurrent device in Nabokov's proper names. In the Russian version of *Glory*, the name of Alla's deceived husband, Chernosvitov, shown shaving in the morning, and his tacky joke about "pryshchemor," a "pimplekill face cream,"[198] form a portmanteau word that is the proper name and the parodic literary origin of the character (Chernomor, the enamored and deceived evil magician in Pushkin's *Ruslan and Liudmila*).[199]

Having already mentioned some of Nabokov's changes to Carroll's text, I would like finally to mention Nabokov's insertions into Carroll's text, since they provide a preview of some of the signature characteristics of his future style. The unexpected "aprelskie utochki" (April little ducks) among the members of the jury[200] in the trial scene might be part of the "intangible estate" of childhood already mentioned above, perhaps some treasured Easter toys. There are other instances in which the insertion of a detail, absent in Carroll's version, is for the sake of idiosyncratic precision: "golubenkie oboi" (the "light-blue wallpaper") in the Rabbit's house,[201] and "goriashchie volchi glaza" ("the burning wolverine eyes") of the Queen.[202] Such insertions should not be surprising when one remembers Nabokov's concern for detail in his fiction: sometimes sheerly delightful, sometimes reaching the level of "crazy ingenuity," in the words of Michael Wood.[203]

As it often happens in translation, the idiosyncratic eccentricities of the original, refracted and reflected through the prism of another language and the congenial talent of the translator, made Nabokov's own idiosyncrasies loom large. The last two of Nabokov's insertions into Carroll's text would otherwise remain quite unmotivated.

Alice's sister pictures how Alice, a "grown woman," would amuse other children with her adventures, "remembering her own child-life and the happy summer days."[204] Nabokov replaces Carroll's two neutral attributes with three three-syllable adjectives separated by the languid pause of a comma: "dlinnye, sladkie letnie dni" ("long, sweet summer days," a dactylic line). Since the Russian attribute "sladkii," when denoting things other than taste, resonates with lingering nostalgia, the last sentence of Nabokov's *Ania* acquires a prolonged quality, a continuum, a *durée*, both elegiac and personal, that Carroll's last passage suppressed but probably suggested. Shortly before the end, Alice's older sister envisions her little sister in her dream: "once again the tiny hands were clasped upon her knee."[205] The unexpected eroticism of Ania's "tonkie ruki, obkhvativshie goloe koleno"[206] in Nabokov's translation—her "thin arms clasping around her bare knee"—sends distant regards to the many underage heroines of Nabokov's fiction and, eventually, to Lolita.

## NOTES

1    Brian Boyd, *Vladimir Nabokov: The Russian Years* (Princeton: Princeton University Press, 1990), 197.

2    Liuis Kerroll [Lewis Carroll], *Ania v strane chudes*, perevod V. Sirina (V. Nabokov); illiustratsii S. Zalshupina (Berlin: Izdatelstvo "Gamaiun," 1923).

3    Lewis Carroll, *Alice's Adventures in Wonderland*, illustrated by J. Tenniel/ *Ania v strane chudes*, perevod V. Nabokova; risunki L. Kerrolla, vstupitelnaia statia i kommentarii k tekstu N. Demurovoi (Moscow: Raduga, 1992). All references to Nabokov's translation and Carroll's original hereafter will be from this edition. All quotations will be noted as *"Alice/Ania"* with a page number.

4    See Warren Weaver, *Alice in Many Tongues: The Translations of "Alice in Wonderland"* (Madison: University of Wisconsin Press, 1964).

5    Nina M. Demurova, "Golos i skripka. (K perevodu ektsentricheskikh skazok Liuisa Kerrolla)," *Materstvo perevoda*, sb. 7 (1970): 159. Nina Demurova, Russian translator and scholar, published her own translation of *Alice* in 1967: Liuis Kerroll, *Prikliucheniia Alisy v strane chudes. Skvoz zerkalo i chto tam uvidela Alisa ili Alisa v zazerkale*, perevod N. M. Demurovoi, stikhi v perevode S. Ia. Marshaka i D. T. Orlovskoi (Sofia: Izdatelstvo literatury na inostrannykh iazykakh, 1967).

The second version of her translation was brought out in the series "Literary Landmarks" by Nauka publishing company in Moscow in 1978. However, mostly for ideological reasons, Nauka suppressed some of the appended materials that later appeared in the second amended edition: Liuis Kerroll, *Prikliucheniia Alisy v strane chudes. Skvoz zerkalo i chto tam uvidela Alisa ili Alisa v zazerkale*, perevod N. M. Demurovoi, stikhi v perevode S. Ia. Marshaka, D. T. Orlovskoi i O. A. Sedakovoi; illustratsii Dzh. Tenniela (Moscow: Nauka, 1990).

Among the previously suppressed materials were essays by W. H. Auden, J. B. Priestly, excerpts from Elizabeth Sewell's *The Field of Nonsense*, and Demurova's own page in which she "compared the end of the Wonderland trial scene with the final pages of Nabokov's *Invitation to a Beheading*, seeking to establish a similarity, and, perhaps, an influence" (cited in Nina M. Demurova, "Alice Speaks Russian: The Russian Translations of Alice's Adventures in Wonderland and Through the Looking Glass," *Harvard Literary Bulletin* 5.4 [Winter 1994-1995]: 19). Demurova points out that she was able to draw this comparison only in her Foreword to the Raduga Publishing two-language edition of *Alice* (in Sirin/Nabokov's translation), "Alice on the Other Shores" (an obvious reference to the Russian title of Nabokov's memoir). See N. M. Demurova, "Alisa na drugikh beregakh," *Alice/Ania*, 7-28. More recently, Demurova's analysis of Nabokov's translation appeared as an article: Nina Demurova, "Vladimir Nabokov, Translator of Lewis Carroll's Alice in Wonderland," in *Nabokov at Cornell*, ed. Gavriel Shapiro (Ithaca and London: Cornell University Press, 2003), 182-191.

6   To name just one, the Pigeon who accuses little girls of being snakes because, like girls, they also eat eggs, in Nabokov's version is male: his sitting on eggs is certainly comic, from an ornithological point of view. Nabokov also shifts from formal to informal "you" within one dialogue without any psychological reason for such change (*Alice/Ania*, 206).

7   Vladimir Nabokov, "Translator's Foreword," in Mikhail Lermontov, *A Hero of Our Time*, trans. Vladimir Nabokov in collaboration with Dmitri Nabokov (Ann Arbor: Ardis, 1988), xiii, xix.

8   A. N. Rozhdestvenskaia, *Prikliucheniia Alisy v strane chudes. Zadushevnoe slovo* 49, issues 1-7; 9-21; 22-33.

9   The editions used for reference hereafter are: *Sonia v tsarstve diva* (Moscow: Tipografiia A. Mamontova i Ko., Montievskii per. d. 3, 1879); M. Granstrem (trans.), *Prikliucheniia Ani v mire chudes*, sostavleno po L. Karroliu M. Granstrem (St. Petersburg: Izdatelstvo E. A. Granstrem, 1908); A. N. Rozhdestvenskaia (trans.), *Prikliucheniia Alisy v strane chudes Liuisa Kerrolia*, perevod A. N. Rozh-destvenskoi s predisloviem i vstupitelnoi statei (St. Petersburg and Moscow: Izdanie t-va M. O. Volf, bez daty [no date]); and Allegro (Poliksena Solovieva) (trans.), *Alisa v strane chudes*, *Tropinka* 2-5, 7-15, 17, 19-20 (January–March 1909; April–July 1909; September 1909; October 1909). All quotations

from these editions will be noted hereafter in the notes by a reference to, respectively, *Sonia*, Granstrem, Rozhdestvenskaia, and Allegro with a page number.

10 Nina Demurova mentions a "minor sensation" in 1990 when a Moscow mathematician, A. M. Rushailo, discovered a "hitherto unknown translation of *Alice*." It was published as a supplement to the children's magazine *Zolotoe detstvo* (The Gold Childhood) without the title of the magazine, name of publisher or illustrator, and publication date. Since then the illustrator has been identified as Harry Furness and the translation dated late 1913-early 1914. The name of the translator remains a mystery, though Rushailo suggested it might be Mikhail Chekhov, the younger brother of the writer Anton Chekhov, who was both a publisher of and contributor to the magazine and often translated from English and French. See Nina M. Demurova, "Alice Speaks Russian," 14; also see A. M. Rushailo, "Iubilei *Alisy v strane chudes*," in *Prikliucheniia Alisy v strane chudes* (1990), v-vi.

11 See Simon Karlinsky, "Anya in Wonderland: Nabokov's Russified Lewis Carroll," *TriQuarterly* 17 (Winter 1970): 310-315.

12 See Nabokov, *Selected Letters*, 519.

13 Efim Etkind, *Poeziia i perevod* (Moscow and Leningrad: Sovetskii pisatel, 1963), 347.

14 Poliksena Sergeevna Solovieva (1867-1924) was a daughter of the historian S. M. Soloviev and sister of the poet and philosopher Vladimir Sergeevich Soloviev. Together with N. Manaseina, she published the children's magazine *Tropinka* (24 issues per year) from 1906 to 1912. The body of contributors and illustrators of *Tropinka* is a constellation of names important to Russian culture: Zinaida Vengerova, Aleksandr Blok, Dmitrii Merezhkovskii, Zinaida Gippius, Sergei Gorodetskii, Viacheslav Ivanov, Aleksandr Kuprin, Fedor Sologub, Aleksei Tolstoi, Vsevolod Uspenskii, and Kornei Chukovskii formed part of the "literature department" of *Tropinka*. Such important artists as Mikhail Nesterov, Elizaveta Kruglikova, and Mariia Sabashnikova contributed to the "art department." Solovieva (Allegro), herself a poet, contributed her own verse to *Tropinka*. Issues 21-22 (1909), for example, contain her own (mediocre) tale in verse, "The Little Birch Tree's Birthday."

15 Julian W. Connolly, *Nabokov's Early Fiction: Patterns of Self and Other* (Cambridge: Cambridge University Press, 1992), 314.

16 Julian W. Connolly, "*Ania v strane chudes*," in *The Garland Companion to Vladimir Nabokov*, 19.

17 This has been observed by Julian W. Connolly with, in his turn, reference to the observations of Gennady Barabtarlo. Connolly calls Nabokov's *Ania* an "adaptation" or "transposition" (*perelozhenie*). See Connolly, "*Ania v strane chudes*," 19.

18 *Mashenka* (*Mary*, 1970) was written in 1925 and published in 1926, soon to be followed by *Korol, dama, valet*, 1928 (trans. as *King, Queen, Knave*, 1968).

19   Gilles Deleuze, *What is Philosophy?*, trans. Hugh Tomlinson and Graham Burchell (New York: Columbia University Press, 1994), 54, 58.

20   Gilles Deleuze, "The Schizophrenic and Language: Surface and Depth in Lewis Carroll and Antonin Artaud," in *Textual Strategies: Perspectives in Post-Structuralist Criticism* (Ithaca: Cornell University Press, 1979), 280.

21   Deleuze, "The Schizophrenic and Language," 285.

22   Jean-Clet Martin, "The Eye of the Outside," in *Deleuze: A Critical Reader*, ed. Paul Patton (Oxford: Blackwell Publishers, 1996), 19.

23   Cited in Deleuze, "The Schizophrenic and Language," 283.

24   See Boyd, *Vladimir Nabokov: The Russian Years*, 257.

25   See Gleb Struve, *Slavonic and East-European Review* (1934): 436-44. Cited in Norman Page (ed.), *Nabokov: The Critical Heritage* (London, Boston, Melbourne and Henley: Routledge and Kegan Paul, 1982), 49.

26   Gleb Struve, *Russkaia literatura v izgnanii* (Parizh: YMCA-Press, 1965), 279.

27   See Karlinsky, "Anya in Wonderland: Nabokov's Russified Lewis Carroll"; and Connolly, "*Ania v strane chudes.*"

28   Demurova, "Alice Speaks Russian," 13.

29   Rozhdestvenskaia, iv.

30   Ibid.

31   Ibid., 29.

32   Ibid., 52.

33   Ibid., 31.

34   Ibid., 24.

35   *Alice/Ania*, 262-263.

36   Allegro, 599.

37   Ibid., 292-293. Nabokov, no doubt, would not miss a chance to define the mushroom's species and genus with torturous precision, as he did in Chapter Two of his *Speak, Memory*: baby *edulis*, genus *Boletus*.

38   *Alice/Ania*, 202-204. Nabokov puns here on "ugrevatyi nos" (nose strewn with blackheads) and "ugr" (the eel that the old uncle, to the surprise of his inquisitive nephew, managed to balance on the end of his "ugrevatyi nos"). "Ugr'" means both a "blackhead" and an "eel."

39   Ibid., 218.

40   *Sonia*, 18.

41   Connolly, "*Ania v strane chudes,*" 20.

42   Demurova, "Alice Speaks Russian," 20.

43   Allegro, 158.

44   Ibid., 162.

45   Rozhdestvenskaia, 52.

46   *Alice/Ania*, 86.

47   Allegro, 330, and Rozhdestvenskaia, 110. Connolly praises a later translator of *Alice*, Aleksandr Shcherbakov, for finding a neat solution for the "axis/axes" pun (Connolly, "*Ania v strane chudes,*" 22), yet his "vam-to pora/topora" (it's

time for you/ an axe) seems to be merely a modification of Rozhdestvenskaia's and Allegro's solution.

48  See Zinaida Vengerova, "O tom, kto napisal 'Alisu'," *Tropinka* 22 (November 1909): 825. Translation is mine.

49  Ronald Reichertz, *The Making of the "Alice" Books: Lewis Carroll's Uses of Earlier Children's Literature* (Montreal, Kingston, London, and Buffalo: McGill-Queen University Press, 1997), 21.

50  Ibid., 22.

51  See Iurii Lotman, *Besedy o russkoi kulture: Byt i traditsii russkogo dvorianstva XVIII-nachala XIX veka* (St. Petersburg: Iskusstvo—SPb, 1994), 62.

52  *Plutarkha Khersoneiskogo o detovodstve, ili vospitanii detei nastavlenie. Perevedennoe s ellino-grecheskogo iazyka S[tepanom] P[isarevym]* (SPb [St. Petersburg], 1771).

53  Lotman, *Besedy o russkoi kulture*, 62.

54  Diana Greene, "Mid-Nineteenth-Century Domestic Ideology in Russia," in *Women and Russian Culture: Projections and Self-Perceptions*, ed. Rosalind Marsh (New York and Oxford: Berghahn Books, 1998), 79.

55  Ibid., 92-93.

56  *Speak, Memory*, 76.

57  Ibid.

58  ". . . his mother loathed the Russian magazine for children *Zadushevnoe slovo* (The Heartfelt Word), and inspired in him such aversion for Madame Charski's young heroines with dusky complexions and titles that even much later Martin was wary of any book written by a woman, sensing even in the best of such books an unconscious urge on the part of a middle-aged and perhaps chubby lady to dress up in a pretty name and curl up on the sofa like a pussy cat.... Russian children's literature swarmed with cute lisping words, when not committing the sin of moralizing." See Vladimir Nabokov, *Glory*, trans. Dmitri Nabokov in collaboration with the author (New York: Vintage International, 1991), 3.

59  M. O. Volf, Tovarishchestvo, *Polnyi katalog izdanii tovarishchestva 1853-1905*; Tovarishchestvo M. O. Volf, *Sistematicheskii katalog noveishikh knig po belletristike i vsem otrasliam znaniia* (St. Petersburg and Moscow, 1913).

60  Ibid., 221.

61  Greene, "Mid-Nineteenth-Century Domestic Ideology in Russia," 86.

62  Ibid., 84-87.

63  See M. I. Fundaminskii, "O pervykh detskikh entsiklopediiakh v Rossii," *Kniga v Rossii XVII—nachala XIX v. Problemy sozdaniia i rasprostraneniia* (Leningrad: Biblioteka Akademii Nauk SSSR, 1989), 146. For more details on Russian encyclopedias for children, see V. Iu. Kirianova, "Detskaia entsiklopedicheskaia kniga v dorevoliutsionnoi Rossii," *Sovetskaia pedagogika* 10 (1984): 198-112; and N. V. Chekhov and A. K. Pokrovskii, *Materialy po istorii russkoi detskoi literatury (1750-1855)*, vypusk 1 (Moscow: Institut metodov vneshkolnoi raboty, 1927).

64 Fundaminskii, "O pervykh detskikh entsiklopediiakh v Rossii," 156.

65 *Tropinka* 17 (September 1909).

66 Granstrem, 9.

67 Karlinsky, "Anya in Wonderland," 311.

68 Granstrem, 20. All "re-translations" into English are mine.

69 In line with the self-congratulatory turn of the educational system to the pre-revolutionary past in Russia in the 1990s, excerpts of this text were reintroduced into the literature curriculum of many Russian *lycées*. See, for example, N. N. Tolokonnikov, sostavitel, *Kolosok: Kniga dlia vneklassnogo chteniia v nachal'noi shkole*. Vtoroi klass (Moscow: Bukman, 1996), 49-54.

70 Granstrem, 53.

71 Ibid., 58.

72 Ibid., 161.

73 Ibid., 79.

74 Reichertz, *The Making of the "Alice" Books*, 32.

75 Zhukovskii's "Liudmila" and Katenin's "Olga," 1808 and 1816 respectively, can be termed as "translations" of Gottfried August Bürger's "Lenore" only very loosely. Russified heroines of the ballads dictated the Russification of other realia. Thus the betrothed of Katenin's Olga sets out to join Peter the Great's army.

76 Susan Bassnett-McGuire, *Translation Studies* (London and New York: Methuen, 1980), 71.

77 Ibid., 73.

78 Weaver, *Alice in Many Tongues*, 60-61. Since then, a copy of this edition has been acquired by the Fales Library of New York University.

79 Simon Karlinsky, in his essay on Nabokov's *Ania*, calls Weaver's misinterpretation of the title "a rather lame exegesis" (Karlinsky, "Anya in Wonderland," 315). However, ironically, Karlinsky misinterpreted it even further as *Son v tsarstve detstva* ("A Dream in the Kingdom of *Childhood*"). See ibid.

80 See John Francis McDermott (ed.), *The Russian Journal and Other Selections from the Works of Lewis Carroll* (New York: E. P. Dutton & Co, 1935). Of his impressions of Russian children, Carroll writes: "After the Russian children, whose type of face is ugly as a rule, and plain as an exception, it is quite a relief to get back among the Germans and their large eyes and delicate features" (cited in Morton N. Cohen, *Lewis Carroll: A Biography* [London: Paremac, an imprint of Macmillan Publishers Ltd, 1995], 271).

81 D. M. Urnov, a Russian scholar, wrote: "Who was it? Possibly Olga Ivanovna Timiriaseva, cousin to K. A. Timiriasev, the well-known scientist. Her brother left a memoir in which he tells us about their family, who were on good terms with Pushkin and his circle. He says that in his childhood he and his sister read much in European languages, English included, the books being selected by Zhukovsky himself. Indeed, *Sonia in the Kingdom of Wonder* follows the tradition of the literary fairy tale which was started by Pushkin

and Zhukovsky" (cited in Demurova, "Alice Speaks Russian," 11). See also D. Urnov, "Put k russkim chitateliam," posleslovie k knige Dzh. Viterikh (John T. Winterich), *Prikliucheniia znamenitykh knig*, sokrashchennyi perevod s angliiskogo E. Skavaiers (Moscow: Kniga, 1955), 219-233.

82  See Maurice Friedberg, *Literary Translation in Russia: A Cultural History* (University Park: Pennsylvania State University Press, 1997), 61-62.

83  Ibid., 62.

84  See Kornei Chukovskii, *Vysokoe iskusstvo: O printsipakh khudozhestvennogo perevoda* (Moscow: Iskusstvo, 1964), 294. Also see Friedberg, *Literary Translation in Russia*, 62.

85  Kornei Chukovskii and Andrei Fedorov, *Iskusstvo perevoda* (Leningrad: Akademiia, 1930), 27. Also see Friedberg, *Literary Translation in Russia*, 62.

86  *Sonia*, 109.

87  Fan Parker, *Lewis Carroll in Russia: Translations of Alice in Wonderland 1879-1989* (New York: Russian House Ltd, 1994). The book makes the astonishing claim that all of the translations she discusses, including Nabokov's, were "individual expressions and did not exemplify any particular theories of translation" (ibid., 4). Parker dismisses Demurova's outstanding translation as "plebian in tone and nuance, the choice of words and idioms taken solely from poor Soviet stock" (ibid., 32). Parker's attacks on Demurova seem too personal and unsubstantiated for the "first critical study of the Russian translations of *Alice*," which she claims her book to be (ibid., 3). Her argument is reduced to rhetorical laments about the "vulgarization and impoverishment of the Russian language during the decades of Soviet rule" (ibid., 32) and such claims as "though impossible to convey to the non-reader of Russian, the banality of her [Demurova's] translation is overwhelming" (ibid., 34). However, in the only two instances she adduces to substantiate these claims, she is either unconvincing or simply wrong. Parker claims that the use of the informal *ty* (second person singular) instead of the formal *vy* (equivalent to the French *vous*) diminishes Alice's status as a person. Meanwhile, other translations (among them Nabokov's, which Parker praises unreservedly) are far less consistent in the use of either of the forms. Nabokov himself shifts inexplicably from the formal to the informal form. In the other instance, when Parker tries to prove the alleged vulgarity of Demurova's translation, she seems to be unaware that the Russian verb *rugat* may mean not only "to swear" (which of course would be quite incompatible with a proper English miss), but also "to reprimand" or "to scold" (ibid., 35).

88  Ibid., 9.

89  Ibid., 10.

90  Ivan Krylov, the famous nineteenth-century fabulist, makes extensive use of *skaz* in reworking La Fontaine's fables. His fables were staple reading for school children; that is, they belonged to the not yet fully developed "children's literature." When one takes a close look at the narrator's voice

in his canonic fables, like "The Crow and the Fox," one sees the model and inspiration for the translator of *Sonia*: "Vdrug syrnyi dukh Lisu ostanovil:/ Lisitsa vidit syr.—Lisitsu syr plenil./ Plutovka k derevu na tsypochkakh podkhodit;/ Vertit khvostom, s Vorony glaz ne svodit/ I govorit tak sladko, chut dysha:/ Golobushka, kak khorosha!" See I. A. Krylov, *Basni* (Moscow: Detgiz, 1951), 5. Cf. the following passage about Sonia's discovering of the mushroom: "Sonia poshla, gliadit po storonam; to podoidet k tsvetku, osmotrit listia, to zaglianet v travu,—net nichego i pokhozhego, chto mozhhno bylo siest. Idet dalshe, vidit pered neiu sidit grib, kak raz s nee rostom; ona oboshla krugom griba, vnimatelno osmotrela ego, zaglianula emu pod shapochku." (*Sonia*, 52). That Krylov was very much on the translator's mind is confirmed later in the text when, ultimately defeated in his/her struggle with the original, the translator cancels the "trial scene" of the last chapter by merely quoting Krylov's fable "The Quartet" (*Sonia*, 163).

91   *Sonia*, 1.
92   Ibid., 3.
93   Ibid., 8.
94   Ibid., 9.
95   Ibid., 22.
96   Ibid., 42.
97   Ibid., 11.
98   Ibid., 63.
99   Ibid., 43.
100  Ibid., 8.
101  Ibid., 90.
102  Ibid., 51.
103  Ibid., 11.
104  Ibid., 17.
105  Ibid.
106  Ibid., 106.
107  Ibid., 8.
108  Ibid., 17.
109  Ibid., 7.
110  Ibid., 163.
111  The "crossed-eyed hare." The word *kosoi* in a certain context may come close to the madness attributed to the March Hare: it might be associated with the state of drunkenness.
112  It is interesting that Nabokov, rendering the Mock-Turtle's song about the soup of the evening (Carroll's parody of "Star of the Evening," words and music by James M. Sayles), resorts to another regionalism: *lokhan*—without a soft sign in the end of the word and masculine instead of the feminine *lokhan'*, with a soft sign (*Alice/Ania*, 263).

113 *Sonia*, 10.

114 Ibid., 72.

115 *Alice/Ania*, 83. In *Sonia*: "A ia prosizhu zdes i nyne, i zavtra i vo veki vekov" (77), which corresponds to "I nyne, i prisno i vo veki vekov"—"Now and always and eternally"—chanted by the deacon at the end of Holy Communion.

116 *Sonia*, 97.

117 Cited in V. Zhirmunskii, *Gete v russkoi literature* (Leningrad: Nauka, 1981), 138.

118 *Sonia*, 22-23.

119 Ibid., 24.

120 Ibid., 39.

121 Ibid., 40.

122 *Alice/Ania*, 65.

123 Reichertz, *The Making of the "Alice" Books*, 47-48.

124 *Sonia*, 44-45.

125 Ibid., 49.

126 Friedberg, *Literary Translation in Russia*, 39.

127 In her Foreword to the Raduga edition, "Alice on the Other Shores," Demurova writes: "Nabokov addressed his translation to children and, most certainly, did not even think that many things in this funny children's book could be understood only by well-educated adults and experts" (Translation is mine; see in *Alice/Ania*, 22).

128 Zinaida Shakhovskaia, "Nabokov v zhizni," in *In Search of Nabokov*, 14.

129 Weaver, *Alice in Many Tongues*, 80-81.

130 See Demurova, "Golos i skripka," 173-185.

131 Ibid., 174.

132 Vladislav Khodasevich, "O Sirine," *Vozrozhdenie* (Paris, 1937). Cited in Vladislav Khodasevich, "On Sirin," trans. Michael H. Walker, ed. Simon Karlinsky and Robert P. Hughes, *TriQuarterly* 17 (Winter 1970): 97.

133 Ibid., 96.

134 *Alice/Ania*, 185.

135 Karlinsky, "Anya in Wonderland: Nabokov's Russified Lewis Carroll," 313; Connolly, "Ania v strane chudes," 19.

136 *Alice/Ania*, 216.

137 Ibid., 217.

138 Ibid., 249.

139 Cf. Freud's *Fehlleistungen*—literally, "faulty acts" or "faulty functions"—parapraxes, one of the earliest subjects of Freud's psychological investigations (mishearings, missayings, misreadings, slips of the pen, slips of the tongue). See lectures II, III, and IV in S. Freud, *Introductory Lectures on Psychoanalysis*, trans. and ed. James Strachey (New York: W. W. Norton & Company, Inc., 1966), 25-79.

140 *Alice/Ania*, 180-181.

141 Ibid., 238.

142  Vladimir Nabokov, *The Annotated Lolita*, ed. with preface, introduction and notes by Alfred Appel, Jr. (New York and Toronto: McGraw-Hill Book Company, 1970), 129.

143  *Alice/Ania*, 123.

144  Ibid., 253.

145  Ibid., 253 (Russian); 123 (English).

146  Ibid., 253.

147  *Sonia*, 141.

148  Allegro, 598.

149  *Alice/Ania*, 249.

150  Nora Buks [Bukhs], *Eshafot v khrustalnom dvortse: O russkikh romanakh Vladimira Nabokova* (Moscow: Novoe literaturnoe obozrenie, 1998), 60. See also Nora Bukhs, "Sur la Structure du Roman de V. Nabokov 'Roi, Dame, Valet,'" *Revue des Etudes Slaves* [Paris], 59-4 (1987): 799-810.

151  Vladimir Nabokov, *Mary* (New York: McGraw-Hill, 1970), xii.

152  Ibid., xiii.

153  Buks [Bukhs], *Eshafot v khrustalnom dvortse*, 35.

154  Ibid., 36.

155  Ibid., 39.

156  *Mary*, 52.

157  *Glory*, xi.

158  Buks [Bukhs], *Eshafot v khrustalnom dvortse*, 61-70.

159  *Alice/Ania*, 138. As we know, the date of the mad tea party Alice attends is May 4, Alice Liddell's birthday: Carroll, in his best book, also coded a lot of biographical information on the subjects concerned.

160  Ibid., 138.

161  See Nikolai Gogol, *The Complete Tales of Nikolai Gogol*, vol. 1, ed. and rev. Leonard J. Kent, trans. Constance Garnett (Chicago and London: University of Chicago Press, 1985), 253.

162  *Alice/Ania*, 268.

163  Ibid., 146.

164  Ibid., 275.

165  *Speak, Memory*, 95.

166  *Alice/Ania*, 27-28.

167  *Speak, Memory*, 79.

168  Virginia Woolf, "Lewis Carroll," in *The Moment, Collected Essays*, vol. 1 (New York: Harcourt Brace & World, Inc., 1967), 254.

169  *Speak, Memory*, 40.

170  *Strong Opinions*, 184. Nabokov might have been describing himself. It is rather interesting that some of Nabokov's critics, such as G. Struve, for example, pointed out his "uncharacteristic cloying sentimentality" in everything that had to do with reminiscences of his childhood. See G. Struve, *Russkaia literature v izgnanii*, cited in *Vladimir Nabokov: Pro et Contra*, 281.

192  *Alice/Ania,* 89.
193  See Demurova's commentary in *Alice/Ania,* 302.
194  *Mary,* 80.
195  See in Buks [Bukhs], *Eshafot v khrustalnom dvortse,* 20.
196  *Glory,* 150.
197  Ibid., 177.
198  Ibid., 31.
199  This was pointed out by Bukhs, *Eshafot v khrustalnom dvortse,* 79.
200  *Alice/Ania,* 274.
201  Ibid., 186. It is interesting, though the connection might be completely coincidental, that Magda/Margot, in *Camera obscura/Laughter in the Dark,* describes "the blue wallpaper" to her blind deceived lover, intentionally changing all colors in another house in which things are not what they seem.
202  Ibid., 237.
203  Michael Wood, *The Magician's Doubts: Nabokov and the Risks of Fiction* (Princeton: Princeton University Press, 1995), 58.
204  *Alice/Ania,* 154.
205  Ibid., 152.
206  Ibid., 281.

171 Vladimir Alexandrov, *Nabokov's Otherworld* (Princeton: Princeton University Press, 1991), 17.

172 Ibid., 14-15. It is interesting that Sergei Eisenstein, reflecting on the structure of his work, took much interest in the passage in his friend Lev Vygotskii's *The Psychology of Art*, "in which the author develops the idea of the great Russian philologist Potebnia that, in the fable, each hero (animal) is univocally defined and functions like a chessman, i.e., he is limited to certain types of moves." See V. V. Ivanov, "Functions and Categories of Film Language," trans. Stephen Rudy, *Film Theory and General Semiotics: Poetics in Translation* 8 (1981): 5.

173 Vladimir Nabokov, *Nikolai Gogol* (New York: New Directions, 1978), 141.

174 *Speak, Memory*, 275.

175 G. W. F. Hegel, *Philosophy of Nature. Being: Part Two of the Encyclopaedia of the Philosophical Sciences* (1830), trans. A. V. Miller, with Foreword by J. N. Findlay (Oxford: Clarendon Press, 1970), 34.

176 Ibid., 35.

177 Ibid., 40.

178 *Speak, Memory*, 275.

179 *Drugie berega*, 442. Translation is mine.

180 *Speak, Memory*, 291-292.

181 Vladimir Nabokov, *Laughter in the Dark* (New Directions, a revised edition, 1960), 143. The passage, absent in its original Russian version, *Camera obscura* (1936), might serve as a good example of how Nabokov gradually arrives at aesthetic formulae, often via the process of translation of his own work; the parallel process is a gradual formulation of his translation principles through his non-fictional writings.

182 Alexandrov, *Nabokov's Otherworld*, 17.

183 *Ada* "is framed as the work of a philosopher whose primary area of study is the nature of time." See Glenn Horowitz (ed.), *Véra's Butterflies: First Editions by Vladimir Nabokov Inscribed to his Wife*, by Sarah Funke, with contributions by Brian Boyd, Stephen Jay Gould, et al. (New York City: Glenn Horowitz Bookseller, Inc., 1999), 247. Part four of Ada, entitled "The Texture of Time," is Van Veen's treatise—his philosophical ruminations on the nature of time, which echo both Henri Bergson and Hegel.

184 Elizabeth Sewell, *The Field of Nonsense* (London: Chatto and Windus, 1952), 46-47.

185 Vladimir Nabokov, *King, Queen, Knave* (New York: McGraw-Hill, 1968), x.

186 Buks [Bukhs], *Eshafot v khrustalnom dvortse*, 41-48.

187 Deleuze, "The Schizophrenic and Language," 280.

188 See Connolly, "*Ania v strane chudes*," 24, and *Alice/Ania*, 27.

189 Tzvetan Todorov, *The Fantastic: A Structural Approach to a Literary Genre* (Cleveland and London: Case Western Reserve University Press, 1973), 25.

190 See Daniel 5:26-28.

191 Connolly, "*Ania v strane chudes*," 56.

## Chapter 2

# THE NOVEL ON TRANSLATION AND "ÜBER-TRANSLATION": NABOKOV'S *PALE FIRE* AND *EUGENE ONEGIN*[1]

$$\text{"non v'accorgete voi che noi siam vermi/}$$
$$\text{nati a formar l'angelica farfalla. . . .}^2$$
(Dante, *Purgatorio*, X, 124-125)

## Formulation of the problem

In his 1937 French essay for the *Nouvelle Revue française*, "Pouchkine, ou le vrai et le vraisemblable" ("Pushkin, or the Real and the Plausible"),[3] Nabokov claimed that the truth of another's life is inaccessible because thought inevitably distorts whatever it tries to encompass. However, the intuitions of a fictionalized biography motivated by love for its subject might convey a "plausible" life bearing a mysterious affinity for "the poet's work, if not the poet himself."[4] This relatively early statement on this subject by Nabokov, made during centennial celebrations of Aleksandr Pushkin's death, becomes poignant in light of Nabokov's novel *Pale Fire* and his monumental endeavor of translation and critical commentary — *Eugene Onegin* — some twenty years later. In *Pale Fire*, John Shade, the author of the eponymous poem, writes: *"Man's life as commentary to abstruse / Unfinished poem.* Note for further use."[5]

Nabokov's four-volume translation of *Eugene Onegin* was published by the Bollingen Foundation in 1964 (a second revised edition came out in 1975) and provoked a variety of reactions, from disbelief ("the raised eyebrow, the sharp intake of breath")[6] and outrage, to admiration and appraisal. The parallels between *Pale Fire*, written simultaneously with Nabokov's work on the *Onegin* translation and published in 1962, and Nabokov's *Onegin* (translation, Commentary, and Index) have attracted many Nabokov scholars to the presence of "some kind of a link-and-bobolink" between the two, to use the words of "Pale Fire" the Poem.[7] *Pale Fire* bears such a striking structural similarity to Nabokov's *Onegin* that it is easy to suggest self-parody. Nabokov worked on Pushkin's verse novel *Eugene Onegin* (1823-1831) from 1949 to 1957. In the published four-volume edition, the translation took up 240 pages, while the Commentary and Index ran to almost 1200. In what could have been a comment on the motivations for Nabokov's extraordinary endeavor of *Onegin*, Brian Boyd writes of *Pale Fire*: "Here the whole situation of Kinbote and Shade—Kinbote's desperation that Shade tell his story in the verse he cannot write himself, his resolving to tell it via a commentary to the poem when he finds Shade has not obliged him—can *only* be fully told in the form Nabokov devises for *Pale Fire*."[8] *Pale Fire* also can be viewed as Nabokov's response to the deficiencies of other translations of *Eugene Onegin*, which he had criticized, as well as to the inequities involved in literary translation.[9] Commentators and interpreters, much like Kinbote himself, are too preoccupied with their own megalomaniac idiosyncrasies, their own environment and tradition, their likes and dislikes, to focus on those of the original they are dealing with.[10] For the sake of bringing the original closer to the target audience, or claiming to "free" or "distill" the pure matter of the authorial intent of the original, they "tell" somebody else's story as they believe it should be told or would have been, if only the original were written in the target language. Similarly, Kinbote thinks he "enhances the poem by revealing 'the underside of the weave,' the much more thrilling story that he pressed Shade so often to tell, that Shade *should* have told and *would* have told had he been free."[11]

Nabokov's translation of *Eugene Onegin*, especially seen in the context of his major work of fiction, *Pale Fire*, raises an unexpected question: was what is generally considered to be a radical change in Nabokov's views of literary translation really a change? On the surface level it seems hard to deny the striking contrast between Nabokov's earlier translations of Fyodor Tiutchev, for example, which he himself later would dub "adaptations," to the unyielding literal behemoth of *Onegin*, fascinating to study but barely possible to read. I would like to suggest a different view: I believe that there is evidence that Nabokov's metaphysical vision defined his literary translation all along, just as it defined his fiction. This vision is the underpinning of all his literary endeavors and did not change much throughout his literary career. With *Onegin* it was just coming to fruition, to the moment of "crystallization." What seems to be a radical change in translation strategy is therefore not a change at all. In other words, what changed was the *way* he deemed appropriate to practice what were essentially the same theoretical postulates.

To paraphrase the famous statement by Carl von Clausewitz, this would be "the continuation of policy by other means." Praxis being what it is, literal translation was basically the expression of the same understanding by other means at other times.

In what follows, I consider Nabokov's metaphysics, linking his novel *Pale Fire*, whose central focus is the process of translation via appropriation of the original, to his translation of Pushkin's *Eugene Onegin*. The central premise on which this chapter hinges is that translation for Nabokov was always a means for expressing his profoundly held ideas about art. I argue that Nabokov's metaphysical uncertainty shapes the allegorical (metonymical) mode of his writing, including translation (the discussion of the metonymical and metaphorical modes continues in Chapter 3). In this light, I look closely at how the Index and Commentary to Nabokov's *Onegin* function, how literalism is achieved, and the criteria for its assessment.

## Nabokov's Metaphysics

The very Western reluctance to accept metaphysics as being at the heart of all of Nabokov's "stratagems" (his word) is understandable. The fatigue and mistrust of metaphysics in twentieth-century Western criticism, in contrast to the opposite vision in Russian literary discourse, can be best illustrated by a relatively recent anecdote. At a joint conference aimed at the advancement of Russian-American cultural exchange, an American poet and professor of humanities warmly praised his Russian guests, representatives of a Moscow literary magazine, some of them themselves poets, for their "courage" in addressing largely metaphysical issues in their work. The Russian visitors exchanged glances of incomprehension. Was it their English? What "courage" was he talking about? What could be more natural than addressing metaphysical issues? In the West, the un-ironic Almighty is not exactly a frequent "visitor" of contemporary poetic creations, often called "texts" rather than "poems." Perhaps Russian literary tradition conspired, as it were, with the very "irreality" of twentieth-century Russian history, premature political "post-modernism" with all its nebulous simulacra, and created the pre-disposition for the opposite fatigue—fatigue of the so called "real," while addressing metaphysical issues became the most natural thing in the world.

The vantage point of the vast majority of Nabokov studies in the West was of Nabokov as primarily a "metaliterary" writer.[12] This reputation started to build rather early, when the writer was still known as Sirin and his fellow Russian émigrés delighted in or cringed at the sight of his unusual talent. His friend and contemporary Vladislav Khodasevich contributed to it by perspicaciously pointing to the role played by literary device in Nabokov's fiction. Nabokobv's foes were upset by this preoccupation with form, perceiving the ostensible lack of concern for grand social issues as "un-Russianness." His American/Western reputation made him a "master of style," a genius of artifice and intertextual play. As his fame grew considerably after *Lolita*, Nabokov himself molded his reputation by projecting his public persona through carefully crafted interviews. Playfulness and mimicry, the two characteristics most often evoked in connection to Nabokov's art, applied to the projected image of the "artist" himself. The undeniable fact is that Nabokov, most likely intentionally, created intricate patterns and coincidences without explicit interpretation. He allows them to be read in diametrically opposite ways: either as "fatidic patterns" (Vladimir Alexandrov's term) or as the deliberate interpolation of the text's artificiality.

However, the evidence that Nabokov's perceived artificiality goes against the grain of his work has always existed in plain view. It was explicitly stated in his poetry (especially his poem "Slava" ["Fame"]) and his public pronouncements, including those in *Strong Opinions* and *Speak, Memory*. There is also the blunt statement by Véra Nabokov in the Foreword to the collection of Nabokov's Russian poetry in 1979, claiming *potustoronnost*—the "otherworldliness," the metaphysical "beyond"—as the main theme of her husband's art, as well as direct assertions in Nabokov's own posthumous "The Art of Literature and Commonsense." Finally, the evidence is everywhere, cumulatively, in Nabokov's own fiction.

The critical approach started to change in the 1980s. One of the early examples is W. W. Rowe's *Nabokov's Spectral Dimension*.[13] The book does a valuable service, as it assembles concrete evidence of specters swarming in Nabokov's fiction. However, it never goes beyond the acknowledgement of specific ghosts, as it were, and the situations in which they usually reveal their presence. Gennady Barabtarlo's and Alexandrov's books reached beyond the specifics and rightfully emphasized Nabokov's metaphysics.[14] Alexandrov characterized Nabokov's transcendental beliefs thus: "an intuition about a transcendental realm of being."[15] Both Barabtarlo and Alexandrov are Russians (albeit American professors), and it might be tempting to dismiss their emphasis on metaphysics as a natural Russian idiosyncrasy. Boyd's excellent studies of *Pale Fire* and *Ada* therefore should be credited for firmly placing Nabokov's metaphysics on the radar of the Western Nabokovian studies. One cannot help feeling grateful to these scholars: no longer does one need to spend time proving that Nabokov's preoccupation with metaphysical issues was profound—as asserted by the author himself. For a concise summation of the "shape" in which the metaphysical reveals itself, I would resort, as many before me, to the much quoted "Fame" of *Poems and Problems*. It talks about a "secret," a motif evoked either vaguely or more or less explicitly in many novels of Nabokov (*Invitation to a Beheading*, *The Defense*, and *The Gift*, to name just a few):

> . . . I am happy that Conscience, the pimp
> of my sleepy reflections and projects,
> did not get at the critical secret. Today
> I am really remarkably happy.
> That main secret tra-tá-ta tra-tá-ta tra-tá—
> and I must not be overexplicit;
> this is why I find laughable the empty dream
> about readers, and body, and glory.
> . . . I admit that the night has
> been ciphered right well
> but in place of the stars I put letters,
> and I've read in myself how the self to transcend—
> and I must not be overexplicit.

Trusting not the enticements of the thoroughfare
or such dreams as the ages have hallowed,
I prefer to stay godless, with fetterless soul
in a world that is swarming with godheads.
But one day while disrupting the strata of sense
and descending deep down to my wellspring
I saw mirrored, besides my own self and the world,
something else, something else, something else.[16]

The secret cannot be made explicit, and it is nothing new. Tiutchev wrote in his famous "Silentium!" (1833): "An uttered thought is a lie."

On the other hand, on those occasions when Nabokov tries to articulate the secret and convey the actual details of the afterlife, his fiction suffers (*Look at the Harlequins* and *Transparent Things*). Metaphysical secrets notwithstanding, Nabokov's explicitly expressed desire to stay "godless" testifies to the impossibility of reducing this metaphysical "something else" to any conventionally understood religion or spirituality. Nabokov squarely avoided being placed with any and all religious denominations: "In my metaphysics, I am a confirmed non-unionist and have no use for organized tours through anthropomorphic paradises."[17] Nabokov's characters are on a quest for glimpses of that metaphysical "beyond." It is the central quest of Shade's life in *Pale Fire*: Shade writes his poem "projecting himself imaginatively beyond death. ..."[18] As a rule however, Nabokov's characters, including Shade, have to admit their failure in such quests, though the quest is never without gratification.

## The "Source" of *Pale Fire*

To tie in issues of metaphysics, fiction, and translation, I would like to use the very title of *Pale Fire* as a symbolic springboard for further investigation. As is well known, on the last day of writing his poem and grappling for the appropriate title, Shade playfully evokes Shakespeare's *Timon of Athens*: "But *this* transparent thingum

does require / Some moondrop title. Help me, Will! *Pale fire.*"[19]
Shakespeare's lines are:

> . . . . I'll example you with thievery:
> The sun's a thief, and with his great attraction
> Robs the vast sea; the moon's an arrant thief,
> And her pale fire she snatches from the sun;
> The sea's a thief, whose liquid surge resolves
> The moon into salt tears.[20]

As attentive readers, we know that despite the mysterious presence of an edition of this play in Kinbote's own life, he spectacularly fails to identify the source of Shade's title. Kinbote's Commentary on his uncle Conmal, a Zemblan translator of Shakespeare, quotes the above passage in "re-translation" from Zemblan into English, in which "pale fire" gets lost in translation.

Whether the Shakespearean title reflects Shade's modesty or wit—whether he claims that his light is pale only compared to the source of Shakespeare (this interpretation would fit well with Shade's image of Shakespeare's ghost being able to light up an entire town in Shade's poem "The Nature of Electricity"!) or he "wittily steals from Timon's denunciation against universal thievery"[21]—we still have to acknowledge that not only Shade's poem but also Kinbote's enterprise and Nabokov's novel as a whole are called *Pale Fire* (a new triad!). The echoes of "pale fire" are present, unbeknownst to Shade, in his daughter Hazel's investigation of the "roundlet of *pale light*"[22] in the Haunted Barn, spelling out a mysterious message that the reader can decode while Kinbote cannot (he also misrecognizes the ghost, thinking it is Shade's friend Hentzner's specter), and, unnoticed by Kinbote, in his account of the "dim light" of his teenage lover's ghost in the tunnel to freedom during the Zemblan revolution. Kinbote says that he "caught [himself] borrowing a kind of opalescent light from my poet's fiery orb. . . ."[23]

While Shakespeare might be a "fiery orb" to the "heroic couplets"[24] of Shade's "Pale Fire," the Poem in and of itself would become this "fiery orb" to Kinbote's Commentary. And Nabokov is obviously the hidden source of "fire" to *Pale Fire* the novel. We are dealing with several stages of removal from the source of creation described in terms of light. To confirm this, here is, interestingly, how Kinbote describes "God's presence": ". . . a faint phosphorescence at first, a pale light in the dimness of bodily life, and a dazzling radiance after it."[25]

The Shakespearean passage from *Timon of Athens* becomes an allegory of writing/translation/commentary and stands ironically as a scrambled version of a metaphysical ladder to the source of light: ". . . To start with, he[man]'d find shadows the easiest things to look at. After that, reflections—of people and other things—in water. The things themselves would come later, and from those he would move on to the heavenly bodies and the heavens themselves. He'd find it easier to look at the light of the stars and the moon by night than look at the sun, and the light of the sun, by day."[26] The Shakespearean model, being circular rather than linear, would not allow a simple Platonic solution to the metaphysical source of light, but becomes sort of a "hall of mirrors," much as Nabokov's novels themselves, always toying with the titillating possibility of *one* solution, but never truly allowing for it. Examples of such moments "on the verge of a simple solution of the universe"[27] are abundant in Nabokov's fiction. The secret of the title is discovered on many different levels in the novel (the ascension to each new level gives a delightful feeling of *jouissance* to the reader), but the Shakespearean source yields one more secret meaning and it applies not just to the intricacies of the plot, nor even to the text as a whole, but to the process of writing as translation on a metaphysical level, as well as to translation/commentary as another degree of removal from the same "source," yet all the same partaking in it.

In *Strong Opinions*, Nabokov described his understanding of a "ladder" to the unknown dimension: "time without conscious-ness—lower animal world; time with consciousness—man; con-sciousness without time—still higher state."[28] Since Nabokov's metaphysics always goes hand in hand with his aesthetics, his accounts of what he called, alternatively, "cosmic synchroniza-tion"[29] and "inspiration" (in "The Art of Literature and Common-sense")[30] concern positioning an artist vis-à-vis time: "while the scientist sees everything that happens in one point of space the poet feels everything that happens in one point of time."[31] The moment of epiphany or "fissure" in the "spherical prison" of time allows for an escape from "smug causality."[32] Jonathan Borden Sisson observed that Nabokov's notion of cosmic synchronization is akin to T. S. Eliot's and Ezra Pound's "holistic experiences related to the creation of poetry."[33] In *Speak, Memory,* inspiration, "in a sudden flash," brings together the past, present, *and* future, and in this flash time stops existing.[34] The initial jolt of inspiration is described by Nabokov in his article "Inspiration" (1972) as "pale fire" of sorts—a "prefatory glow."[35] The whole book is said to "be ready ideally in some other, now transparent, now dimming, dimension. . . ."[36] Over the years, Nabokov's descriptions of his creative process remained surprisingly stable. He went as far as to suggest in a review that creative work is "conservation" rather than creation of the "perfect something which already exists in the somewhere which Professor Woodbridge [the author Nabokov is reviewing] obligingly terms 'Nature.'"[37]

Parallels to Platonic dialectic are, of course, inevitable, but Nabokov always tried to protect himself from being associated with any "big ideas": "I am afraid to get mixed up with Plato, whom I do not care for. . . ."[38] In a jab at Nietzsche, Nabokov says he would have not lasted long in Plato's "Germanic regime of militarism and music."[39] Instead, his is a peculiar kind of Platonism, a metaphysics that comes to terms with Nietzschean repudiation of it. It is strongly filtered through Nietzsche, just as the whole of Symbolist and post-Symbolist Russian culture was. Nabokov *was* undoubtedly the product of the Russian Silver Age, which he himself readily admitted: "the 'decline' of Russian culture in 1905-1907 is a Soviet invention . . . Blok, Bely, Bunin and others wrote their best stuff in those days. And never was poetry so popular, not even in Pushkin's days. I am a product of that period, I was bred in that atmosphere."[40] From that same source (Silver Age and Nietzschean influence) comes Nabokov's distaste for "common sense" — the iron-clad laws of cause and effect, as well as the identification of inspiration, or cosmic synchronization, with the "spirit of free will that snaps its rainbow fingers in the face of smug causality."[41] From that same source comes also the incommunicability of the secret (the "truth")

I have mentioned earlier. In Nietzschean terms, the Dionysiac, as an expression of the unconscious, can never arrive at the fully articulate form either: "that striving toward infinity, that wing-beat of longing even as we feel supreme delight in a clearly perceived reality, these things indicate that in both these states of mind we are to recognize a Dionysiac phenomenon."[42] The truth, in other words, cannot be plainly stated.

To a certain degree, the Nabokovian metaphysical uncertainty resembles most of all the controversial Nietzschean "primordial unity" (Arthur Schopenhauer's term), a sheer pool of unactualized potentiality encompassing the seemingly opposite entities. A good example of how this is achieved in *Pale Fire* is the unity of the perception of art by characters supposed to be in juxtaposition to one another. Shade, by far the most positive character, derives a fair share of autobiographic and aesthetic details from Nabokov's own life and understanding, but so does Kinbote, which makes it impossible to reduce him to a loony. Kinbote, for example, describes what in him reveals a true artist (an "artist and a madman"!) much in the same terms that Nabokov could use in speaking about himself: what he says he *can* do is to "pounce upon the forgotten butterfly of revelation, wean [himself] abruptly from the habit of things, see the web of the world, and the warp and the weft of that web."[43]

By the very nature of the metaphysical, the "beyond" is inextricably related to death (to what lies "beyond") and its representation. In her investigation into the representation of death in *Over Her Dead Body*, Elizabeth Bronfen starts with the interpretive analysis of Gabriel von Max's salon painting "Der Anatom" (1869).[44] A beautiful dead woman is the center of this painting; a seated anatomist gazes intently at her; skulls and other death paraphernalia are posited to the left of the body, while a live moth is to her right. This may interest us primarily because of the butterfly motif. Bronfen writes of the nocturnal butterfly:

> In European folklore, the moth, also called "death bird" because the traces on its body suggest the patterns of a skull, is iconographically read as a figure of death and immortality. Because it is a nocturnal butterfly, often found hovering above graves, classical Greek tradition saw the moth as a figure for

the soul (psyche) departing from a dead body, if death occurred in the hours of the night. The moth is also used as a figure for souls in purgatory or for the good or bad spirits of the deceased, wandering restlessly on earth, which may include demons and witches. Finally, the moth is understood as a messenger carrying oracles or omens, and again due to its colouring and its nocturnal appearance, its presence is thought to presage illness or death.[45]

The image of a butterfly, so central to Nabokov's work and so frequently discussed, is one of the signs, catalogued by Rowe in his book, that signals Nabokov's "spectral dimension." This image goes to the heart of the related questions of fate and pattern, "order concealed behind chance."[46] As I pointed out at the beginning of this chapter, this allows for diametrically opposite hermeneutic possibilities. Nabokov's philosophical review "Prof. Woodbridge in an Essay on Nature Postulates the Reality of the World," from which I quoted earlier, also points to an understanding of creativity that is very Romantic in its essence: the artist is to the world of art as God is to the world of nature. The Romantic notion of art as a "divine game"[47] once again is filtered through the Nietzschean tradition of *homo ludens* (or Dionysiac pessimist—"man of intuition," artist), but does not allow for the Romantic-Nietzschean opposition to the "theoretical man" or scientist (Nabokov the lepidopterist perfectly merged the artist and the scientist—a very twentieth-century hybridity of his own "gift"). Nabokov's study of mimicry in lepidoptery and the intricate patterning and use of "fatidic dates" in his writings (an obsession he shared with Pushkin) echo the theories of mimicry and conscious play of the early twentieth-century occultist Pyotr D. Ouspenski (1878-1947), as Alexandrov has pointed out.[48] The fateful Vanessa, the Red Admirable, appearing in *Pale Fire* a minute before Shade dies, "flashed and vanished, and flashed again, with an almost frightening imitation of conscious play. . . ."[49] Nabokov calls Vanessa a "butterfly of doom" in *Strong Opinions*[50] and ties this to a dubious theory that the Red Admirables had markings resembling the year 1881 (when Tsar Alexander II was assassinated and, supposedly, the butterflies were unusually abundant). This might be one of Nabokov's multiple mystifications, but Vanessas do flutter through many a fateful moment in Nabokov's fiction (*King, Queen, Knave, The Gift, Ada*), making a butterfly one of the most important metaphysical "pointers" in Nabokov. Whatever this transcendental dimension might be, its structurally necessary possibility, "iterability" as it were, features prominently in Nabokov. In Benjaminian terms, the call for "translation" (in every sense of this word, including being transported elsewhere) is posited at the heart of the structure of the work in and of itself.

There are other relevant metaphysical "pointers" in *Pale Fire*, which imply being transported/translated elsewhere; to name a few: iris, number eight or the lemniscate, translation/transformation of zero or even triple zero (nothingness or "triple nothingness") into the sign of infinity. It seems to me that Boyd, in his otherwise excellent analysis, misinterpreted some of these pointers. Thus he writes about Iris Acht, an actress-lover of King Charles the Beloved's grandfather. The King sees her portrait in his room of confinement after the revolution, and her role is important in his escape because the tunnel through which he flees leads to her room in the theater. Boyd adduces rather far-fetched connections between her and Shade's daughter Hazel (who is, in Boyd's search for a unified "author" of *Pale Fire*, a plausible candidate for this role from beyond the grave). The connection he makes is that "iris" points to "hazel" as color because of the "eye association."[51] Much more convincing would be to interpret Acht in light of Nabokov's metaphysical "pointer"—"iris" as the rainbow (the bridge between worlds) and the sign of eternity "8" ("Acht"). Rainbow (*raduga*, in Russian), and as its extension, "iris" (*raduzhka*, the iris of the eye) are among those metaphysical "pointers" that often tie together the themes of death and resurrection (often related to the death of the father) with fate and gift (and, in many instances, Pushkin).[52] "Acht" or "8" is obviously another "pointer." Among the poets of Russian Symbolism, the influence of whom Nabokov acknowledged, Innokentii Annenskii played a special role. (Volumes of Annenskii's poetry are mentioned at the moment of death of Yasha Chernyshevskii in *The Gift*.) Annenskii's metaphysical "deviz tainstvennyi pokhozh na oprokinutoe vosem'" ("the mysterious motto is like an eight turned on its side") was an eloquent example of Symbolist theosophical vision. In other instances, Boyd interprets the unsettling proliferation of the figure eight in the text (such as 1888, for example, the meticulously cited year of Acht's death) only in terms of "the intense chess ambience" of the tunnel scene.[53] Then there is a "lemniscate" allusion in the Poem, describing Shade's dreams as a child ("the miracle of a lemniscate left / Upon wet sand by nonchalantly deft / Bicycle tires").[54] Kinbote, in his turn, interprets this allusion, with the help of "Webster's Second," as a figure eight. As the King (Kinbote) flees through the tunnel, in which he had been thirty years earlier with his teenage lover Oleg, he sees his own "lemniscate"—the thirty-year-old "patterned imprint of Oleg's shoe" in the tunnel. At this point, Boyd arrives at the interpretation of the "lemniscate" as "infinity,"[55] also pointing out that the unwritten last line 1000 of the Poem, with its three zeroes, is a "blank, a triple zero like Hazel's death in one of three conjoined lakes, Omega, Ozero, Zero."[56] It might be interesting to note here the affinity with the childish belief of Lolita that the zeros on the speedometer can all turn back into nines if the car is put in reverse (time can be reversed). Boyd says that Hazel (in the role that he assigns her—that of the unified "author") seems to answer that "in the repeated 1888 she has Kinbote imagine, death is not a triple zero but a triple eight, a triple lemniscate, infinity, upon infinity, upon infinity. . . ."[57] The survival of the original, as it were, is once again possible through being transported (translated) into something else.

Hazel sets out to investigate a mysterious "pale light" in the barn that spells out a famous "Vanessa Atalanta" message, which Kinbote fails to decode. The Nabokovians, of course, decoded it— as a warning to Shade not to go near his neighbor's house (he goes and dies at the hand of a deranged assassin). The precedent for the interpretation was set by Barabtarlo,[58] who correctly noticed the word "Atalanta" (Vanessa) repeated three times. I think it is important to add that, just as in the example of Nabokov's early poem cited above,[59] the message forms the Russian word *talant* (talent, gift) repeated three times as a magic formula. It is also significant that Kinbote himself, trying to interpret the message, comes up with the word *talant*, among other possible "lexical units" ("war," "talant," "her," "arrant," etc.), but dismisses all of them as making no sense.[60]

Because *talant* is the only Russian word among "the balderdash" and tentative English, and because including the "truth" but dismissing it as "silly" or "insignificant" is a favorite strategy of Nabokov's, one can assume that the word is not accidental. *Talant* is arguably the greatest metaphysical mystery of many of Nabokov's works. (One of these works, let us not forget, is actually entitled *The Gift*! In this novel, Nabokov employs a very similar technique: the keyword "gift," initially present in a poem the protagonist is composing, is excluded from the "final version"—the key is "lost," just as the actual key to the apartment).

The issue of *talant* is especially important because of the continuous search for a "unified author" (apart from Nabokov, naturally) of *Pale Fire*. To some extent, this "search for the original" foregrounds interpretation: if one looks at it from the vantage point of Benjamin's discussion of translatability, one realizes that while the original "survives" through translation/interpretation, the interpretation itself is finite, possessing a *Fortleben* rather than *Nachleben*. Finding the "finite" interpretation proves elusive.

The search continued in the 1990s in *The Nabokovian*,[61] as well as on the Internet (in 1997-1998), and pitted the "Shadeans" against the "anti-Shadeans." The "Shadeans" (e.g. Andrew Field, Julia Bader, and Boyd himself, at the beginning of the discussions) argued that the unified author of the text and the inventor of Kinbote and his Commentary was Shade. Boyd admits to having been a "Shadean" for a time, but then rejecting this theory on the basis of textual evidence. The "anti-Shadean" hypothesis is that Kinbote also wrote the "original"—Shade's Poem in heroic couplets.

The hypothesis Boyd pursues in his book, as mentioned previously, posits Shade's daughter Hazel as "dreaming the dream" of the Red King, not unlike Alice in *Through the Looking Glass*, and "dictating" or "orchestrating" both her father's Poem and Kinbote's Commentary. Hazel could be a "prompter from the beyond," the role Boyd tries to ascribe to her, in two mutually opposed cases. One would be if Nabokov shared the theosophical theories that accompanied Russian Symbolism in the late nineteenth century, with their central role for the "eternal feminine." The other would have Nabokov creating a tongue-in-cheek parody of metaphysical certainty, as he often does. (For example, he did it in the case of Shade's discovery that his unified vision of the beyond is predicated on a misspelling in an old lady's article — "mountain"/"fountain.")[62]

As Bronfen wrote, "while Jean-Martin Charcot was experimenting with the use of hypnosis to treat patients for hysteria, spiritualists maintained that at the site of a figuratively deadened feminine body the immaterial realm of the beyond could become visible, a contact between the living and the dead be established and secured, and the boundary between the here and the beyond blurred."[63] The latter part was arguably Shade and Nabokov's quest, but we also know that Nabokov scoffed at well-worn spiritualist theories. Boyd's idea of the poor pudgy Hazel, working in consortium with the tongue-tied (and dead) Aunt Maud, as a medium for a work of genius, is amusingly ironic indeed. Boyd has a vested interest in the validation of this theory, so he carefully collates the clues that *are* present in the narrative. However, this theory can be also undermined, since its vantage point is the identification of Hazel with a Vanessa butterfly, which ties together the "Atalanta" message, the Vanessa from the Poem, and the actual butterfly fluttering teasingly in front of Shade moments before he dies. The fact is that the Vanessa of the Poem explicitly signified Sybil, Shade's wife. Boyd argues that after her death the unattractive Hazel *becomes* Vanessa (i.e. her own attractive mother), but there is no textual evidence to support this bold development. Without such a "metamorphosis," the theory falls apart.

Discussing origin (and thus the "original"), as Benjamin does in relation to translation, attunes one to the notion of history thought of in terms of "life," "survival," and "afterlife" — that is, history profoundly aware of mortality. The ambiguity of the afterlife in Benjamin and Nabokov does not allow for any perfect equivalence or ultimate signification.

Yet there is always a girl or young woman lurking somewhere near the locus and moment of the miraculous transcendence of the world of "here and now" envisioned in terms of imprisonment — as a cage or jail whose bars define the existence of Kinbote, or a man making contact with God in one of Kinbote's accounts, or, for that matter, Humbert in *Lolita*. Kinbote escapes through a closet in his

Zemblan castle only to find himself "surrounded by his fears."[64] He writes of "a personality consisting mainly of the shadows of its own prison bars,"[65] which resonates with an ape allegory that allegedly gave Nabokov a jolt of inspiration for writing *Lolita* (the ape, given an opportunity to paint, comes up only with the pattern of its own cage bars), as well as with the account by Kinbote of "seeing a man in the act of making contact with God" whose "clenched hands seemed to be gripping invisible prison bars."[66] Nabokov, situated between Western and Russian cultures, vacillates between culturally bound significations of women: the redeemer and the "eternal feminine" of Russian culture or an irreducible enigma, the radical Other of Western culture. In both cases woman as a trope is related to death. The woman might have any of the culturally inscribed roles inherent in the semiotization of femininity. As allegory and fetish, nonetheless, the woman always presents as it hides the referent— death and the beyond.

However, I believe that, like many other pointers to the spectral dimension catalogued by Rowe, the woman is the sign, but not the means. Something else is needed to transcend to the metaphysical, some other medium, and this medium would be Nabokov's "secret" (which he evokes mysteriously in poetry and interviews), something that he takes uncharacteristically seriously. This secret might be the gift. It seems to be the narrow passage, a point of criss-crossing of the "giant wings" of time from the Poem: ". . . Infinite foretime and/ Infinite aftertime: above your head/ They close like giant wings, and you are dead."[67] There is a graphic depiction of this "lemniscate," "oprokinutoe vosem," the hourglass placed on its side, the infinity, that ties together all of its three elements (the foretime, the aftertime, and the node in between): it is a butterfly. This is perhaps why butterflies flutter in Nabokov's texts when the "tunnel" to the beyond and the beyond itself are nearby. Just as Eros in Plato's *Symposium* is found to be a spirit and a messenger between the worlds, the gift is a thing "in-between," a messenger. Thus a poem, for example, is a certain "intermediary" between reason and the beyond. It is a certain "instrument" with which knowledge not accessible otherwise is obtained. The Vanessa butterfly that Shade identifies with his wife (love being his Platonic "intermediary," or tunnel, to the beyond) and that Boyd tries—not very convincingly—to identify with Hazel, is, I believe, the same secret formula for the "gift." Like Nabokov's gift, merging the insights of science and art, Nabokov's butterflies are both specimens of his lepidoptery studies and harbingers of the beyond. In a similar fashion, the chiasmic task of translation, according to Nabokov, also bridges the paradox: "a poet's patience and scholiastic passion blent." Butterflies appear in his texts as actual creatures, as the process of metamorphosis, or as names (such as Falter, the character from Nabokov's story "Ultima Thule," who claims to have arrived at the ultimate secret of the universe).[68] By virtue of its very nature as *gift* (whoever or whatever granted it), it is always accepted and greeted with gratitude, which Nabokov expresses again and again—hence, his well known optimism and cheerfulness, his feeling of being made "to measure of something not quite comprehensible, but wonderful and benevolent. . . ."[69] Véra Nabokov wrote about it in the Foreword to his posthumous Russian collection *Stikhi* (1979): "He was involved in this mystery for many years, almost not realizing it; and it was it that gave him his impossible cheerfulness and lucidity even at the time of the biggest hardships and made him completely invulnerable to any and all stupid and evil criticism."[70]

In the "Shadeans" versus the "anti-Shadeans" debate described above, it might be that neither side has a case. The disturbing correspondences between the Poem and the Commentary that Ellen Pifer writes about in *Nabokov and the Novel*,[71] or "the intimacy of relationship between part and part, when at a surface level they indeed appear to be utterly remote" that Boyd evokes,[72] are not due to Shade dreaming Kinbote's dreams or Kinbote dreaming Shade's dreams (or for that matter, a third person, Hazel, in Boyd's theory, dreaming dreams for both of them), but are a result of all three partaking—unbeknownst to them—of the same physical (Nabokov's imagination) and metaphysical sources. "Passion of science and patience of poetry,"[73] already paradoxical in this unlikely formula and transformed hilariously in the novel through parody and self-parody, are, after all, doing a very serious job. And the jobs of science and poetry are ultimately the same. Formulations like these are not to be made, things like this are not intended to be uttered, because they are always under the threat of being trivialized and made a lie by the fact of utterance (as in Tiutchev's "Silentium!"). Therefore, they instead have to be worked into the texture of the novel, made, as in Shade's "revelation" of the nature of the beyond, "not text, but texture,"[74] or, in Benjaminian terms, they make sure that any fixed meaning does not exhaust the intrinsic heterogeneity of language.

The mystery cannot be explained (so the resolute final interpretation is never possible); its presence, however, is made known and felt, and can be re-created. In Neo-Platonic terms, things are good only insofar as they are created by Being (Beyond begins with the initial of Being, rightly notes Boyd).[75] Therefore, partaking of the immutable life of Being is only possible by re-creation of the act of creation. On this, deeply metaphysical level, the gift partakes of the life of Being. Nabokov, as Boyd observes, "did know the twentieth-century fashion for mordant metaphysical skepticism."[76] Instead of postulating metaphysical ideas in a twentieth-century *Symposium*, one can deal with the metaphysics, as well as metaphysical uncertainty, on the "scholiastic" level as Nabokov does in *Pale Fire*—"an intimation of concealed design, the coy expression of an unjustifiable trust, a hint of what might lurk within the intimate texture of things."[77] Hesitation between different hermeneutic possibilities creates the Nabokovian metaphysical uncertainty but does not eliminate the existence of precise patterns of signification. His text is an endless interplay between the stability of meaning and the instability of meaning, with new possibilities opening up every time some stability seems to be achieved.

## The Allegorical Model

Bronfen argues that the moth in the painting mentioned above, depicting an anatomist and a dead woman, introduces a non-metaphorical rhetorical mode—the allegorical. Drawing on Paul de Man's writings on allegory, she points out:

> Traditionally defined as an extended metaphor, allegory informs this painting in the sense that it produces a juxtaposition and tension between all figured relations. What distinguishes the allegorical mode is that it reveals at the same time that it hides,

and so explicitly points to the incommensurability or disjunction between signifier and signified. Based on the Greek *allos*, Other, allegory indicates a figurative speaking, a speaking in other terms, of other things. Its rhetorical turn is such that it articulates the difficulty of determining a conclusive or binding referential relation between signifier, signified and a nonsemiotic reality.[78]

Death itself becomes a signified that defies expression or the realm of nonsemiotic reality altogether.

Preoccupation with death, or more precisely, with a lack of "conclusive referential relation," that is the centrality of allegory in Nabokov's fiction was first pointed out by Pyotr Bitsilli in "The Revival of Allegory," published in *Sovremennye zapiski* in 1935.[79] It provides a remarkable early insight into the nature of Nabokov's art. Commenting on the ending of *Invitation to a Beheading*, Bitsilli points out that

> everything ends with the "cliff-hanging." The point is that there can be no answer to the question, for the question itself cannot be phrased. Death is the end of life. But can we call that state in which Cincinnatus lived "life"? Is it not all the same whether he was decapitated or not? Real life is the movement directed toward some goal, toward self-discovery in intercourse and in strife with real people. Death is the completion of life. Life is the thesis— death the antithesis; after which human consciousness expects some kind of synthesis—some final, extratemporal realization of the sense of a completed life. But if nothing is asserted in life, if life does not propose any thesis, then how can there be an antithesis, and how then is a synthesis possible?[80]

Bitsilli continues to elaborate on the "life is but a dream" theme in Sirin, as he argues in his 1938 review of *Invitation to a Beheading* and *The Eye* that Sirin-Nabokov's "truth" is in glimpsing a vague vision of something essential that lies *beyond* the horrifying unreality of life: "'Life is but a dream,' and Dream, as it is well-known, has been long considered a brother of Death. Sirin goes to the end into this direction. If so, then life itself means death."[81] The opposites are conjoined in one.

Life and death/"the beyond" in Nabokov are articulated through repetition, the recurrent motifs and literary devices, just as the disappearance and return in Sigmund Freud's "economic" model of the avoidance of un-pleasure and its replacement with "production of pleasure" in his *Beyond the Pleasure Principle* (exemplified in the *fort-da* game played by a child), are predicated on loss and repetition. Repetition is seen as a "form of control, as a return to self-assertion in response to an endangering moment of absence."[82] In Jacques Lacan's reading of the game described by Freud,[83] the production of meaning, which in his interpretation is the aphanisis (disappearance, fading) of the subject (not just the disappearance of the mother as Freud states), is tied to the difference between two opposites. The opposites are represented (*fort-da*), but at the center of the child's game is self-identification of the subject with a lack of the object of reference. The aim of the game is its end; the aim of life becomes death itself. In Benjaminian terms, while translation deals with the afterlife of the original, translation in and of itself does not signify immortality because it is finite and cannot be translated further; translation is the end of translation.

As Boyd points out, the production of meaning in *Pale Fire* happens in its most prominent conflict: the conflict between the two opposite minds—Shade's and Kinbote's, that of creator/poet and that of translator/commentator.[84] Boyd insightfully observes that this clash extends beyond the creator's death. The great inversion of this novel is the inversion of roles: instead of the sacred insanity of poetry and scholarly rationality and dryness, one faces a romantic, mad commentator and a pleasantly, if a bit insipidly, rational poet. Boyd interprets these roles as two ways of dealing with *loss*.[85]

The unsettling "withdrawal from any semantically fixed encoding"[86] was known to the Romantics as the chiasm in the expression of the sublime. An example would be the striking rhyme of "prekrasen/uzhasen" (awesome/awful) in reference to Peter I on the battlefield in Pushkin's "Poltava."[87] The uncanny effect is similar to Freud's *unheimlich*—two opposites, anxiety and desire or familiar and strange, conjoined in one. In the case of the violence of death, the experience is made sharable through the process of *translation* into representation. Death as a signified defies representation; it is a "receding, ungraspable signified, invariably pointing back self-reflexively to other signifiers."[88] As in the poem "On Translating

*Eugene Onegin,*" translation is made possible only by the violent death of the original. However, the violence done to the original by the process of translation is sublated by acknowledging the limitation of language and producing an allegorical model, the Other, the Commentary. The allegorical model speaks in other terms, of other things. Bronfen adds: "It always also articulates the occulted signifier, present though under erasure."[89] The Greek *diaballo* means "to translate, as well as to split, cause strife and difference, reject, defame, deceive."[90] In a sense, speaking again in psychoanalytic terms, one recognizes violence inevitably done to the original and deals with it by giving it "a fixed position," confining it to the Commentary.[91] The beginning of Kinbote's "translation" of Shade's poem into his own text requires the violent death of the author. Indeed, in his poem "On Translating *Eugene Onegin,*" Nabokov conceptualizes translation as "profanation of the dead" and describes the process as parasitically feeding off the helpless original. The critic/translator's freedom, as he gets rid of the "original" author (as happens literally in *Pale Fire*), produces an unreliable or lucidly mad narrator/interpreter.

In discussing translation as the allegorical mode, we should be attuned to the notion of repetition. Jean Baudrillard discusses repetition as emerging from a position of liminality between life and death, a rhetorical strategy that, according to him, involves doubling (another characteristic motif of Nabokov's fiction)—the reanimation of a model, the return of the "original" in its artificial copy.[92] While the motif of doubling in Nabokov is truly inexhaustible, *Pale Fire* alone gives plenty of relevant examples.[93] Masha Levina-Parker addresses the motif of repetition inherent in Nabokov's fiction, interpreting it specifically in a context close to that of translation and allegory:

> The use of motif repetition, especially in *Bildungsroman,* autobiography, or pseudo-autobiography, is usually perceived precisely as a return . . . to some original element of narration, be that a subject, a hero, an event, or a discussion. Repetition therefore always presupposes the presence of a source or a beginning, which is positioned outside the system of repetitions, but which establishes it and defines its composition and function.

> Such a point of departure is an "original" of sorts, while the subsequent repetitions are its more or less faithful copies.[94]

However, these "copies/repetitions" are never "ideal" copies; the process of approximation is a series of unfolding attempts, pointing to some elusive but ultimately unattainable referent positioned outside the text. The possibility of absolute repetition is illusory and meaning is endlessly suspended.

In relation to translation as "profanation of the dead," it is interesting and perhaps significant to note that Kinbote argues that his name is not an anagram of Botkin, but that it means *regicide* in Zemblan.[95] Its obvious source of reference is Shakespeare's "bare bodkin," which kills the king. Disa, the rejected queen of Charles II, bears the name that "echoes Dis, the kingdom of the dead."[96] Reiterating the notion of feeding off of the original, Sybil, Shade's wife, calls Kinbote "an elephantine tick; a king-sized botfly; a macaco worm; the monstrous parasite of a genius."[97] One would not notice this on the first reading, but Sybil's vision is artfully echoed when Botkin is defined in the Index as "American scholar of Russian descent . . . : king-bot, maggot of extinct fly that once bred in mammoths and is thought to have hastened their phylogenetic end."[98]

In the post-modernist context, one asks the chicken and the egg question: is the copy equal to the original? Does the original produce its reading or does the reading produce the original? Trying on this kind of approach with *Pale Fire*, Boyd even entertains a theory of Kinbote as Shade's invention, "a mirror-inversion of himself (exile rather than stay-at-home, lonely homosexual rather than happily married man, vegetarian rather than meat-eater, bearded rather than clean-shaven, left- rather than right-handed, and so on),"[99] but eventually has to reject this theory on the basis of "literary merit," as it were: if Shade were indeed capable of concocting such complex narratives, he would have shown, at his age of sixty-one, the ability to write fiction. Kinbote, on the other hand, claims to be the "only begetter" of the Poem "Pale Fire," the "prompter behind."[100] This, however, is a conclusion based solely on the sense of his own importance: on his claimed closeness to the author and the alleged fact of providing Shade with the theme, the setting,[101] and the meaning (himself and his misfortunes as an exiled king of Zembla). The meanings are often inversions, mirror images of sorts. An example of such inversion in interpretation is Kinbote's complaints in the Commentary that Sybil constantly stood in the way of his great friendship with Shade, preventing Kinbote from seeing the poet. Kinbote perversely finds the proof for such claims in Shade's expression of love for his wife in "Pale Fire": "And all the time, and all the time, my love, / You too are there. . . ."[102] The Index, with just one page dedicated to him compared to two pages about Kinbote, shows how the poet matters only insofar as he is interpreted, invented, or seen by the commentator in light of his own life, work, and circumstances.

Of course, in Nabokov's "hall of mirrors" the unsettling reality is that the Commentator himself might be an invented figure. This points straight to Nabokov's understanding of both fiction (in all senses of this word) and translation, as well as their relationship with one another. It is not accidental that Nabokov's painstaking work on the *Eugene Onegin* Commentary was done between the years when he started *Lolita* and finished *Pale Fire*. De Man's notion of all reading as a form of allegory makes one think of what one does when one performs the reading: it is not literate but interpretive, and in the case of *Pale Fire*, it is a radical *misreading*. One is also tempted to think about the contrast between Shade, always attuned to the world outside the self, and the self-obsessed Kinbote:[103] the contrast provides insight into the "fiction" of translation being concerned with the Other (which always ends up in the self) and its crucial difference from the creative effort of fiction reaching beyond the self.

As the allegorical model of Nabokov's novels stands in direct relation to his interest in the beyond (and, because of this, in death), allegory becomes the preferred mode by means of which death is "rhetorically articulated in language."[104] As Nabokov's endeavors of writing and translating became intertwined due to circumstances and necessity, the allegorical model was extended to literary translation itself. I think it would be accurate to suggest that it accounts for Nabokov's trajectory towards literal translation. His practice of translation seems to change radically, yet his adherence to the idea of some "true" "metaphysical" language—ever elusive and ever present—remains surprisingly constant (the "ideal" referent positioned outside the text). While Nabokov's defense of the technical implications of literalism is well known from the theoretical squabbles that ensued after *Eugene Onegin*'s publication, it is important to remember that philosophically, literalism is related to the absolute: any claim of ultimate accuracy excludes any form of relativity. In the following symptomatic comment, Nabokov directly related this philosophical agenda to the practical choices he was making while translating *Onegin*. In his commentary to verses 1-4 of stanza XXXIX of Canto IV, Nabokov makes a connection between Pushkin's stanza and an autobiographical allusion disguised as a translation of André Chénier. (The allusion is to a specific illicit relationship Pushkin had with a peasant girl on his Mikhailovskoe estate.) Nabokov, defending his translation of the object of Onegin's bucolic affections as "a white-skinned girl"—a strange and least obvious choice—writes:

> Pushkin's line 3 ["poroi belianki chernookoi . . ."] is, by the by, an excellent illustration of what I mean by literalism, literality, literal interpretation. I take "literalism" to mean "absolute accuracy." If such accuracy sometimes results in the strange allegoric scene suggested by the phrase "the letter has killed the spirit," only one reason can be imagined: there must have been something wrong either with the original letter or with the original spirit, and this is not really a translator's concern. Pushkin has literally (i.e. with absolute accuracy) rendered Chénier's "une blanche" by belyanka, and the English translator should reincarnate here both Pushkin and Chénier. It would be false literalism to render belyanka ("une blanche") as "a white one"—or, still worse, "a white female"; and it would be ambiguous to say "fair-faced."[105]

Such understanding of "absolute accuracy," in which unified vision becomes a hall of mirrors, whose reflections double and triple *ad infinitum,* is very much in line with Nabokov's unusual metaphysics. Allegory as a strategy allows the translator to partake of the same "gesture" as the original by signifying difference, by focusing on other things (commentary, criticism). The in-betweenness points to the "central aporia" of the allegory, the gap "inscribed in all production of meaning."[106] While other existing English translations of *Eugene Onegin*—by Charles Johnston, Oliver Elton/[Anthony David Peach] A. D. P. Briggs, James E. Falen, and Walter Arndt—could be called metaphorical, in the sense that they are meant to be "like the original" (just in another language) and that they are meant to be read, Nabokov's idiosyncratic translation is an undertaking of a different nature—allegorical or, more specifically, metonymical, related to the original by spatial contiguity rather than complete identification with it. It can only be studied (and in fact the four volume "mammoth" grew out of a "little book" intended for teaching purposes). On the one hand, the literal translation itself functions as a scholarly source for exact quotes. The entire text of *Eugene Onegin* becomes one giant quotation. On the other hand, the Commentary paradoxically takes on the function of a translation and becomes in English what Pushkin's text is supposed to be in Russian. In Goethe's terms, it exists not instead (*anstatt*) of the original, but rather in its place (*an der Stelle*). In *Westöstlicher Diwan* (*West-Eastern Diwan*), Goethe assesses what a "perfect" translation might be. It can be "identical" to the original, but the identity is "functional," not absolute. A return to the original is still necessary and access to it should be open.[107] The Commentary and Index in *Pale Fire* parody this metonymical mode of translation by distorting it through a comical and tragic mirror and turning it into its opposite, the metaphorical: translation becomes appropriation since everything can be substituted for everything else. As translation disintegrates into madness, the parody becomes a diagnosis of total metaphoricity.

Nabokov proudly claims that his *Onegin* is just a "pony" for students.[108] He sacrifices rhyme (retaining only the iambic meter) and brings his translation closer to prose. Structural parallels to *Pale Fire* demonstrate especially well how the translation and Commentary together reclaim Pushkin's text as a novel. The prose aspect of Nabokov's *Onegin* cannot be accidental if we consider it in the light of the allegorical (metonymical) mode of translation. In "Two Aspects of Language and Two Types of Aphasic Disturbances,"

Roman Jakobson draws on the competition of metonymical and metaphorical devices in the symbolic process of signification: "Similarity in meaning connects the symbols of a metalanguage with the symbols of the language referred to. Similarity connects a metaphorical term with the term for which it is substituted. Consequently, when constructing a metalanguage to interpret tropes, the researcher possesses more homogeneous means to handle metaphor, whereas metonymy, based on a different principle, easily defies interpretation."[109] Jakobson argues that the functioning (or rather, malfunctioning) of two major linguistic mechanisms—the metaphorical and the metonymical—are responsible for the two aphasic afflictions: the "similarity disorder," predicated on the incapability of selection and substitution, and the "contiguity disorder," hinged on the agrammatical augmentation of words into a "word heap."[110] The prevalence of one mechanism over the other also defines literary and artistic trends. "The primacy of the metaphoric process in the literary schools of Romanticism and Symbolism" might account for the prevalence of poetry in these two literary trends, whereas Realism follows "the path of contiguous relationships" and "synechdochic details."[111] In the context of the allegorical/metonymical mode of Nabokov's translation, it is especially significant that prose, unlike poetry, "is forwarded essentially by contiguity."[112]

## The Allegorical Model at Work: The Nature of the Index, the Nature of the Commentary

Upon careful consideration, one cannot fail to notice that Nabokov's aesthetic apparatus is at work both in his Index to *Eugene Onegin* (and *Pale Fire*) and the Commentary, as much as it is at work in his fiction. In other words, translation and its apparatus are not just what they seem to be, but also vehicles for expressing Nabokov's original ideas about the nature of creativity and art. Nabokov's Index to *Onegin*, while certainly serving its necessary utilitarian purposes (as an integral part of any scholarly work of such dimension), also fulfills the interpolating function of patterning. One is reminded of the "hidden pictures" described by Nabokov in the ending of the Russian version of his memoir, *Drugie berega* (*The Other Shores*). The "camouflage" of the cityscape entangles the details of a magnificent ship in the distance that the eye at first refuses to register—the ship that would carry Nabokov, in the third act of exile, to America. Nabokov likens this vision to "hidden pictures" ("Naidite, chto spriatal matros"—"Find what a sailor has hidden") and writes: "odnazhdy uvidennoe ne mozhet byt vozvrashcheno v khaos nikogda" ("what is once seen, can never be returned back into chaos").[113]

It is a fundamental creative principle that points in two directions simultaneously: first, the discovery lies within the picture itself, not outside it ("not text, but texture," to quote "Pale Fire"); and second, once one "sees" the "answer," one is able to see *only* it—the entanglement of "texture" will be destroyed. Of course, in the ending of The *Other Shores*, this principle deals with the pattern of the personal fate of the author, but the same principle is applicable to Nabokov's poetics—patterning and repetition rather than ideological interpolations (such interpolations would be the method of Lev Tolstoi, for example). The Index, used in both *Pale Fire* and *Onegin*, is a fascinating device of double nature: whereas it feigns being merely a helpful apparatus to the main text, it actually hides; and, as it creates certain patterns or "signal words" that might have remained concealed even throughout the Commentary, it discloses.

Just as most of Nabokov's plots create "chaos" that seems to be devoid of any order until patterns and repetitions "pull out" a thread that has been previously concealed, the chaos of the Index seems at first glance to be plotless, as any reference apparatus would be: "Flora," "Florence," and "Florida," for example, coexist for no reason other than the alphabetical order of references. However, the "signal words" trace a hidden path through the apparent chaos of the apparatus. If one takes, for example, the word "Abyssinia (Ethiopia)" in Nabokov's Commentary to *Onegin*, one first finds it as a reference to Pushkin's interest in his pedigree and Ethiopian descent (also explored in Pushkin's poem "My Pedigree" ("Moia rodoslovnaia"), the issues raised in the commentary to the first stanza of *Onegin*. Abyssinia, however, has nothing to do with the indexed stanza about Onegin's uncle, just as the poem "My Pedigree" bears no relation to it, except for certain affinity of meter and rhyme. This seemingly unrelated commentary then veers off into tracking "My Pedigree" (Onegin's uncle and the relevant stanza now totally forgotten!) back to the imitation of Pierre-Jean de Béranger's "Le Vilain" and ends in a surprising pronouncement, revealing more about Nabokov than Pushkin: "This can only be explained by Pushkin's habit of borrowing from mediocrities to amuse his genius."[114] (This becomes especially poignant in light of the revelations in 2004 of Nabokov's "plagiarism" in *Lolita*—his alleged borrowings from an obscure German writer, Heinz von Lichberg.) The next reference to Ethiopia emerges in the commentary to line 14 of the same Canto I ("but harmful is the North to me")—Pushkin's allusion to his exile to Bessarabia, where *Eugene Onegin* was started. "Ethiopian" here appears as a reference to Pyotr Viazemskii's pun in his letter to Alexander Turgenev, calling Pushkin "bes arabskii" ("Arabian devil"), a pun on "the Bessarabian" ("bessarabskii"). It should actually be "arapskii," explains Nabokov patiently, referring to "arap" or "Blackamoor." However, this "Ethiopian" reference is marginal to the commentary; it actually discusses how "Pushkin often alludes to personal and political matters in geographical, seasonal, and meteorological terms."[115] The next reference to Abyssinia has very little to do with the commentary to Canto X, stanza IV. This commentary discusses at length Alexander I's title of "head of kings"[116] after the defeat of Napoleon. The ending of the commentary, however, is: "*Negus nagast*, the title of Abyssinian emperors, means 'king of kings.'"[117] Since "Abyssinian" is a "signal word," an unmistakable reference to Pushkin, it not only establishes Pushkin's primacy over the actual emperor of his time,[118] but it immediately calls to mind for the Russian reader an entire hidden "chain" of obvious references—one of Pushkin's perennial motifs, "Poet—Tsar," as in the famous "You are Tsar—live alone."[119] Thus the "Abyssinian" thread, inextricably related to Pushkin himself, through commentary barely relevant to the referenced lines of translation, leads one through Nabokovian aesthetics to the bliss and freedom of creative solitude—one of Nabokov's most persistent and important themes. All of the remaining "Abyssinian" references occur in Nabokov's Appendix One, about Pushkin's ancestor Abram Gannibal. Having painstakingly traced all available sources to check a rather dubious hypothesis of Pushkin's descent from Ethiopian royalty, Nabokov concludes Gannibal's story with a semi-absurd final paragraph, in which the very last "Abyssinian" reference occurs.

> We recall Coleridge's Abyssinian maid (*Kubla Khan*, 1797) singing of "Mount Abora," which (unless it merely echoes the name of the musical instrument) is, I suggest, either Mt. Tabor, an amba (natural citadel), some 3000 feet high in the Siré district of the Tigré, or still more exactly the unlocated amba Abora, which I find mentioned by the chronicler Za-Ouald (in Basset's translation) as being the burial place of a certain high official named Gyorgis (one of Poncet's two governors?) in 1707. We may further imagine that Coleridge's and Poncet's doleful singer was none other than Pushkin's great-great-grandmother; that her lord, either of Poncet's two hosts, was Pushkin's great-great-grandfather; and that the latter was a son of Cella Christos, Dr. Johnson's Rasselas. There is nothing in the annals of Russian Pushkinology to restrain one from the elaboration of such fancies.[120]

Not only does this remind one of Nabokov's own scholarly mystifications (one wonders whether anyone has ever checked out all these rather improbable chroniclers Nabokov refers to), but it also points to the key theme of the failure at interpretation in *Pale Fire* and in Nabokov's Pushkin lecture of 1937: the attempts to construct a "plausible" life of a poet with a mysterious affinity for "the poet's work, if not the poet himself." One is also reminded of the famous mystification in *The Gift*, when a gullible Russian, returning to Petersburg after a long time abroad and not being aware of Pushkin's death in 1837, is shown an elderly gentleman at the theater and told that he is Pushkin. The whole alternative life of Pushkin (or what it might have been, had he not been killed) suddenly grows out of nothing, out of a bubble of mystification, in which amusement is mixed with piercing sense of chance, possibility, and loss.

The dynamics of the Index become even more clear if one takes a look at its parody in *Pale Fire*. The agenda of the Index in

*Pale Fire* is of course made much more obvious by the mere fact that *Pale Fire* is a work of fiction, masquerading as a poem with accompanying scholarly apparatus. The original (the Poem) is being "translated"/appropriated by the Commentary; the Index makes the task of appropriation complete. The Commentary as translation makes choices about *how* and *what* to comment on, thus forcing the resisting original into the Procrustean bed of interpretation; but the Index bares the mechanism of translation to its "bones," so to speak, since it maintains control *entirely* by selection. In the Commentary, two struggling voices still have to co-exist out of necessity—that of Shade and that of Kinbote; in the Index, Kinbote, as Boyd puts it, "has no competition: no other voice can be heard."[121] By creating order within the scholarly framework, the Index legitimizes Zembla, "almost seeming to verify its validity and refute our recent dismissal, until we remember that it confirms only the relentless method of his [Kinbote's] particular madness."[122] The most obvious example of this selective method would be the "cast" of characters from the Index. G, K, S, as we are informed, "stand for the three main characters in this work," that is, Gradus, Kinbote, and Shade.[123] By the time the reader reaches the Index, he or she has supposedly realized that two of the three "main characters" mentioned are madmen. This, one might think ironically, sets the right tone for the Index! Shade's wife Sybil gets a reference in *"passim,"* and Shade's daughter Hazel gets two lines full of cruel irony, since we know that her suicide had been caused by her perceived physical ugliness (according to Kinbote, she deserves "great respect, having preferred the beauty of death to the ugliness of life").[124] Shade himself is indexed in about one page, but most of the entries describe him as seen through the eyes of Kinbote: "his first brush with death as visualized by K, and his beginning the poem while K plays chess at the Students' club, 1," or "the complications of K's marriage compared to the plainness of S's, 275."[125] Shade's major works are not indexed at all (the exception is "his work on *Pale Fire* and friendship with K").[126]

Kinbote, defined as "an intimate friend of S, his literary adviser, editor and commentator,"[127] gets two full pages—considerably more than the author he is supposed to be editing and commenting on. Kinbote's entries describe minute details of his life and character, bringing out his obsessions, his homosexuality, his misogyny, and absurdly infusing completely unrelated lines of the Poem with "his modesty, 34"; "his anxieties and insomnia, 62"; "his sense of humor, 79"; his own "boyhood. . . , 162,"[128] etc. Of all other residents of New Wye, only Botkin makes a disconcerting appearance. Apart from the reader's guess that this eccentric Slavic professor might be the insane Kinbote in "real life" (the notion of "real" now so far removed that the actual existence of this nebulous campus can be put into question), Botkin is not even a character in the novel! The last line of his entry, however, makes a sly reference to Hamlet (by defining "botkin, or bodkin, a Danish stiletto,"[129] etc.), thus obliquely evoking Hamlet's famous "to be or not to be" soliloquy and its puzzling over the beyond.

The general method of the Index is to inundate, by slight of hand and outlandish fabrications, Shade's work with Zembla, its king (Kinbote is the "King" of the Index!), and Kinbote's personal obsessions. For example, an entry for Gradus claims that line 596 of the Poem mentions his name in an unpublished variant and talks of Gradus's wait in Geneva.[130] However, when we return to the Poem, we plainly see that there is nothing there about Gradus: the stanza is about the difficulty of talking to "our dear dead" in our dreams, in which a long dead "old chum" might be not at all surprised to see us at the door, and "points at the puddles in his basement room."[131] The matter is complicated, however, by the fact that what the Index is actually "indexing" is not the line itself, but rather Kinbote's Commentary on this line. This commentary suggests that "Lethe leaks in the dreary terms of defective plumbing"[132] and offers a "variant," fabricated by Kinbote, which mentions "Tanagra dust." As readers, we are supposed to put the three last letters of the first word and the first two of the second word together, get the name Gradus, and become convinced that it was, as the entry "Variants" in the Index informs us, "a remarkable case of foreknowledge."[133] Finally, the Index as a whole symbolically concludes with the entry of "Zembla," "a distant northern land" (the "North" where Pushkin had so much trouble!), with no references to any lines of the Poem at all. The absence of references makes sense because Zembla is mentioned only once in the Poem, and even this mention is a joking reference to Pope, which bitterly disappoints Kinbote. There is another reason for the absence as well: there is no need to make references; every single line of the Poem has *become Zembla* by now, as the act of the Poem's appropriation has been completed. In his Foreword, Kinbote unambiguously states that it is the commentator who has the last word. He means that his "word" outweighs that of the author, and he indeed transforms Shade's text into a text about Zembla: he does have the last word, as it literally becomes the *last* word of the book. Shade's Poem famously lacks its last line, but Kinbote has provided it for the novel as a whole: the last line of the *novel* is "Zembla."

Nabokov's creation of patterns is equally important in his Commentary to *Onegin*, with its multiple examples of the "fatidic" dates tying biographical information in with the translated text. For example, the comment on Baron Anton Delvig, in relation to Canto VI, stanza XX, references the "marvelous coincidence "of Delvig dying" on the anniversary of death of the fictional Lenskii (who is compared to him here on the eve of a fatal duel)."[134] Nabokov further notes that the wake for Delvig was held by his friends—Pushkin, Viazemskii, Evgenii Baratynskii, and Nikolai Iazykov—on January 27, 1831, exactly six years before Pushkin's own duel.[135] The death of the author, like the death of the father, forever looms at the heart of Nabokov's work. In *Pale Fire*, for example, Shade, Kinbote, and Gradus (the author, the commentator, and the assassin), all share the same birthday—July 5, and Shade is killed on Nabokov's father's birthday—July 21. This, among other things, allows Boyd to argue that Nabokov in *Pale Fire* transforms his father's death into the "shambolic farce" of Shade's assassination, just as he "turns his father's death into a cosmic chess game" in the "margins of his autobiography."[136] Nabokov's father was fatally shot in an assassin's attempt on the life of another man—Pavel Miliukov, Nabokov's father's former ideological adversary from the State Duma. Kinbote calls Shade's assassination in lieu of his own "the farce of fate."[137]

Nabokov treats Pushkin's art and life as an ethical and aesthetical paradigm. In "Pushkin, or the Real and the Plausible," Nabokov talks of Pushkin's truth being different both from truth as brilliant illusion and from "Russian truth," with its inexorable impetuosity. Pushkin's truth is the aesthetic truth—the truth of art. It is significant that Nabokov's friend Khodasevich thus defined the central aspect of Pushkin's art: "Pushkin subjugated both himself and all coming Russian literature to the voice of internal truth. To follow Pushkin is to share this burden. Pushkin was first to judge himself in his art by final judgment and bequest to a Russian writer a fateful liaison between man and artist, between personal life and creative fate."[138] Another aspect of Pushkin's work also noted by Khodasevich—that of "profanity" as a combination of the serious and the funny—is remarkably similar to Nabokov's "comic/cosmic" juxtaposition, hinged only on the difference of one consonant.

Fate and life intertwine in many ways, and mimicry and patterning are Nabokov's devices of choice to herald this intertwining. Life imitating art, Nabokov's favorite theme related to the issues of mimicry and conscious play, is what he dubs a "classical case of life's playing up to art" in the *Onegin* Commentary.[139] Thus Lenskii's actions before his fateful duel are synchronized in Nabokov's Commentary with Lord Byron's life (Byron being one of Lenskii's prototypes). While Lenskii is going to his last ball, writing his last elegy, and fighting the duel (January 12, 13, and 14, 1821, respectively), Byron actually makes corresponding entries in his diary in Ravenna, Italy, about seeing masked revelers singing and dancing, "for tomorrow they may die," about only gods knowing whether life or death is better, and, finally, about "firing pistols— good shooting."[140] The patterning extends itself beyond plots and dates to the patterning of Pushkin's *Onegin* stanza on a sonnet, as well as the alliterative order of his poetic language. For example, Nabokov comments on the "alliterative magic that our poet distills"[141] from lining up the characters of popular French, German, and English novels (such characters as Julie Wolmar, Malek-Adel, Gustave de Linar, Werther, Sir Charles Grandison). Nabokov thinks it to be a perfect example of how the artist finds "a poetic pattern in pedestrian chaos."[142]

A characteristic example of a fatidic date in the Commentary, Pushkin's birth in 1799, also brings together Nabokov's ideas on the relation of life and art. The date in question comes up as part of a comment on Nikolai Karamzin that bears an uncanny resemblance to Shade's *"Life is a message scribbled in the dark. /* Anonymous."[143] Nabokov explains how in a bouts-rimés exchange Karamzin made a "New Year prophesy for 1799," presaging the appearance of the greatest Russian poet: "To sing all things, Pindar will be reborn."[144] The peculiar and perhaps significant characteristic of this comment on Karamzin, Pushkin's important older friend and the famous author of the *History of the Russian State*, is that the only other detail about him that Nabokov found necessary to include was his epigram that Nabokov translated thus: "Life? A romance. By whom? Anonymous. / We spell it out; it makes us laugh and weep, / And then puts us / To sleep." ("Chto nasha zhizn? Roman.— Kto avtor? Anonim. / Chitaem po skladam, smeemsia, plachem . . . spim.") This inclusion of Karamzin's epigram can only be explained by it itself being the source of Shade's lines in *Pale Fire*.

Nabokov's commentaries are delightfully personal and, as those of Kinbote, reflect much of the commentator's biography (or "fictional" biography). For example, Nabokov discusses the "fancies of the British Muse" that "disturb the sleep of the *otrokovitsa*" (maiden). (Pushkin mistakenly includes the French *Jean Sbogar* by Charles Nodier, 1818, in these British "fancies.") Nabokov makes the following ironic comment on the dangerously attractive "amateur communist" Sbogar: "He is interested in the redistribution of riches. But I am not an *otrokovitsa*, and at this point Sbogar ceased to disturb my sleep."[145]

However, just as Kinbote's Commentary is not reliable, Nabokov's Commentary should not be trusted. It serves too many purposes at once: it is a serious philological study; it serves the less serious purpose of self-parody; and it settles scores with critics, literary enemies—past and present—and former friends. In one instance, Nabokov directly explains his choice of emphasis on a particular word in his translation by an autobiographic detail. Putting emphasis on *Why* (it literally should translate as *What for*) in "Zachem vy posetili nas?" (Tatiana's letter to Onegin), Nabokov translates line 22 of the letter as *"Why* did you visit us?" explaining his emphatic, *pathétique* "why" as the product of a "wonderful record (played for me one day in Talcottville by Edmund Wilson) of Tarasova's recitation of Tatiana's letter."[146] This comment, however, is itself a parody of the genre of "personal" *pushkinistika* (Pushkin studies) in general and of Wilson's innocent trust in various interpreters of Pushkin (especially Soviet) in particular.[147]

Family legends also play a big part in Nabokov's Commentary. For example, the history of Pushkin's duel with Kondratii Ryleev (part of the commentary on verse 4-6, Canto IV, stanza XIX) on Ryleev's estate Batovo, which later belonged to the Nabokovs, becomes carefully orchestrated with Nabokov's own childhood memories of his strolls along a wooded path known as "Le Chemin du Pendu."[148] While Nabokov objects on multiple occasions to dragging biography into hermeneutic efforts, he does engage in this practice both by inscribing the codified biographical information into his fiction and, for example, by discovering Pushkin's biographical details (his affair with a peasant girl that produced an illegitimate child) behind the veil of Chénier, forming a "marvelous mask, the disguise of a personal emotion."[149]

The debate about the legitimacy of or faithfulness in translation is also considered within the framework of metaphysical certainty (or uncertainty). In *Pale Fire* this problem is refracted through the teasing possibility of one unified author in the novel and the reliability of its multiple narratives. The unreliability of the narrator is one of the main thematic nodes of *Pale Fire*. The unreliability of commentaries is also treated by Nabokov at length in the Commentary to *Onegin*, especially whenever he deals with the Soviet or Russian commentators.[150] Such would be his comment to, Canto III, stanza XII, verse 10, which is rather amusing in light of Rowe's approach to Nabokov's metaphysical dimension: that is, his cataloguing of situations that lead to the appearance of ghosts in Nabokov's fiction. Nabokov talks of ghosts appearing in inept criticism, but the only ghosts that make their appearance are "bibliographic spooks . . . the references to nonexistent authors and works"[151] in notes on *Onegin* by the Russian commentator Dmitrii Chizhevskii. In a similarly funny twist, in *Pale Fire* we encounter the two "Shadeans": "inept" professors from Kinbote's Index, whom Sybil is trying to impose on Kinbote as co-editors of her late husband's manuscript, and whom Kinbote showers with contempt. Boyd explains that they are doubling in the novel as

"Andronnikov and Niagarin" (and the second time as "Niagarin and Andronnikov"), haplessly pursuing the disappeared jewels of the King. Kinbote writes in the Index: "two Soviet 'experts' still in quest of a buried treasure, 130, 681, 741; see Crown Jewels."[152] All this confusing doubling has perhaps yet another layer concerning commentary and criticism: Iraklii Andronikov was a popular Soviet commentator of Lermontov.

Finally, the Commentary becomes the site of Nabokov's polemical vision of the genesis of Pushkin's art: systematically uncovering Pushkin's foreign sources, Nabokov demonstrates how appropriation and borrowing, in Pushkin's case, had the uncanny ability to generate a new origin. In a characteristic example, Nabokov writes in his Commentary about Pushkin's defense of the Gallicisms. Pushkin exclaims: "Where are our Addisons, La Harpes, Schlegels? . . . Whose [Russian] critical works can we use for reference and support?" Viazemskii chimes in: "You did well to come out in defense of Gallicisms. Someday we must really say aloud that metaphysical Russian is with us still in a barbaric state. God grant it may acquire form someday similarly to the French language, to that limpid, precise language of prose, i.e., to the language of thought."[153] Nabokov shows how Pushkin's Gallicisms formed new Russian expressions in their own right, such as the "liubeznaia nebrezhnost" ("aimiable abandon") that characterizes Tatiana's writing style. Most of European literature came to Russia through translations from French and occasionally from German, rendering the very idea of authorship problematic. Reading Samuel Richardson, for example, the Russian reader was in fact reading the abbé Antoine François Prévost with his understanding of "elegant taste." If the notion of authorship is inherently problematic, what are we reading in the case of Nabokov's translation?

## *Eugene Onegin*: Nabokov's Literalism

Perhaps what we are reading is a "foundation myth" of Nabokov's own writing.[154] It is widely known that Nabokov attributed mystical importance to the fact of having being born on the same day as Shakespeare (Shakespeare being another "foundation myth" that served as a genesis and model to many of Nabokov's English-language novels, just as Pushkin served to the Russian ones—a sort of an "English-language double" of Pushkin) and one hundred years after Pushkin. According to A. Bessonova and V. Viktorovich, Nabokov acted as the first Nabokovian scholar when, in his translation and Commentary, he made a "non-sentimental journey" to his own literary sources.[155] Pushkin provides the framework for Nabokov's Russian fiction. *Mary* starts with a quote from *Onegin*'s Canto XLVII. *The Gift*, the last of Nabokov's Russian novels, ends with a sonnet written in *Onegin* stanza, reiterating the "open ending" of Pushkin's novel. In *The Gift*, "s golosom Pushkina slivalsia golos otsa" ("with Pushkin's voice merged the voice of his father").[156] The antithesis and antidote to the "truth" of the "dry labor" of Chernyshevskii's life in *The Gift* is Pushkin and his truth. The architectonics of *The Gift* (as those of Pushkin's own *Onegin* and Nabokov's *Pale Fire*) are those of a meta-novel: the "metaplot" of creativity, of a writer's work, which brings into focus in the denouement of the novel all of the separate plot-lines of fate, art, love, and death.[157] Nabokov's English novels also use specific asides and digressions from Pushkin's "free novel," as the poet called his *Onegin*, often inverting them for parody and turning them into expressive details or plots, or even specific situations within plots. Thus, for example, in *Ada*, Demon and Marina's supposedly salacious encounter in the intermission between the acts of a play, plainly modeled on *Onegin*, becomes funniest and most dubious if read against the events taking place in the respective acts of the play; the incestuous situation of *Ada* might be viewed as a parodic transformation of Onegin's response to Tatiana's declaration of love: "I love you with a brother's love / and maybe still more tenderly."[158] Characters in Nabokov's English novels (be they *The Real Life of Sebastian Knight*, *Lolita*, *Ada*, or *Pale Fire*) are also preoccupied or even obsessed—literally or metaphorically—with the process of accessing the truth of the original, or finding a perfect copy, a double of the elusive original—in short, with the process of translation.

Apart from the literalism of his translation per se, Nabokov's "trespassing" on the boundaries of scholarly genre caused controversy and lengthy public polemics in the West, and his challenge to Pushkin as national myth caused and is bound to cause further controversy in Russia.[159] Since Vissarion Belinskii's assessment of *Eugene Onegin* in the nineteenth century as an "encyclopedia of Russian life and a national work of art to its highest degree," a truism that generations of Russian middle school students have learned by heart, Pushkin has served as "the weightiest testimony of authenticity, of the primacy of national Russian culture."[160] Nabokov's meticulous search for Pushkin's European sources made all the "sacred cows" of Russian cultural nationalism look like cultural appropriations: even the Russian winter, the melancholic Tatiana and her old *niania* (nanny)—all sacrosanct cultural icons—turn out to be metamorphed renditions of their French, German, and English cultural prototypes.[161] In his "Description of the Text" that precedes the translation itself, Nabokov writes (in a description that makes one think of the setting of *Ada*): "It is not a 'picture of Russian life'; it is at best the picture of a little group of Russians, in the second decade of the last century, crossed with all the more obvious characters of western European romance and placed in a stylized Russia, which would disintegrate at once if the French props were removed and if the French impersonators of English and German writers stopped prompting the Russian speaking heroes and heroines."[162]

Nabokov is sublimely uninterested in the social aspects of the novel, which had been the emphasis of nineteenth-century Russian criticism (e.g. Belinskii or "naturalnaia shkola" ["naturalist school"]) and, similarly, of Soviet criticism. Nabokov's cultural archeology presages certain aspects of Iurii Lotman's scholarship. But the center of his effort is the novel's "creative history and genesis of *Onegin* as a work of language."[163] As Nabokov wrote in his *Gogol*, Gogol's work, "as all great literary achievements, is a phenomenon of language and not one of ideas."[164] Echoing this pronouncement, he observes in the "Description of the Text": "The paradoxical part, from a translator's point of view, is that the only Russian element of importance [in *Eugene Onegin*] is this speech, Pushkin's language, undulating and flashing through verse melodies the likes of which had never been known before in Russia."[165]

It makes little sense—if any—to get incensed, as Wilson did, because Nabokov chose the strangest or most obscure words (such as "prognostications" or "tears of conjurement") and to argue whether one could do better substituting "tit for tat." Instead, in the remaining part of this discussion I aim to investigate exactly how literalism is achieved and by what criteria we might assess the result. Boyd claimed that syntactical quaintness, which characterized Nabokov's literalism, was aimed at making the reader meet Pushkin "face to face," at drawing the reader's attention to the original.[166] This makes sense, since the translation grew out of teaching the text and, certainly, according to Nabokov himself, ideally should read parallel to the original or should inspire the reader to learn the language of the original.[167] Alexander Dolinin provides a different theoretical explanation. His theory is based on Shklovskii's effect of *ostranenie*, as he maintains that Nabokov deliberately violates the division of a line into syntactical units normal for English versification to make it "strange."[168]

Dolinin's approach might be indebted to Mikhail Gasparov's excellent article on another, much earlier example of literalism in translation, namely the famous poet-Symbolist Valerii Briusov's translations of *The Aeneid*.[169] Briusov attempted to translate *The Aeneid* many times: his first translations were accomplished when he was still a teenager, a student in a gymnasium; later, in 1899, he translated Books II and IV of the *Aeneid* in expert hexameters. In 1913, Mikhail Sabashnikov (a publisher with whom, by a twist of fate, Nabokov's father was to fight in a duel) offered to publish Briusov's *Aeneid* in his series "The Monuments of World Literature." Sabashnikov's edition never came out due to the upheavals of Russian history, but Briusov's translation, some notes, and a foreword to that translation do exist. Briusov rejected the versions he had written before and started anew, this time making his translation as literal as possible. According to Gasparov, a comparison of Briusov's different versions allows one to understand "Briusov's path to literalism."[170] The progress of Briusov's work from version to version, described by Gasparov and substantiated with multiple examples, provides insight into the procedures of any literary translator, including Nabokov, adopting *bukvalizm* (literalism) as his or her approach.

Briusov called his first, earliest version "not a translation but a paraphrase."[171] This is similar to Nabokov's own term. Briusov makes a transition to "poetic translation" by making paraphrases and images more precise, bringing them closer to the original. The second stage of his work ("so that an artistic translation can serve at the same time as an artistic crib") involves bringing grammatical forms closer to the original, changing the word order to that of the Latin original, and shifting stresses in proper names to make them sound as they did in Latin and not as is culturally accepted in Russian.[172] The result is decisively strange and barely readable: even a culturally prepared reader has to make an effort to follow unusual syntax while at the same time making sense of multiple names that no longer resemble their culturally established Russian counterparts.

Further discussion of literalism may go (and does go, in Gasparov's article) into two different directions. One direction is defining what literalism in translation is; the other is articulating the motivation and theory of literalism's practitioner. The former, in Gasparov's formulation, may provide a valuable insight into Nabokov's literalism. Gasparov makes use of a notion that exists in the theory of non-literary translation—that of the "length of context" (a unit of the original text of such length for which one can find in a translation an equivalent unit of absolute or near absolute correspondence). Depending on the length of context, non-literary translations are divided into roughly "word-to-word," "syntagm-to-syntagm," "phrase-to-phrase."[173] Gasparov suggests applying this notion to literary translation as well, pointing out that the "length of context" in this case might vary from word, to verse, to stanza, to paragraph, and even to a work as a whole.[174] Thus translations may follow the original with a word-to-word precision, even by including in italics or brackets those words that were not present in the original, but were added in translation out of necessity (as is the case in some translations of the scriptures); or translations might become *Nachdichtungen* (adaptations). Many translations of the eighteenth or early nineteenth century, with titles such as "From Horace" or "From Anacreon," for example, aimed at conveying only an emotional impulse of the original.[175] The translation program of the mature Briusov, the program of *bukvalizm*, is thus that of the "shortening of 'length of context.'"[176] If we were to apply the "length of context" approach to Nabokov's translation of *Onegin*, we would have to agree that the length of context Nabokov aimed at was that of the line. He himself claimed a "closer line-by-line fit (entailing a rigorous coincidence of enjambments and the elimination of verse transposal)" as the "technical" criterion for perfecting his literalism.[177]

Nabokov asked himself in the Foreword, "can a rhymed poem like *Eugene Onegin* be truly translated with the retention of its rhymes?" His answer was "of course . . . no."[178] So what does Nabokov sacrifice, apart from what he dismissively called "pleasure-measure"? According to him, pretty much everything except iambic meter:

> In transposing *Eugene Onegin* from Pushkin's Russian into my English I have sacrificed to completeness of meaning every formal element save the iambic rhythm: its retention assisted rather than hindered fidelity; I put up with a greater number of enjambments, but in the few cases in which the iambic measure demanded a pinching or padding of sense, without a qualm I immolated rhythm to reason. In fact, to my ideal of literalism I sacrificed everything (elegance, euphony, clarity, good taste, modern usage, and even grammar) that the dainty mimic prizes higher than truth. Pushkin has likened translators to horses changed at the posthouses of civilization. The greatest reward I can think of is that students may use my work as a pony.[179]

Nabokov estimated that the text of *Evgenii Onegin* contained 5,523 iambic lines,[180] whose stanza—Pushkin's invention in Russian—is based on a sonnet form "with a regular scheme of feminine and masculine rhymes: ababeecciddiff."[181]

Despite the quaintness of certain aspects of Nabokov's translation, it still retains what Liuba Tarvi called "'iambic' harmony and wholeness," perhaps since it was the only element consciously preserved by Nabokov as a translator.[182] Dolinin claimed that Nabokov actually created "perfect iambic clones," "mirror reflections" of Pushkin's tetrameters.[183] Dolinin estimated a rather high percentage of such clones, about 14 percent of all the lines. Tarvi undertook a very interesting experiment to verify this empirical estimate of Dolinin by developing a set of rigorous criteria, such as number of syllables in a line; rhythm (i.e. the variety of tonal arrangements in a line—the way stresses are imposed on the metric composition of the line and its coincidence with Pushkin's arrangement; this criterion also shows whether Pushkin's and Nabokov's lines coincide in their masculine/feminine rhyme); semantic parameter (the category on which Nabokov insisted himself);[184] and, finally, syntactical parameter (i.e. preservation of the order of words in a line). Tarvi's methodical application of these criteria to all 5,523 lines of the text yields a result substantially lower than Dolinin's estimate—213 "imperfect clones," i.e. 3.8 percent, while in only 14 lines was the coincidence according to all four criteria complete and resulted in "perfect clones."[185] An example of such a "perfect clone" can be either a line consisting mostly/only of names, which makes it a natural clone (e.g. Canto VIII, stanza XXXV, verse 4: "Mme de Stael, Bichat, Tissot"), or those rare ones in which English lexical equivalents by chance and by choice contain the same number of syllables, same stresses, and thus can be syntactically arranged in a perfect equivalent (e.g. Canto III, stanza I, verse 14: "pro dozd, pro len, pro skotnyi dvor" as "of rain, of flax, of cattle yard").

Tarvi convincingly demonstrates how Nabokov, having chosen the poetic line as the main building block of his literal translation, consistently works at perfecting the interlinear correspondence between the original and his translation in the 1975 edition. For example, to create a closer interlinear correspondence to the Russian line, Nabokov eliminates the verb (thus making the syntactical structure unusual for an English sentence) in Canto I, stanza XXXVI, verse 8: "and next day same as yesterday" (instead of "twill be the same as yesterday," in the edition of 1964). On the basis of methodical analysis of such changes in the second edition, made in 30 percent of the selected 213 lines, Tarvi expresses her justified doubts at Dolinin's idea of *ostranenie* as the reason for Nabokov's syntactical "quaintness." One might add that Nabokov's reference in the "Translator's Introduction," to his translation as a "crib" (i.e. line-by-line translation) with no fake modesty or any attempt at self-deprecation, is a mere statement of what was for him fact. Tarvi, however, goes on to formulate a bold hypothesis of Nabokov's "stikhoProza" ("versoProse") and Pushkin's "prozoStikhi" ("prosoVerse"). The essence of this hypothesis is that Nabokov created a translation of *Eugene Onegin* that came remarkably close to Pushkin's prose. Comparing Nabokov's translation of stanza XXVIII of Canto I, written down *in continuo*, to a fragment of Pushkin's prose, she points out striking affinities in their syntax and style.[186] Thus the empirical impression of "truth" and "harmony" of the translation might actually turn out to be confirmed by the optimal approximation to the "source" text (or the "next best thing," as metonymical contiguity, once again, suggests), in this case, Pushkin's own prose.

This interesting hypothesis is especially significant in light of Mikhail Lotman's analysis of Nabokov's technique in *The Gift*.[187] Discussing the place and role of poetry in *The Gift*, Lotman states the following: the most fundamental problem of studies of verse and versification is the problem of defining what verse *is*.[188] One of the experiments Nabokov conducts in *The Gift* is testing whether the reader is capable of detecting verse that is not graphically "highlighted" as such in the stream of prose. Lotman says that the abundance of seemingly "accidental" iambic passages is suspect in Nabokov's case. The confirmation for these passges not being accidental is Nabokov's own conclusion that the iambic passages within Pushkin's prose texts are intentional as a designing principle: "Uchas metkosti slov i predelnoi chistote ikh sochetaniia, on dovodil prozrachnost prozy do iamba i zatem preodoleval ego"[189] ("Learning precision of words and extreme purity of their combination, he carried the transparency of prose to iambic [meter] and then transcended it").[190] One of Nabokov's goals, concludes Lotman, is to overcome the linear juxtaposition of prose and verse: prose text includes clear fragments of rhymed verse, then metamorphs again into prose or unrhymed verse (at one point in *The Gift*, a mock reference to the stratagems of Andrei Bely's metric prose, his "cabbage hexameter," underscores the notion that all these complex arrangements are also a conscious design on the part of Nabokov).[191]

The other aspect of Gasparov's article on *bukvalizm* discussed above is *why* Briusov was doing what he was doing; that is, the theoretical premises of literalism. In Gasparov's formulation, all significant events in culture can be characterized by something that they have in common (insofar as they are the product of human creation) and something individual (insofar as they differ in terms of their time, place, and civilization).[192] The young Briusov, creating a pantheon of great personalities and heroes in the poems of his early collections, underscores the common element all cultures share. This vision is also reflected in his "Fialki v tigle" ("The Violets in the Crucible"), a relatively early article on literary translation, in which Briusov insists on being true to the whole of the meaning of the original at the expense of being true to the letter of translation. In the years of the first Russian revolution, Briusov's faith in the supreme unity of culture was dealt a severe blow, and Briusov was compelled to perceive, almost physically, that he and his contemporaries were standing on the fault line of two cultures, one dying and the other, alien and incomprehensible, that was yet to come, that of the "coming Huns."[193] His "The Coming Huns," a poem written at that time, spoke of the death of culture and the savage rejuvenation of the world. As Gasparov puts it, Briusov's understanding was now that of individual civilizations replacing one another but not as heirs to their predecessors, unable to appreciate or assess one another, just like the European culture and what was to come in its stead.[194] "Rejection of the theory of progress and transition to the theory of civilizations, closed onto themselves,"[195] are symptomatic of the time and are later theoretically summed up by Oswald Spengler. Thus, when Briusov in the 1910s writes his "Roman novels," such as *The Altar of Victory*, he fills them with exotic archeological details and lexical Latinisms. His translations from the Romans also strive for the "distancing effect": the reader had to be aware at every given moment that he or she was dealing with a text from a foreign and distant culture.[196] Briusov's principles of translation are best summed up in his article on the translations of the *Aeneid*: "Perevod . . . dolzhen byt prigoden i dlia tsitat po nemu" (literally, "Translation . . . should be also usable for the purpose of drawing quotations [of the original] from it").[197] In other words, if one were translating, for example, an English novel and encountered a quote from Shakespeare in it, one's first impulse would be to go to the accepted and established translation of Shakespeare for the translation of the quote. However, the existing translation might not necessarily be helpful for this purpose: the principles of translation of a short quote and a whole play are different (because the "length of context" is different) and the particular meaning in the quote might have been sacrificed in the process. Thus the approach Briusov advocated in his translation of the *Aeneid* was to create a source of "giant quotations" of sorts.[198]

One might argue that Nabokov's *Onegin*, as a translation devised in the process of teaching (hence the need for accurate quoting), might have shared Briusov's reasons for the shortening of the "length of context" to the individual line, thus constructing *Onegin* as a source for giant quotations. However, given Nabokov's ill disposition towards utilitarianism, one would reasonably doubt that this was the whole story. For all the reasons analyzed before, one might suspect that the less utilitarian, more metaphysical source of Nabokov's literalism is closer to what Anna Akhmatova meant when she wrote: "And perhaps Poetry itself / is one magnificent quotation."[199] It is possible to conceive an inversion of Nabokov's formula of carrying prose to the iambic meter and transcending it, used in *The Gift* and discussed earlier—his recipe for the creation of ideal prose, which is, of course, Pushkin's "harmonious" prose. Such inversion might help to capture the nature of Nabokov's translation of *Onegin*. Going in reverse order through the steps of the formula, one transcends mimicry ("wondrous likeness of difference," which Nabokov, an ardent anti-Darwinist, always understood as a "non-utilitarian" and thus artistic gift) on the way to complete metamorphosis (the complete internal affinity of the unlike, a "metaphysical gift").[200] This process, from mimicry to metamorphosis, shows mechanisms of concealed design and patterns of signification, strikingly similar to those of *Pale Fire*—the metaphorical tension within the metonymical (allegorical) model of the triad, Poem-Commentary-Index, as a whole.

# NOTES

1     A part of this chapter was published as an article as Julia Trubikhina, "Metaphysical 'Affinity of the Unlike': Strategies of Nabokov's Literalism," *Intertexts*, Special Nabokov Issue, 12/1 (2008): 55-72.

2     "Do you not understand that we are worms,/ each born to form the angelic butterfly..." Dante Alighieri, trans. Mark Musa (New York: Penguin Books, 1985), 111.

3     Vladimir Nabokoff-Sirine, "Pouchkine, ou le vrai et le vraisemblable," *La nouvelle revue française* 48 (1937): 362-378.

4     Vladimir Nabokov, "Pushkin, or the Real and the Plausible," trans. Dmitri Nabokov, *New York Review of Books* (31 March 1988): 40. See also Alexandrov, *Nabokov's Otherworld* (Princeton: Princeton University Press, 1991), 34.

5     "Pale Fire" the Poem, lines 939-940. See Vladimir Nabokov, *Pale Fire* (New York: Vintage International, 1989). Hereafter, all references to *Pale Fire* will indicate the novel's part (Poem, Commentary, or Index) and reference it by the line or page number, respectively.

6     Cited in Clarence Brown, "Nabokov's Pushkin and Nabokov's Nabokov," in *Nabokov: The Man and His Work*, ed. L. S. Dembo (Madison: The University of Wisconsin Press, 1967), 196.

7     *Pale Fire*, Poem, line 812.

8     Brian Boyd, *Nabokov's Pale Fire: The Magic of Artistic Discovery* (Princeton: Princeton University Press, 1999), 67.

9     Ibid., 68.

10     Ibid., 69-70.

11     Ibid., 43.

12     Alexandrov, *Nabokov's Otherworld*, 3.

13     W. W. Rowe, *Nabokov's Spectral Dimension* (Ann Arbor: Ardis, 1981).

14     See Alexandrov, *Nabokov's Otherworld*. Also see Gennady Barabtarlo, *Aerial View: Essays on Nabokov's Art and Metaphysics*, American University studies, Ser. XXIV, vol. 40, American Literature (New York: Peter Lang Publishing, 1993).

15     Alexandrov, *Nabokov's Otherworld*, 4.

16     See "Fame" ("Slava"), 1942, in Nabokov, *Poems and Problems*, 111-112. The quoted passage from the poem in the Russian original reads as follows:

> . . . Ia schastliv, chto sovest moia,
> sonnykh myslei i umyslov svodnia,
> ne zatronula samogo tainogo. Ia
> udivitelno schastliv segodnia.
> Eta taina ta-ta, ta-ta-ta-ta, ta-ta,
> a tochnee skazat ia ne vprave.
> Ottogo tak smeshna mne pustaia mechta
> o chitatele, tele i slave. . . .

Priznaius, khorosho zashifrovana noch,
no pod zvezdy ia bukvy podstavil
i v sebe prochital, chem sebia prevozmoch,
a tochnee skazat ia ne vprave.
Ne doverias soblaznam dorogi bolshoi
ili snam, osviashchennym vekami,
ostaius ia bezbozhnikom s volnoi dushoi
v etom mire, kishashchem bogami.
No odnazhdy, plasty razumenia drobia,
uglubliaias v svoe kliuchevoe,
ia uvidel, kak v zerkale, mir i sebia,
i drugoe, drugoe, drugoe.

[17] Nabokov, *Speak, Memory*, 297.
[18] Boyd, *Nabokov's Pale Fire*, 122-123.
[19] *Pale Fire*, Poem, lines 961-962.
[20] William Shakespeare, *Timon of Athens*, 4.3.435-440.
[21] Boyd, *Nabokov's Pale Fire*, 33.
[22] *Pale Fire*, Commentary, 347.188.
[23] *Pale Fire*, Commentary, 42.81.
[24] It is interesting and perhaps significant that Nabokov chose the form of heroic couplets for Shade's Poem in the first place, since it was translations of Ovid that signaled the development of heroic couplets in the English language. This points to Nabokov's preoccupation with Ovid and metamorphosis in a broad sense of the word.
[25] *Pale Fire*, Commentary, 549.227.
[26] Plato, *The Republic*, Book 7: 516a-b.
[27] Vladimir Nabokov, *Pnin* (New York: Avon, 1969), 58.
[28] Vladimir Nabokov, *Strong Opinions* (New York: McGraw-Hill, 1973), 30.
[29] See *Speak, Memory*, 218.
[30] See Alexandrov, *Nabokov's Otherworld*, 30.
[31] *Speak, Memory*, 218.
[32] *Strong Opinions*, 95.
[33] See Alexandrov, *Nabokov's Otherworld*, 28. Alexandrov draws on Jonathan Borden Sisson's doctoral dissertation, "Cosmic Synchronization and Other Worlds in the Work of Vladimir Nabokov" (University of Minnnesota, 1979).
[34] *Speak, Memory*, 378.
[35] Cited in Alexandrov, *Nabokov's Otherworld*, 28.
[36] *Strong Opinions*, 69.
[37] Vladimir Nabokov, "Prof. Woodbridge in an Essay on Nature Postulates the Reality of the World," *New York Sun*, 10 December 1940.
[38] *Strong Opinions*, 69.
[39] Ibid., 70.

40  See Vladimir Nabokov's letter to Edmund Wilson concerning his misinformed comment about the decline of Russian culture in *Correspondence Between Vladimir Nabokov and Edmund Wilson, 1940-1971*, ed. Simon Karlinsky (New York: Harper & Row, 1979), 220.

41  Vladimir Nabokov, "The Tragedy of Tragedy," cited in Alexandrov, *Nabokov's Otherworld*, 42.

42  Friedrich Nietzsche, "The Birth of Tragedy," in *The Birth of Tragedy And Other Writings*, ed. Raymond Geuss and Ronald Speirs (Cambridge: Cambridge University Press, 1999), 114.

43  *Pale Fire*, Commentary, 991.289.

44  Elizabeth Bronfen, *Over Her Dead Body: Death, Femininity and the Aesthetic* (New York: Routledge, 1992).

45  Ibid., 9.

46  Boyd, *Nabokov's Pale Fire*, 146.

47  Vladimir Nabokov, *Lectures on Russian Literature*, ed. Fredson Bowers (New York: Harcourt Brace Janovich/Bruccoli Clark, 1981), 106.

48  See in Alexandrov, *Nabokov's Otherworld*, 227-234.

49  *Pale Fire*, Commentary, 993-995.290.

50  *Strong Opinions*, 170.

51  Boyd, *Nabokov's Pale Fire*, 160.

52  As early as 1922, in his collection *The Cluster*, the young Sirin says in a poem "Molchi, ne vspenivai dushi . . ." ("Silence; Do Not Froth Up the Soul . . ."), written as a second part to another poem, "Paskha" ("Easter"), dedicated to his father's memory: ". . . dar luchezarnyi, dar stradania,—/ zhivuiu radugu, rydania . . ." (". . . a radiant gift, a gift of suffering,—/ a live rainbow, sobs . . ."). The Blokian formula from his drama "The Rose and the Cross," "radost-stradane" (joy-suffering) and, as noted M. Malikova, the repeated sound formation of "dar" ("gift") become an enormous funnel of references, sending one back to the motif of knighthood (knighthood, or "*rytsarstvo*," was underscored in all obituaries of Nabokov's father), Blok's "Rytsar-Neschaste" (The Knight of Misfortune), and Briusov's translation of Paul Verlaine's "Bon chevalier masqué qui chevauche en silence . . ." (1880). See M. Malikova, "Obraz Pushkina u Nabokova: Neskolko nabliudenii," in *A. S. Pushkin and V. V. Nabokov: Sbornik dokladov mezhdunarodnoi konferentsii 15-18 aprelia 1999 g.* (St. Petersburg: Dorn, 1999), 257-258. The latter text, very different from its original, also calls the "chevalier" the Knight of Misfortune and ends thus: ". . . kak vsiakii, kto vidit videne, s kem iavno beseduet Bog" ("as any one who is seeing a vision and with whom God is openly conversing") (cited in Malikova, 258). For any Russian poet, the final destination of any such reference of the explicit conversation with God is Pushkin's "The Prophet" (1826). Nabokov's poem "On the Death of A. Blok" calls Pushkin "a rainbow over the entire earth" (cited in *A. S. Pushkin and V. V. Nabokov*, 79).

53  Boyd, *Nabokov's Pale Fire*, 182; see also 169.

54  *Pale Fire*, Poem, lines 136-138.

55  Boyd, *Nabokov's Pale Fire*, 186-187.

56  Ibid., 187.

57  Ibid.

58  Barabtarlo, *Aerial View*, 207.

59  See note 52.

60  *Pale Fire*, Commentary, 347.189.

61  *The Nabokovian* is the twice-yearly publication of the International Vladimir Nabokov Society featuring news of the field, annual Nabokov bibliography, annotations to Nabokov's works, abstracts, books, dissertations, photographs, illustrations, notes, and queries. Edited by Stephen Jan Parker, Department of Slavic languages and Literatures at the University of Kansas.

62  As Shade describes in his Poem "Pale Fire," he suffers a heart attack while delivering a lecture entitled "Why Poetry is Meaningful to Us." In his near-death experience, Shade has a vision of a white fountain. Some time later, he reads a story of "a Mrs. Z" in a magazine, in which she describes her "beyond the veil" experience as also featuring a white fountain. This prompts Shade to seek her out only to learn that the article about her experience contained a misprint: it was a *"mountain,* not *fountain.* The majestic touch" (*Pale Fire,* Poem, 801-802).

63  Bronfen, *Over Her Dead Body*, 4.

64  Boyd, *Nabokov's Pale Fire*, 105.

65  *Pale Fire*, Commentary, 549.227.

66  Ibid., 47-48.88.

67  *Pale Fire*, Poem, lines 122-124.

68  One of the latest examples of this would be Nabokov's paraphrase of Nikolai Gumilev's poem "Ia i Vy" ("I and You") in his own poem of identical meter speaking of his own death in *Stikhi*: "I umru ia ne v letnei besedke/ ot obzhorstva i ot zhary,/ a s nebesnoi babochkoi v setke/ na vershine vysokoi gory . . ." ("And I will die not in a summer pavillion/ of overeating and heat,/ but with a celestial butterfly in my net/ on the top of a high mountain . . ."). Translation is mine, unless otherwise stated. See Vladimir Nabokov, *Stikhi* (Ann Arbor: Ardis, 1979), 297. The poem is dated 1972. Gumilev's poem reads: "I umru ia ne na posteli,/ Pri notariuse i vrache,/ A v kakoi-nibud dikoi shcheli,/ Utonuvshei v gustom pliushche . . ." ("And I will die not in my own bed/ in the presence of a doctor and lawyer,/ but in some wild crevice,/ overgrown with ivy . . .") (Nikolai Gumilev, *Stikhotvorenia i poemy* [Leningrad: Sovetskii pisatel, 1988], 286).

69  *The Gift*, 177.

70  The translation is mine. The Russian quote from Véra Nabokov's introduction to Nabokov's posthumous Russian collection is: "Etoi taine on byl prichasten mnogo let, pochti ne soznavaia ee, i eto ona davala emu ego nevozmozhnuiu

zhizneradostnost i iasnost dazhe pri samykh tiazhelykh perezhivaniiakh i delala ego sovershenno neuiazvimym dlia vsiakikh samykh glupykh i zlykh napadok." See *Stikhi,*1979.

71  Ellen Pifer, *Nabokov and the Novel* (Cambridge, MA: Harvard University Press, 1980), 110-118.

72  Boyd, *Nabokov's Pale Fire,* 275.

73  *Strong Opinions,* 7.

74  *Pale Fire,* Poem, line 808.

75  Boyd, *Nabokov's Pale Fire,* 144.

76  Ibid., 286.

77  Ibid., 258.

78  Bronfen, *Over Her Dead Body,* 8-9.

79  Pyotr Bitsilli, "Vozrozhdenie allegorii," *Sovremennye zapiski* LXI (1935): 191-204. See also "The Revival of Allegory," trans. Dwight Stephens, *TriQuarterly* 17 (Winter 1970): 102-118.

80  See Bitsilli, "The Revival of Allegory," 113-114.

81  See Pyotr Bitsilli, "V. Sirin. *Priglashenie na kazn.*—Ego zhe. *Sogliadatai,*" Paris, 1938, *Sovremennye zapiski* LXVIII (1939): 474-477. Cited in *V. V. Nabokov: Pro et Contra,* 253-254. Translation is mine.

82  Bronfen, *Over Her Dead Body,* 23.

83  Jacques Lacan, *The Four Fundamental Concepts of Psycho-Analysis* (New York: Norton, 1981).

84  Boyd, *Nabokov's Pale Fire,* 72.

85  Ibid., 74.

86  Bronfen, *Over Her Dead Body,* 45.

87  Aleksandr Pushkin, *Sobranie sochinenii v desiati tomakh,* ed. Dmitrii Blagoi, Sergei Bondi, Iurii Oksman. Tom 3. *Poltava.* (Moscow: Gosudarstvennoe izdatelstvo "Khudozhestvennaia literatura," 1960), 228.

88  Bronfen, *Over Her Dead Body,* 54.

89  Ibid., 183.

90  Ibid., 69.

91  See Julia Kristeva's analysis of the connection between death drive and signification in *Revolution in Poetic Language* (New York: Columbia University Press, 1984).

92  See Jean Baudrillard's analysis in *L'Echange symbolique et la Mort* (Paris: Gallimard, 1976).

93  The reader would undoubtedly notice the doublets of Mr. Campbell and Monsieur Beauchamp (in this case the doubling of names occurs in translation), the guards of the King whose carelessness while playing a chess game allows the King to flee through a tunnel; the King's red reflection in the lake suddenly moving by itself; Charles II himself envisioned as the Red King (these references are, of course, to *Alice* and her "tunnel," the rabbit hole, and the chess game in *Through the Looking Glass,* as well as to the claim that Alice

is only a dream of the Red King); Shade's daughter Hazel's love for "mirror words"; Hazel doubling as Sir Walter Scott's "Lady of the Lake"; Zembla being called the "land of reflections," etc.

94  Masha Levina-Parker, "Povtorenie. Répétition. Repetitsiia? Ob odnoi povestvovatelnoi strategii u Nabokova i Belogo," in *Imperiia N: Nabokov i nasledniki*, 487.

95  *Pale Fire*, Commentary, 894.267.

96  Boyd, *Nabokov's Pale Fire*, 164-165.

97  *Pale Fire*, Commentary, 247.171-172.

98  *Pale Fire*, Index, 306.

99  Boyd, *Nabokov's Pale Fire*, 123.

100  Ibid., 44-45.

101  "How persistently our poet evokes images of winter in the beginning of a poem which he started on a balmy summer night" (*Pale Fire*, Commentary, 34-35.79).

102  *Pale Fire*, Poem, lines 949-950.

103  Boyd, *Nabokov's Pale Fire*, 72-73.

104  Bronfen, *Over Her Dead Body*, 229.

105  *Eugene Onegin* (1964, 1975), Volume 2, 464-465. Herein, all references will be from the 1964 edition, unless otherwise stated.

106  Bronfen, *Over Her Dead Body*, 229.

107  Cited in Emad, "Thinking More Deeply into the Question of Translation," 338-339.

108  *Eugene Onegin*, 1975, Volume 1, x.

109  Jakobson, "Two Aspects of Language and Two Types of Aphasic Disturbances,"113.

110  Ibid., 109.

111  Ibid., 111.

112  Ibid., 114.

113  Nabokov, *Drugie berega*, 508.

114  *Eugene Onegin*, Volume 2, 34.

115  Ibid., Volume 2, 37.

116  Ibid., Volume 3, 323.

117  Ibid., 324.

118  It inevitably brings out Pushkin's own *"Exegi monumentum,"* with the monument Pushkin erects for himself rising "taller . . . than Alexander's column" — the famous column in front of the Winter Palace.

119  Reference to Pushkin's famous 1830 poem "Poetu" ("To a Poet").

120  *Eugene Onegin*, Volume 3, 441.

121  Boyd, *Nabokov's Pale Fire*, 63.

122  Ibid.

123  *Pale Fire*, Index, 303.

124  Ibid., 312.

125 Ibid.
126 Ibid. Also see Kinbote's "Foreword" in *Pale Fire*, 13-29.
127 *Pale Fire*, Index, 308.
128 Ibid.
129 Ibid., 306.
130 Ibid., 307.
131 *Pale Fire*, Poem, line 596.
132 *Pale Fire*, Commentary, 231.
133 *Pale Fire*, Index, 315.
134 *Eugene Onegin*, Volume 3, 23.
135 Ibid.
136 Boyd, *Nabokov's Pale Fire*, 123.
137 *Pale Fire*, Commentary, 1000.294.
138 Vladislav Khodasevich, "Okno na Nevskii," in *Sobranie sochinenii v chetyrekh tomakh*, vol. 1 (Moscow: Soglasie, 1996), 490.
139 *Eugene Onegin*, Volume 2, 546.
140 Ibid.
141 Ibid., Volume 2, 342.
142 Ibid.
143 *Pale Fire*, Poem, lines 235-236.
144 *Eugene Onegin*, Volume 3, 145.
145 Ibid., Volume 2, 358-359.
146 Ibid., Volume 2, 391.
147 Wilson often "tortured" Nabokov in his letters, inquiring about his opinion on different Pushkin scholars, whom Nabokov had not read or did not respect. I am thankful to Vera Proskurina's article, which prevented me from being "duped" by this touching autobiographical detail in Nabokov's Commentary. See Proskurina, "Nabokov's *Exegi Monumentum*," 34.
148 *Eugene Onegin*, Volume 2, 433-434. "Path of a hanged man": Ryleev, a Decembrist, was hanged in 1826 for his leading role in the Descembrist revolt against the Tsar in 1825.
149 Ibid., Volume 2, 463.
150 Nabokov obviously does not speak about his own unreliability since, as a translator, he is convinced in his essential fidelity to Pushkin. Nabokov's understanding of "fidelity" does not necessarily extend to "others."
151 *Eugene Onegin*, Volume 2, 355.
152 *Pale Fire*, Index, 311.
153 *Eugene Onegin*, Volume 2, 378.
154 A similar idea was expressed by A. Bessonova and V. Viktorovich in "Nabokov—interpretator 'Evgeniia Onegina,'" in *A. S. Pushkin and V. V. Nabokov*, 279-289.
155 Ibid., 284.
156 *The Gift*, 98.

157 See Bessonova and Viktorovich, "Nabokov—interpretator 'Evgeniia Onegina,'" 281.
158 See *Eugene Onegin*, Volume 1, 189. The translation is Nabokov's.
159 The Commentary to *Eugene Onegin* has been translated into Russian: see Vladimir Nabokov, *Kommentarii k "Evgeniiu Oneginu" Aleksandra Pushkina* (Moscow: NPK "Intelvak," 1999).
160 See Bessonova and Viktorovich, "Nabokov—interpretator 'Evgeniia Onegina,'" 285.
161 Ibid., 286.
162 *Eugene Onegin*, Volume 1, 7.
163 See Bessonova and Viktorovich, "Nabokov—interpretator 'Evgeniia Onegina,'" 287.
164 Nabokov, *Nikolai Gogol*, 150.
165 *Eugene Onegin*, Volume 1, 7-8.
166 Brian Boyd, *Vladimir Nabokov: The American Years* (Princeton: Princeton University Press, 1991), 335.
167 *Eugene Onegin*, "Translator's Introduction," Volume 1, 8.
168 Alexander Dolinin, "Eugene Onegin," in *The Garland Companion to Vladimir Nabokov*, 122.
169 Mikhail Gasparov, "Briusov i bukvalizm (Po neizdannym materialam i perevodu 'Eneidy')," in *Poetika perevoda: Sbornik statei* (Moscow: Raduga, 1988), 29-62.
170 Ibid., 34.
171 Ibid.
172 Ibid., 41.
173 Ibid., 45.
174 Ibid., 46.
175 Ibid.
176 Ibid., 48.
177 See *Eugene Onegin*, 1975, Volume 1, xiii.
178 Ibid., Volume 1, ix.
179 Ibid., 1975, Volume 1, x.
180 Ibid., "Description of the Text," Volume 1, 4.
181 Ibid., 10.
182 Liuba Tarvi, "Pushkin and Nabokov: Iz opyta po klonirovaniiu oneginskoi stroki na angliiskom," in *A. S. Pushkin and V. V. Nabokov*, 299.
183 Dolinin, "Eugene Onegin," 122.
184 *Eugene Onegin*, 1975, Volume 3, 185.
185 Tarvi, "Pushkin and Nabokov," 300-301.
186 Ibid., 311-313.
187 See Mikhail Iu. Lotman, "A ta zvezda nad Pulkovym...: Zametki o poezii i stikhoslozhenii V. Nabokova," in *V. V. Nabokov: Pro et Contra*, 213-226.
188 Ibid., 221.

189  Cited in ibid., 222.

190  The translation is mine, since the existing translation does not convey the literal meaning. See the equivalent line in the English version of the novel in *The Gift*, 97. Khodasevich's poem "Peterburg" ("Petersburg," 1925), much admired by Nabokov, provides an indirect confirmation of the use of Russian prose as the designing principle for verse. Khodasevich writes about his major poetic achievement: "And, *driving each verse through prose*,/ uprooting my every line,/ I succeeded in grafting the classical rose/ onto the Soviet wilding" (The italics are mine.) The Russian original reads as follows:

> I kazhdyi stikh gonia skvoz prozu,
> Vyvikhivaia kazhduiu stroku,
> Privil-taki klassicheskuiu rozu
> K sovetskomu dichku.

191  Lotman, "A ta zvezda nad Pulkovym…: zametki o poezii i stikhoslozhenii V. Nabokova," 224-225.

192  Mikhail Gasparov, "Briusov i bukvalizm," 49.

193  Ibid., 50-51.

194  Ibid., 51.

195  Ibid., 51-52.

196  Ibid., 53.

197  Cited in ibid., 53. The English translation is mine.

198  Ibid., 54.

199  The translation is mine. The Russian original is: "I mozhet byt, Poeziia sama—/ odna velikolepnaia tsitata."

200  These definitions of mimicry and metamorphosis in the context of Nabokov derive from Sergei Davydov, "Nabokov: Geroi, avtor, tekst," in *V. V. Nabokov: Pro et Contra*, 323.

## Chapter 3

## "CINEMIZING" AS TRANSLATION: NABOKOV'S SCREENPLAY OF *LOLITA* AND STANLEY KUBRICK'S AND ADRIAN LYNE'S CINEMATIC VERSIONS[1]

## Struggle for the Narrative: Nabokov's and Kubrick's *Lolitas*

As Alfred Appel effectively demonstrated in *Nabokov's Dark Cinema,* cinematographic allusions and references are omnipresent in Nabokov's fiction.[2] *Lolita,* however, is a special case not only because it employs multiple cinematic correlations and images, but also because of Nabokov's involvement in 1959-1960 in the "cinemizing"—to use his own term—of his famous novel. The result of his well-known collaboration with Stanley Kubrick was the acclaimed motion picture *Lolita* (which left Nabokov with a "mixture of aggravation, regret, and reluctant pleasure" as well as the discovery that "Kubrick was a great director")[3] based on Nabokov's original screenplay, of which very little remained in the film. Nabokov's cinematic aspirations came to fruition solely in *Lolita*'s case. "Never V. Nabokov, movie hack" he wrote in his poem "Pale Film."[4] In the introduction to the published version of his screenplay, Nabokov enunciated the *auteur* theory in his approach to cinema:

> By nature I am no dramatist; I am not even a hack scenarist; but if I had given as much of myself to the stage or the screen as I have to the kind of writing which serves a triumphant life sentence between the covers of a book, I would have advocated and applied a system of total tyranny, directing the play or the picture myself, choosing settings and costumes, terrorizing the actors, mingling with them in the bit part of guest, or ghost, prompting them, and, in a word, pervading the entire show with the will and art of one individual—for there is nothing in the world that I loathe more than group activity.[5]

Nabokov was nonetheless the author of several plays, taught drama at Stanford, and at some point in the thirties had seriously aspired to a collaboration with Lewis Milestone. Yet as Appel points out, *Lolita* remains his only complete screenplay.

Since Kubrick's film *Lolita* is a result of a palimpsestic process — Kubrick's and Nabokov's struggles for the control of the narrative in the course of writing the screenplay — this chapter will deal with the two *auteurs'* collaboration and correspondence. Discussing Nabokov's screenplay in the framework of translation, this chapter will focus on those elements, which are transferable/transferred from one medium to the other, and other elements that resist transfer. Inevitably, we will deal not only with narrational techniques, but also with manipulation of time and space, which do not coincide in text and film. As Keith Cohen observes, in the case of film, there are three kinds of time we deal with: "abstract, chronological time and psychological, human time—Henri Bergson's 'scientific time' and '*durée*,'" plus, as in literature, "the time involved in experiencing the work."[6] While the first part of this chapter is concerned primarily with the dynamics between the novel and the screenplay, in the second part, dwelling on the notions of metaphor and metonymy and the tension their relationship produces in the symbolical workings of the novel, we will attempt to show how the redeployment of cinematic codes shaping the narrative structure of each film version of *Lolita* (Kubrick's and Adrian Lyne's) works vis-à-vis their literary source.

Nabokov was not the first author of the *Lolita* script. In 1958, when Kubrick and James B. Harris initially solicited the film rights to the book, Nabokov received a cautious and courteous letter from Doris Billingsley, Harris's secretary, expressing interest in the motion picture rights to Lolita and asking to arrange to send Harris-Kubrick Pictures a copy. Nabokov's pencil note in the margin says: "17 August, Putnam" and—in Russian—"to send them Lolita (letter from me)."[7] Nabokov ended up selling them the rights for the tidy sum of $150,000 plus 15 percent of the producers' profit but rejecting their offer to write the script himself. The first screen adaptation was written in 1959 by Calder Willingham (Kubrick's collaborator on the *Paths of Glory*) but rejected by Kubrick. Censorship pressures, emanating both from the Roman Catholic Church's Legion of Decency and Hollywood's Production Code, constrained Willingham so gravely that he contemplated an eventual marriage between the nymphet and her insatiate pursuer. Describing the political and moral ambience of the time, Richard Corliss writes: "In 1956 the Legion had condemned Elia Kazan's *Baby Doll* (also about a middle-aged man whose child bride is stolen away by a wilier rival), and in 1955 the Production Code withheld approval from Otto Preminger's *The Man with the Golden Arm*, a film about heroin addiction. But no major-studio picture had yet flouted condemnation from both groups."[8]

Kubrick's telegram to Nabokov in Milan of 8 December 1959 (addressed, incidentally, to Mr. "Nabakov"—ironically, Nabokov's name, through years of back-and-forth exchange with Kubrick and Harris, undergoes multiple "Nabokovian" distortions, ranging from Nabakov to Natsokov) reads: ". . . Stop Willingham screenplay not worthy of book most serious fault not realizing characters [stop] Convinced you were correct disliking marriage [stop] Book a masterpiece and should be followed even if Legion and Code disapprove [stop] Still believe you are only one for screen play [stop] If financial details can be agreed would you be available quick start for May 1 production appreciate cable Kubrick Unfilman Universal City California Regards to you and Mrs Nabakov Stanley Kubrick."[9] Nabokov responds with a cable (10 December 1959) saying he might consider it and promising a letter to follow. After some miscommunication (Kubrick's letter addressed to "Mrs. V. Nabakov" of 21 December 1959), Véra finally suggests in her letter of 31 December 1959 that Kubrick "should make him [Nabokov] now in writing the best final offer you can, which would be either accepted or rejected by him."[10]

This letter also starts a litany of complaints, queries, and worries on both sides about possible interferences from a third party, an issue that would color the Nabokov-Kubrick correspondence up to the very release of the motion picture. This first letter, for example, voices concerns that other motion pictures based on *Lolita* that might be produced in Europe and, in particular, mentions "a Mr. Alberto Lattuada, whose picture will be called 'The Little Nymph.'"[11] After promises that "Mr. Lattuada" will be handled by Kubrick's lawyers, worries about more and more "Lolitas" arise in Véra's letters. She forwards Kubrick her translation of an excerpt from *Nurnberger Zeitung*, which promises that "we shall certainly soon see various Lolitas on the screen which will put out of business all the good little Romys, Heidis and Sabinchen with their childish little mugs and high-pressure erotics."[12] Further correspondence mentions "two pictures that came in today's mail, with a letter in Italian, explaining that this young girl is acting (or studying) under Sofia

Loren's husband [Carlo Ponti] and that she would like to play either the main or a secondary part in *Lolita*."[13] Notoriously secretive about his projects, Kubrick warns Nabokov about the dangers of "leaks" through "typing services" when Nabokov asks him to recommend a typist to retype the script.[14]

Further correspondence shows a growing familiarity between the two parties involved (graduating from "Dear Mr. Nabokov/ Kubrick" to "Dear Vladimir/Stanley"). The Nabokovs even ask Kubrick "to give our son a chance to sing the 'Lolita' song" in the film,[15] as well as for an introduction of Dmitri Nabokov to "Kubrick's wife's uncle, Mr. von Karajan," for an audition "which might lead (if Dmitri qualifies) to an engagement at the Vienna opera."[16] The former was rebuffed by Harris with characteristic elusiveness: "At this stage we are not sure how such a thing would fit in with the film."[17] The latter proved to be a Nabokovian situation at best, for Kubrick writes to Nabokov: "I think you are a bit confused about the name of my wife's uncle, which is, in fact, Gunther Rennert. He is, I believe, a figure of equal stature to Mr. von Karajan in the opera world."[18] However, Kubrick was happy to oblige all the same and his offer was gratefully accepted.[19]

In the process and upon the completion of the production, Nabokov (via Véra) alternately asks for instructions about interviewers and their questions ("coordination is desirable")[20] and disclaims rumors that he has met with a "youngster" from Claude Otzenberger's agency to "envisager un reportage photographique" of the shooting. "You realize, I hope," writes Véra "that my husband is not interested in publicity." Nabokov inserts the word "personal," in relation to publicity, in the margin.[21] In the fall of 1961 Véra even agrees to handle clippings from newspapers and journals around the world dealing with Nabokov's career, which—with the exception of a Persian and an Israeli article "whose contents remain a mystery"—Kubrick asks her to send him for publicity purposes.[22]

By the end of 1961, things start to go awry and the relationship gradually deteriorates over financial matters and the quiet desperations of the Nabokovs about what they see as Kubrick's inconsiderateness. Nabokov starts complaining of not being informed about the distributors and subdistributors, and about the dates of release in different countries: "Since I am entitled to a percentage of the profits I would have thought that that kind of information would be sent to me as a matter of course. I apologize for putting all this griping in your lap but it is the only lap available to me." He also asks Kubrick to return the clippings.[23] Kubrick is elusive, citing the "notoriously loose and inadequate organizational aspects of any film project."[24] The Nabokovs grow annoyed when, after their reminders about the clippings (citing Nabokov's intention to write a book about *Lolita*'s "trials and tribulations"), Kubrick's secretary Angela C. Petschek returns the wrong ones.[25] The souring of the relationship was somewhat assuaged by the enthusiasm of the press and success of the world premiere. A telegram Stanley Kubrick sends Nabokov on 2 May 1962 says: "reactions from the magazine critics who are shown the film two months before opening have been a clear sweep of enthusiasms and superlatives including many comments about the accurate sense of the book having been translated to film."[26] A short-lived coziness ("Dear Stanley" — "Dear Vladimir"), due to the film's obvious success and Nabokov's travel to the London premiere financed by MGM, is soon followed by legal and financial squabbles. Nabokov informs Kubrick that he is prepared to take legal action against Seven Arts and Harris-Kubrick Corporation, but apparently still hopes to solve the matter in a friendly way: he addresses his letter "Dear Stanley" and asks to keep him informed and pay him his due — 15 percent of the net profit of the producer's share.[27] Kubrick maintains that he is leaving for six months for London to make *Dr. Strangelove*, and a little later requests a personal telephone conversation to clear things up.[28]

After that things become "curiouser and curiouser." Nabokov writes that he "abhor[s] telephone conversations, especially long distance" and suggests, idiosyncratically, that Kubrick should talk to Véra while Nabokov remains at her side during the talk.[29] Kubrick could not call on the designated day and requested another phone "appointment." He remained civil and polite but distant and, having moved on to the next project, preferred to deal through his attorney. Characteristically, the next document in their correspondence is a letter of 5 February, 1963 with a ten-page memo from Kubrick's attorneys.[30] Nabokov complains bitterly that "so many companies are shifting the responsibility onto each other's shoulder" that he was obliged to hire a lawyer "in order to obtain any information whatever from your lawyers, Messrs. Blau and Schwartzman."[31] Kubrick responds reluctantly and a little disingenuously: "I am in the midst of filming and I honestly haven't had time to keep track of the discussions between Blau, Lazar and your attorneys."[32] Slyly, Kubrick reiterates the argument of his attorney that, had they sold their interest "for an inadequate sum (say $100,000) and thereafter declared your share to be $15,000," and if the film "went on to gross an enormous amount of money," Nabokov would have claimed that his interest "was not tied in with the disposal of our rights but instead based on 100% of the 'producer's share of the profits' coming from the distribution."[33] The two artists parted ways and their personal relationship was transformed into dull carbon copies of multiple memos full of legalities sent back and forth by their lawyers. The last letter of Nabokov to Kubrick is a dry request to inform him "which rights in the *Lolita* screenplay belong to MGM and which remain the property of Harris and Kubrick," for Nabokov was preparing to publish his "original" screenplay.[34] The screenplay, dedicated "to Véra" (as was everything that Nabokov wrote), indeed was published with a note: "This is the purely Nabokov version of the screenplay and not the same version which was produced as the motion picture *Lolita*, distributed by Metro-Goldwyn-Mayer, Inc."

## Film Adaptation and Translation

Christian Metz once said that the reader "will not always find *his* [the reader's] film, since what he has before him in the actual film is now somebody else's phantasy."[35] Nabokov, who held that the privilege of the best writers was to create his own, new type of reader, had to confront a double anxiety faced with the prospect of turning *Lolita* into a film: not only was any film adaptation "somebody else's phantasy," but his new reader, shaped and nurtured by his own radically novel artistic sensibility, risked being snatched away. Creating his own adaptation was a compromise motivated by a desire to give it some kind of form that would protect it from later intrusions and distortions. Nabokov's compromise was to reimagine his own screen adaptation on the same terms as he would later think of his translation of *Eugene Onegin*: namely, as a genetically related subspecies ("all thorn, but cousin to your rose"). Indeed, Véra's copy of the published screenplay had a "brilliantly attired hand-drawn butterfly (likely a tropical Brushfoot) on the half-title, cleverly named to make the screenplay a subspecies of the *Lolita* species, of the 'Verinia' genus: *Verinia lolita cinemathoides/ V/April 1974.*"[36]

Just before the premiere of Kubrick's *Lolita*, Nabokov recalled the process of adaptation in an interview: "Turning one's novel into a movie script is rather like making a series of sketches for a painting that has long ago been finished and framed. I composed new scenes and speeches in an effort to safeguard a *Lolita* acceptable to me. I knew that at best the end product in such case is less of a blend than a collision of interpretations. . . . From my seven or eight sessions with Kubrick during the writing of the script I derived the impression that he was an artist, and it is on this impression that I base my hopes of seeing a plausible *Lolita*. . . ."[37] Nabokov, glancing back at Aleksandr Pushkin, called his adaptation "a vivacious variant of an old novel,"[38] and, as Michael Wood puts it, he is thereby "both telling the precise truth and understating his achievement."[39] Wood sees Nabokov's adaptation in terms of a new, invented genre: "However literal and practical his intentions in writing the screenplay, Nabokov ultimately invented a subtle new genre: the implied film, the work of words which borrows the machinery and landscape of film as a dazzling means to a literary end."[40]

Since action in the novel *Lolita* is "mainly linguistic," to use Appel's term, any question of interpretation, including cinematic, raises the issue of what is eventually represented and what *can* be represented. It is worth remembering that Nabokov had always resented graphic representations of Lolita on the covers of his novel's editions ("And no girls," as he wrote in one of the letters to his publisher in 1958). To put the issue of the representational in the perspective of translation, the question that arises is the relation of the authorial intent behind the original to its subsequent version. Nabokov's authorial intent is clearly authoritarian; in the Foreword to his screenplay he readily admits to a "system of total tyranny" that would "grant words primacy over action."[41]

To discuss this in terms of translation is not at all far-fetched. In the Foreword to the published script Nabokov, grappling with the modifications and omissions of entire scenes in Kubrick's film, speaks of the script in terms of translation's fidelity and freedom in regard to the original. He writes: ". . . all sorts of changes may not have been sufficient to erase my name from the credit titles but they certainly made the picture as unfaithful to the original script as an American poet's translation from Rimbaud or Pasternak."[42] Such a comparison of film adaptation with translation is pervasive in the majority of existing studies on film adaptations. Even as Brian McFarlane, in his important study *Novels to Film: An Introduction*, claims to offer an alternative to "impressionistic comparisons [to translation] endemic in discussions on the phenomenon of adaptation," he still speaks of "distinguishing between what can be transferred from one medium to another (essentially, narrative) and that which, being dependent on different signifying systems, cannot be transferred";[43] furthermore, he uses Eugene Nida's term "functional equivalents," and admits to leaving out of his analysis such issues as authorship and cultural and historical contexts. However, these issues too are within the orbit of translation studies.[44]

Since the inception of the Academy Awards in 1927-1928, according to Morris Beja,[45] "more than three fourths of the awards for 'best picture' have gone to adaptation," but the film remains all too often merely "a conscientious visual transliteration of the original."[46] Similarly to the debates on fidelity between the original and its translation in translation studies, as Christopher Orr points out, "the concern with fidelity of the adapted film in letter and spirit to its literary source has unquestionably dominated the discourse on adaptation."[47] As it happened in translation studies, the criteria for evaluating fidelity and freedom in film adaptations are shifted and reconsidered depending on a variety of reasons, as well as the cultural and historical context. Since a film adaptation, after all, is a selective interpretation of the original source by the filmmaker— "in the hope that it will coincide with that of many other readers/ viewers"—one is faced with familiar issues.[48] In the case of film adaptation, what is fidelity to the source? Should the cinematic version be faithful to the "letter" or to the "spirit" of the literary source ("the main thrust of the narrative," in the words of Michael Klein and Gillian Parker)?[49] Does the novel possess more authority because it comes first? Is the film merely reinterpreting the novel, or "deconstructing the source text," or regarding it "as simply an occasion for an original work"?[50] Beja formulates similar questions: "What relationship should a film have to the original source? Should it be 'faithful'? Can it be? To what?"[51]

Some scholars create their own taxonomies to frame the issue of fidelity and freedom, leaning heavily on those existing in translation studies. Dudley Andrew proposes the following categories as components of successful adaptations: "borrowing, intersection, and fidelity of transformation."[52] Geoffrey Wagner classifies the types of adaptations: transposition, commentary, and analogy.[53]

Film adaptations of canonical literary texts do not limit themselves to adapting the literary text alone: staging, directing, lighting, and photography, as Pattrick Cattrysse notes, "may well have been governed by other models and conventions which did not originate in the literary text and did not serve as a translation of any of its elements."[54] The relationship with the preceding films "remains implicit":[55] does Lyne's *Lolita*—or any subsequent cinematic version, for that matter, that might be created in the future—translate Nabokov's "canonical" literary text, and possibly even Kubrick's film as well?

Finally, there are the relationships between adaptations and their markets, and between adaptations and their historical contexts. Cattrysse suggests the polysystem approach to the study of film adaptation as "a more or less specific kind of translation of previous discursive practices as well as experiences in real life."[56] McFarlane notes that "modern critical notions of *intertextuality* represent a more sophisticated approach, in relation to adaptation, to the idea of the original novel as a 'resource,'" rather than the *source*.[57]

Many scholars draw on the visual thrust that unites the modern novel with film. Thus Alan Spiegel, in *Fiction and the Camera Eye*, talks of the "concretized form" of modern novels—starting with

Gustave Flaubert and Henry James—as a form providing a lot of visual information, the congruence of image and concept being the main goal.[58] In a similar vein, Cohen's study is concerned with the "process of convergence" between art forms. He believes that the emphasis on showing rather than narrating in the works of Joseph Conrad and Henry James breaks down the nineteenth-century representational novel.[59] He also shows the actual influence of film on the modernist novel (Virginia Woolf, Marcel Proust) to suggest, in the words of McFarlane, "how the modern novel, influenced by the techniques of Eisensteinian montage cinema, draws attention to its encoding processes in ways that the Victorian novel tends not to."[60] The visual, rather than being presented diegetically, is fragmented, and the object is shown from altering points of view.[61] Incidentally, drawing on diegesis in film, Robert Stam chooses *Lolita* as his example: "The diegesis of the Nabokov novel *Lolita* and its filmic adaptation by Stanley Kubrick . . . might be identical in many respects, yet the artistic and generic mediation in film and novel might be vastly different."[62] McFarlane, in his turn, notes the paradox that, despite the use of devices anticipating "cinematic techniques" by the modern novel, it "has not shown itself very adaptable to film."[63] Similarly, modern plays, in his words, "which seem to owe something to cinematic techniques, have lost a good deal of their fluid representations of time and space when transferred to the screen."[64] Both modern social theory and psychoanalysis (Karl Marx, Sigmund Freud) resorted to the cinematic as a metaphor (Freud's dream process as projection is just one example). However, as Cohen has noted, it is rather "the technological constitution of the cinematic process—from recording to editing to projecting," which becomes "a model for the relation between the configurating signifiers of art and the signifying apparatus."[65]

## The Screenplay and the Novel

What underwrites the process of writing and rewriting the screenplay is the very notion of repetition, which involves inherent and irreducible difference of text from itself and from its original source. An exploration of this palimpsestic process shows which elements are carried over (translated), how they are carried over, and which resist transfer. The Nabokov-Kubrick correspondence during their work on the screenplay provides a fascinating insight into the extent to which Kubrick was shaping this new text against the resistance of the author, a self-admitted control freak. Among the materials in the Berg Collection, there are three versions of the *Lolita* screenplay. There is version 1 (typescript "Lolita: a Screenplay" unsigned and dated Spring 1960, 155 pp) with a holograph note on the title page: "Short version of 1960. This is the version as presented to Kubrick in spring 1960 and in autumn 1971 (through Lazar)."[66]

Version 2 (typescript—mostly carbon—unsigned and dated Summer 1960, 200 pp) is a longer version, and is essentially the one that Nabokov published in 1974.

Finally, the third version, which was displayed in the Nabokov centennial exhibition at the New York Public Library, is the longest typescript (410 pages, 85 previously unpublished) and contains scenes not included in either of the two versions previously mentioned. Some of the scenes (30 pages out of 85) were published and analyzed by Wood in *Véra's Butterflies*.[67] Dieter Zimmer intended to publish a German edition of the complete longest version, which was, apparently, everything that Nabokov sent to Kubrick between March and August 1960. Wood maintains that "the interest of the long, unpublished version is that it brings us closest to Nabokov at work, caught in the very act of re-imagining an already spectacularly imagined story."[68] Wood justifies his selection of the scenes he published in terms of best projecting "Nabokov's feeling for mischief, his delight in additional detail and afterthought" and "Nabokov's satire of American manners" that "translates exceptionally well into dialogue form."[69] These include the end of Act 1 with an extended scene of Humbert and Charlotte Haze's fight over Lolita's future; a scene of Humbert's interaction with Dr. Byron about the sleeping pills (ending in the explicit evocation of the author of *Alice in Wonderland*, whose lurking presence often only implicitly pervades the published *Lolita*s in both its screenplay and fiction incarnations), and the sound of the ambulance presaging the future accident.[70]

Then follows a scene in which Humbert, with the help of a forged date on Charlotte's snapshot, persuades the Farlows that he is Lolita's biological father (this melodramatic scene is the end of Act 1 in the 155-page version); and a grotesque scene of Humbert with Jack Beale, "Mr. McFate's nephew," who ran Charlotte over (this farcical scene is at the end of Act 1 in the 410-page version). Other scenes, all from Act 3, include Lolita blackmailing Humbert into letting her participate in the play; Humbert's rather awkward conversation with the headmistress at Beardsley, Miss Pratt; a scene with Clare Quilty and Vivian Darkbloom in the schoolyard, in which Quilty (winner of the Poltergeister Prize!) hangs by one hand, "ape-like," from a horizontal bar and Vivian actually speaks (she does not, in Kubrick's version); and, finally, scenes on the road, all tainted by Quilty's passing presence: on a picnic ground, at a trailer park, on a mountain path. It is noteworthy that the Beale episode was actually used by Kubrick as the grotesquely smiling guy who shows up offering pay the funeral expenses (Humbert lying in the bathtub with his scotch). Big chunks of exchanges between Miss Pratt and Humbert regarding Lolita's sexual development, on the other hand, found their way into Lyne's version.

Boyd characterized the long version as a "draft screenplay," "diffuse and often strangely pedestrian."[71] The extravagances bordering on farce, a "Nabokovian funhouse of comic visual effects," Boyd complains, are the result of trying to "transfer too much of the novel onto the screen" or just to explicate what was only suggested at in the novel.[72] Examples vary from Quilty wearing a mask in the death scene to a theatrical gala in Elphinstone (the town where Quilty steals Lolita from Humbert), where everybody is wearing a mask and Quilty masquerades as "Dr. Fogg" to physically examine Lolita in Humbert's presence.

The significant difference in length between the versions of 1960 suggests changes made to accommodate different issues, not the least of them being time. It was "the best screenplay ever written for Hollywood," according to Harris and Kubrick, but it was also impossible, in the words of Harris in 1993, "to *lift* it."[73] Kubrick's film, long as it seems now, ran 152 minutes, while Nabokov's script, if shot as written, would have run for over four hours.

Nabokov's screenplay is an attempt at "pervading the entire show with the will and art of one individual," as he himself avowed.[74] He tries to distill the "movie-matter" out of the novel, including scenes from the unused material for the novel (such as that of Diana Fowler, the chair's wife at Beardsley, and her niece Nina starting what could have become the next Charlotte/Lolita cycle in Humbert's life). While the "garbling of [his] best finds, the omission of entire scenes, the addition of the new ones"[75] all distressed Nabokov, he also undoubtedly felt unexpected pleasure in applying his talent to movie-making, as well as a "reluctant pleasure"[76] in Kubrick's interpretation—a vision of the novel that was not his own. Nabokov's "vivacious variant of an old novel"[77] is not stage-bound and story-friendly. The authorial voice, so strong in Nabokov's fiction, interferes with he cinematic storytelling: even though, as McFarlane notes, "by exercising control over the mise-en-scène and sound-track or through the manipulations of editing, the filmmaker can adapt some of the functions of . . . narrational prose," there is no readily available commentary on the action unfolding.[78] Nabokov's narration, however, always "indicates adverbially," commentary being one of his narration's most idiosyncratic features, which culminates eventually in a novel written entirely as a commentary to one long poem—*Pale Fire*.[79]

In his assessment of *Lolita* the screenplay (and this is relevant both for the published version and the longer version), Boyd suggests that "the best things . . . seem to be the unfilmable stage directions where Nabokov's own imagination tints the details he selects."[80] For example, after arriving at N 342 Lawn Street and seeing an "unattractive white clapboard suburban house," Humbert notes in *"vocal brackets"*: "What a horrible house."[81] Later, a dog appears in a "cameo role," as it were: "Dog (*perfunctorily*): Woof."[82] Elsewhere, Vivian Darkbloom blows Lolita a kiss "darkly blooming."[83] Quilty's hands are "meatily clapping."[84] "Something reptilian and spine-chilling" is supposed to be in Humbert's stare as he coldly observes the floundering Charlotte.[85] As he cannot count on the novel's "hidden resonances and delayed inferences," Nabokov's film directions, mostly unstageable, take on a considerable part of the novel's verbal glee.[86]

Nabokov's camera itself is an ironic commentary on film as text, as well as a futile exercise in total control. As McFarlane notes, "It is, however, too simple to suggest that the mise-en-scène, or its deployment by the cinematic codes (notably that of montage), can effortlessly appropriate the role of the omniscient, inaudible narrator, or that the camera . . . replaces such [a] narrator."[87] The "Nabokamera," as Corliss called it, curiously "glides around," "dips into," and "with a shudder withdraws."[88] All films are omniscient in a sense because the viewer is "aware of a level of objectivity."[89] However, in the case of Nabokov's prose, the readers are not aware of this, and the only omniscient narrator orchestrating the effects is the author himself. With film, the omniscient narrator's privileged position is lost; he can no longer stay inside the text. "The Camera," McFarlane notes, "is outside of film." It "denotes its operator metonymically."[90]

Nabokov's ubiquity in the book (less obvious and therefore more powerful in *Lolita* than in his less inspired novels, like *Bend Sinister* or *The Defense*, in which the author, with a final flourish, changes the course of the denouement and allows for the characters' escape into the metaphysical) takes on the form of "injecting" himself into the screenplay. He hides in the anagrammatic and ever-present Vivian Darkbloom. In "Pale Film," Nabokov points this out directly: "The larval author lurking in costume, / As Hitchcock did, or Vivian Darkbloom."[91] Corliss aptly calls this character "the drag in which he [Nabokov] masqueraded as Clare Quilty's mistress."[92] For some time, or so it is said, Nabokov even considered publishing *Lolita* under this "pseudoplume or nom de nymph."[93] In the screenplay, he even literally and rather pointlessly wanders straight into the text as a "nut with the net," in Lolita's parlance, whom Humbert and Lolita meet on a mountain path and who does not know the road to Dympleton. Here is Nabokov in action, trying to implement the "system of total tyranny" à la Alfred Hitchcock, which he advocated in the Foreword to his published screenplay, not only "directing the play or the picture [himself]," but also "terrorizing the actors, mingling with them in the bit part of guest, or ghost."[94] Incidentally, having failed to rescue his screenplay from Kubrick's alterations, Nabokov wistfully describes himself as being mistaken for Hitchcock by the fans ("the placid profile of a stand-in for Hitchcock") at the premiere of *Lolita*.[95]

When Nabokov cannot entirely control the cinematic narrative as an *auteur*, he tries to relegate this function to his protagonist. Especially interesting and symptomatic, therefore, are those rare moments when Humbert himself becomes an invisible director of the film, instructing the camera where to "look." For example, narrating his love story with Annabel (the first-person narration), Humbert orders: "I would like a shot of two hands."[96] The shot obligingly appears; the hands of the young Humbert and Annabel meet—"a pretty scene for the subtle camera."[97]

Trying to invent the film alternative to the linguistic flair of the original, Nabokov thrives on the visual. He delights in effects (that were not yet trite at that time) and engages in inventive hermeneutic exercises opening the many parentheses and sketchy asides of *Lolita* the novel. For example, he literally opens up what, according to Tom Stoppard, was the best parenthetical aside in literature: "My very photogenic mother died in a freak accident (picnic, lightning). . . ."[98] The cut after Humbert's voice narrates the story of a "freak accident" in the Maritime Alps provides a Fellinesque vision: raindrops strike the "zinc of a lunchbox" and a lady in white is felled by a "blast of livid light," her "graceful specter" soaring above the rocks with a parasol, blowing kisses to her husband and child standing below hand in hand.[99] In another example, Humbert reading Charlotte's love letter appears "in one SHOT" as a "gowned professor, in another as a routine Hamlet, in a third, as a dilapidated Poe."[100] At the end of this stage direction Nabokov allows: "He also appears as himself."[101] Such visual "compensation" for *Lolita*'s linguistic flair in its screen translation did not suit Kubrick; he methodically eliminated all the effects in which Nabokov took such delight. Humbert ultimately was allowed to appear in the film *only* as himself.

In yet another example, the "synchronous conflagration that had been raging all night in [Humbert's] veins" as the ironic reason for the real storm that burns down the McCoos' residence and lands Humbert at Charlotte's in the novel,[102] turns into a fully-developed thunderstorm in Act 1 of the screenplay, with "gesticulating black trees, rain drumming the roof, thunder, lightning printing reflections on [the] wall" and loud sounds of fire engines,[103] and also into an excited exchange with the Farlows about the events of the night. In the novel, Humbert notes that, bored and disappointed as he was, he, as a polite European, set out to see the lodging recommended by the distraught Mr. McCoo, "feeling that otherwise McCoo would devise an even more elaborate means of getting rid of [him]."[104] The screenplay vividly demonstrates what he meant, turning a suggestion into a fully developed scene: "the grotesque humor turns upon McCoo's conducting a kind of guided tour through a non-existent house."[105] McCoo's effort to make Humbert see through "architectural ghosts" ("the camera escorts them") is in and of itself an ironic comment on the failure of the visual: what a viewer is urged to see is just not there.[106]

The same translation of narrative exposition into visual tricks manifests in the offensive overuse of photographs and diagrams coming alive and turning into *mise-en-scènes*. After Charlotte's death in a car accident, a police photographer takes a picture of the scene; meanwhile, a police instructor with a pointer in a projection room shows the still to a group of policemen. Then a diagram appears, with dotted lines and arrows showing everybody's trajectory. Eventually everything in the still comes to life.[107] This mimetic duplication dwells on a paradox of representation ("image" and "imitate," Jacques Derrida once pointed out, are etymologically related): the cinematic image is supposed to be "faithful" to its referent, but by "doubling its referent, like a mirror, it exposes both its pure supplementarity and its profound difference, its potential deformation of that referent."[108]

Similarly, a snapshot of Annabel and young Humbert comes alive as Humbert "takes off his white cap as if acknowledging recognition, and dons it again."[109] Nabokov indicates that Annabel is supposed to be the same actress as the one who plays Lolita: a metaphor of "the same child" that Humbert believes he sees in Lolita when he first meets her is metonymically extended to proliferate visual sameness, to create a visual double. Neither Kubrick nor Lyne followed through with this idea.

The important challenge for Nabokov was to externalize Humbert, to translate Humbert's intense and perverse inner world into an external vision of his perversity and intensity—Humbert as seen by the other. This includes not only the pre-story of Annabel, the root of his peculiar "illness," but also Humbert's side of the story: from his own perspective, he might see the beauty of the enchanted land in which Lolita is safely "solipsized," while seen from the outside, his story threatens to take on the ugly shape of the illegal transfer of an abused minor across state borders. As far as the pre-story (Annabel) is concerned, Nabokov resorts to a compromise: he lets Humbert narrate it, illustrating his narrative with visual sequences of their young hands touching, their rendezvous in the garden (with "emblematic silhouettes of long leaves"),[110] and Annabel's departure. This is basically illustration as translation, with first-person narration acting as captions. Humbert's brief marriage is rendered in the same fashion, the only difference being that Dr. Ray, the psychiatrist, does the "captions." Dr. Ray provides "captions" to film sequences illustrating Humbert's fascination with young girls (showing in succession: a young roller-skater, chattering schoolgirls at a bus stop, two nymphets playing marbles on a sidewalk, and pale orphans in a garden of an orphanage). He also makes a speech from the point of view of a psychiatrist on Humbert's case and the "moral leprosy" that goes with it. It is, of course, a mock interpretation: even in the screenplay Nabokov could not leave Freud or social philistines alone. In a sense, it turned out to be easier for Kubrick to "externalize" Humbert for the screen precisely because there was less to externalize: he dropped these complicated psychological motivations along with Humbert's past altogether. Characteristically, the prologue of the screenplay abounds in diegesis—the first-person narration ("Humbert's voice") explicating Humbert's condition, perversion, and love. The further Nabokov gets in the screenplay (and, perhaps, the more he is driven to reshape his text due to his exchanges with Kubrick), the more dialogic and less narrational it becomes.

One of the weaknesses of Nabokov's screenplay is the inconsistent nature of its first-person narration: it disappears in the later parts of the screenplay, along with, for the most part, the character of Dr. Ray, to reappear only in the very end, in the epilogue. Dr. Ray's presence, in general, is ambiguously unresolved, as if Nabokov questioned whether his role in the screenplay was to be that of the narrator or of one of the characters.

Nabokov's own work on the script shows the difficulties he experienced dealing with certain key points of the narrative. In his letter to Kubrick of 25 April 1960, upon the completion of Act 2, he wrote: "The concatenation of scenes proved to be very troublesome and I don't know how many times I rewrote the motel sequence."[111] Earlier (March 1960), he wrote to Kubrick about Act 1 that though "still very rough and incomplete . . . structurally it does hang together rather neatly. You will note the seeds I have planted and followed up (the dog, the gun, etc.)."[112] Among the troubles Nabokov encounters, one is finding a balance between the tones of the designated narrators. In the novel, as we know, Dr. Ray's introduction and Nabokov's Afterword ("On a Book Entitled *Lolita*") frame the confession, which is entirely Humbert's. Faced with the inevitable necessity of externalizing Humbert, as it were, for the screen (because Humbert on screen would be primarily *seen*), Nabokov assigned Dr. Ray a larger role. In the letter to Kubrick of June 25, 1960, Nabokov wrote: "As you will see, I have let Humbert talk about his first love but no matter how I fussed with it in my own mind I could not get him to discuss his marriage without encroaching upon the tone of his scenes with Charlotte. Therefore I have had Dr. Ray take over again (p. 20a) after Humbert has finished with Annabel. It seems to me that it is very trim this way but if you still object to Ray's handling of the Valeria scenes, we can have another discussion and try to find another way."[113] In the version of the screenplay that Nabokov eventually was allowed to publish, as we know, Dr. Ray (who is Humbert's psychoanalyst and whose leg he pulls during his sessions with such delight—yet another one of Nabokov's poisonous excursions into the domain of the "Viennese charlatan") "bizarrely intrudes in the voiceover," to use Boyd's expression.[114] Thus in the scene between Humbert and Valeria in the taxi, apart from psychoanalytic remarks on his patient's state of mind, he also comments on the technical condition of the taxi ("needs good brakes") and the itinerary. Closer to the end of Act 3, Dr. Ray provides the narration of the hiatus (both in terms of time and action), from the moment of Lolita's disappearance to Humbert's reinstallment at Beardsley. Here again, as in the taxi episode, Dr. Ray bizarrely claims a larger role—that of a character rather than mere narrator. The information on his marriage to a "very strong analyst," Dr. Christina Fine, whom Humbert "kept trying to hypnotize,"[115] is as irrelevant to the action as Nabokov's own presence in the screenplay as a "nut with a net." If anything, it is a device from a different genre—characters in search of an author, or else, the author in search of characters. It sometimes played out the other way around. Kubrick was convinced (and Nabokov was not) that Mona "might be built up enough to play a part in the development: Lolita might send her a letter for HH. . . ." Nabokov, as Véra puts it, "seems to have convinced K. that reading of inconspicuously received letter in class is better."[116] Kubrick was particularly fond of Mona's "virgin wool" remark (Lolita notes that her sweater is of virgin wool; Mona cynically suggests that this is the only "virgin" thing about Lolita), so he kept toying with Mona's possible role and future destination (college) before assigning her a modest fate of being the Farlows' daughter at Ramsdale with whom Lolita is sent off to Camp Climax.

To somehow bring Humbert and Dr. Ray together in the prologue, Nabokov makes both of them guest speakers at a women's club. (While Humbert lectures on Romantic poetry, Dr. Ray is supposed to be speaking on "the sexual symbolism of golf.") Humbert engages head-on in an explanation of his nymphet concept. As Nabokov has Humbert suffer a breakdown in front of the women's club audience (as well as in front of the film audience), he provides a visual effect of macabre elastic transformations of the female faces in the audience, "changing to eighths and snapping in a distorted mirror; others, lean and long, developing abysmal décolletés; others again blending with the flesh of rolling bare arms, or turning into wax fruit in arty bowls."[117] Supposedly, this is not only the translation of Humbert's illness and perversity into strikingly visual terms but also, perhaps, a metaphor for his distorted vision of adult femininity. To note parenthetically, though none of this found its way into Kubrick's film, a similar distorted mirror effect (along with a Dick Tracy mask) is used by Lyne when the scene of Humbert and Lolita's ferocious lovemaking dissolves into Humbert's nightmare: the tapping on the door, voices, and giggling, terrifying strangers mocking him as he, naked, opens the door. All faces, including Humbert's, are violently stretched and elastically distorted, but the device is used to serve a different end—to become a visual metaphor for his guilt and shame.

A big part of our reluctant fascination with Humbert's inner world in the novel comes from Humbert's/Nabokov's feverish, literary-minded imagination, that of "an artist and a madman, a creature of infinite melancholy."[118] Corliss suggests that, even though a film constructed in a flashback form might include Humbert's "backstory," it would still lack a "suitable equivalent to Humbert's voice."[119] What he means is not the sound of it, not the words per se, but the tone: "His prose is in perpetual state of ecstasy: for Lolita, first and last, but also for whatever he sees and feels. He is aroused by all things, physical, tactile, ethereal, ephemeral; they alight on his erect palp and he comes alive so intensely that his heart could burst. (Which it does.) *Lolita* is rapture rekindled."[120]

Nabokov's biggest challenge, perhaps, came from a dumbing-down effect of film intended for a mass audience. If we consider the relationship between the language of fiction and the language of film as parallel to the relationship between one's native language and a foreign one (for which the framework of translation certainly allows), then the ability one loses first in a foreign language is the ability to quote. Films do quote films; literary allusions, however, slip through one's fingers when transferred on screen. Those subtle literary webs and delicate echoes, aesthetics' substitution for the ethical—a part and parcel of Romanticism—are Humbert's main, in fact, *only*, justification for what he had done. Pointedly, this Romantic stance of the prevalence of aesthetics over ethics makes for the last (and arguably most beautiful) lines of the novel: "I am thinking of aurochs and angels, the secret of durable pigments, prophetic sonnets, the refuge of art. And this is the only immortality you and I may share, my Lolita."[121] Nabokov chooses to supply first-person narration once more in his screenplay to quote these lines verbatim. One can transfer the lines, *l'énoncé*, as it were, but *l'énonciation* proves difficult to reproduce.

What film theory refers to as the enunciated and enunciation (*l'énoncé* and *l'énonciation*—terms originating with the linguist Emile Benveniste) describe a difference between what is "uttered" or enacted in film and the way the "utterance" or a set of events is shaped and mediated.[122] McFarlane further distinguishes between narrative and narration as between story and discourse. (The terms derive from the Formalist theory and the distinction it makes between *fabula* and *siuzhet*.) Whatever the terms, however, as Metz points out in *Imaginary Signifier*, "film gives us the feeling that we are witnessing almost a real thing," but still cinematic enunciation is always present.[123] McFarlane observes that film enunciation, in relation to the transposition of novels to the screen, "is a matter of adaptation proper, not of transfer."[124] There are things that, as he puts it, "are not tied to the semiotic system in which they are manifested,"[125] and therefore are transferable. They are, supposedly, narrative. Nonetheless, those that are tied to the semiotic system of the original text are enunciation: they cannot be transferred, though they can—to a larger or lesser degree—be adapted. Thus enunciation for McFarlane means the totality of expressive methods that govern both presentation and reception of the narrative.

Nabokov's effort to direct enunciation by the same means that he used in writing fiction is, it appears, a highly quixotic and, by virtue of this, futile undertaking. The signifying system of a novel relies on verbal signs that work conceptually, that have a high symbolic value but, to use McFarlane's term, "low iconicity," in comparison to cinematic signs that have "uncertain symbolic function" and high "iconicity" and work perceptually.[126] As Appel writes, "Nabokov's remark about Joyce's giving 'too much verbal body to words' (*Playboy* interview) succinctly defines the burden the post-Romantics placed on the word, as though it were an endlessly resonant object rather than one component in a referential system of signs."[127] Humbert puts it in his own way: "Oh, my Lolita, I have only words to play with!"[128] Among other things, *Lolita* is a book about the limitations of language. However, for the Humbert of the screenplay even words to play with are luxury. The intricate web of wordplay and referentiality cannot be transferred, and adaptation, inevitably, takes on the shape of a "story inside a story" (form inside form): a lecture on Edgar Allan Poe and obsession; Humbert's jotting down a dream of himself, the Dark Knight, and Lolita/Alice riding deeper into the Enchanted Forest;[129] the tape-recording of Humbert's lecture "Baudelaire and Poe."[130]

Among all literary allusions in the novel, Poe is perhaps the most significant presence, for it is through Poe, at least in part, that Nabokov (and Humbert) speak about language and art. As Appel testifies in *The Annotated Lolita*, Poe is referred to more than twenty times (followed by Prosper Mérimée, William Shakespeare, and James Joyce).[131] One can only empathize with Nabokov's quixotic attempt to inflict such appreciation on the film's audience. All the subtleties of "Lo-lee-ta"/Annabel Lee/Annabel Leigh are reduced to Humbert's dictating and playing back of his recorded lecture that evokes Poe's marriage, Humbert's fairly straightforward musings in a faltering voice ("And now Annabel is dead, and Lolita is alive . . ."), and the actual quoting of Poe's poem: "my darling—my life and my bride."[132] Later, as if to sneak in one last parallel, the maid picks up the phone: "No, there's no Miss Lee here. You must have got the wrong number."[133] Humbert's acrimonious forays into psychoanalysis are also brought in via his recorded lecture: "Other commentators, commentators of the Freudian school of thought. No. Commentators of the Freudian prison of thought. Hm. Commentators of the Freudian nursery school of thought. . . ."[134] The theme of the celebrated lovers, Tristram and Iseult, and of yet another Tristram, Laurence Sterne's *Tristram Shandy* (both important references in the novel), is slipped in as two allusions that—provided they found their way into film—would have been most likely wasted on the audience. One is *Stan and Izzie*, a movie that, Lolita claims, gave her ideas about love philters.[135] The other is yet another prophetic dream of the screenplay: Charlotte's premonition of Humbert's betrayal. Right after her near-drowning Charlotte recollects the dream she had the previous night: "You were offering me some pill or potion, and a voice said: Careful, Isolda, that's poison."[136]

The very play on Humbert's name, which occupies such an important place in the novel, bringing in new and unexpected connotations, is brought up in a painfully straightforward fashion. Lolita loathfully distorts his name into the clownish "Humlet Hambert" and "Omlette Hamburg," while Humbert retorts: "Or plain 'Hamlet.'"[137] Similarly, Nabokov's complex ideas on literature are "smuggled in" only as fleeting remarks, such as in the conversation with Mona: "We live in an age when the serious middlebrow idiot craves for a literature of ideas, for the novel of social comment."[138]

It is interesting how Kubrick encourages Nabokov to deal with the issue of doubling. In translating his novel into a screenplay, one of the most difficult problems for Nabokov was the issue of Quilty's role as Humbert's elusive double and the interpretation of the relationship of all three participants of the drama. The effect of doubling in film, as Kubrick sees it, should be translated into both "visual" doubling (adding Vivian as Quilty's escort) and in repetition. In his letter to Kubrick of 9 July 1960, Nabokov writes: "I am sending you the Third act of the Lolita screenplay. As you will see, I have several scenes between Quilty and the nymphet since otherwise he would have remained a ghostly, uncharacterized and implausible figure."[139] In three pages of Kubrick's suggestions for Act 3 (possibly typed by Véra and returned to him with Nabokov's corrections), many concern Quilty's ubiquitous presence.[140] Some suggestions are crossed out and marked in the margins by Nabokov "*est'*" ("it's there"). Among Kubrick's suggestions that ended up in the film are Quilty being "flanked by Vivian (as he should be throughout play)"[141] and the piano teacher's disclosure of Lolita's missed piano lessons in the conversation with Humbert backstage after the school play. Kubrick also insists on blackmailing Humbert into Lolita's participation in the school play (he suggests that the principal, Miss Pratt, should express the demand that she be psychoanalyzed by school psychiatrist). As we know, eventually Kubrick combined the blackmailer and psychiatrist role in Quilty's phony identity as a school psychologist. Peter Sellers, who portrayed Quilty, was known for his performance of multiple roles (more on this in the second part of this chapter), so the added irony was that only Humbert could possibly be left in the dark about his visitor's identity. However, Kubrick insisted that Quilty should remain a "figure in the shadows"[142] when Lolita and Humbert are on the road. He writes: "We do not know how and where she [Lolita] went when she does go."[143]

As far as Vivian is concerned, Nabokov not only agreed to make her flank Quilty but also gave her some lines—a ghost brought to life. It is perhaps significant for illuminating the nature of adaptation as translation that Nabokov lays bare his own device: he calls the viewer's attention to her anagrammatic nature, therefore explicitly offering an interpretation. Quilty explains: "My collaborator, my evening shadow. Her name looks like an anagram. But she's a real woman—or anyway a real person."[144]

Nabokov's Russian translation of *Lolita* invites some parallels to this explicatory activity: in numerous instances Nabokov inserts reminders to the reader to help decipher the chronology of the events, laying out the clues, as it were, whereas the English reader is left to his or her own devices. In the same vein, Dr. Braddock, a participant in the doctors' convention in the screenplay, offers an explicit interpretation of the mural in the Enchanted Hunters Hotel: "The hunter thinks he has hypnotized the little nymph but it is she who puts him into a trance."[145] The metaphor of Humbert who has drugged Lolita and will take advantage of her only to be enthralled by her forever is interpreted and ready for consumption.

Nabokov, apparently, was struggling with translating Quilty's shadowy ubiquity into the screenplay. Page three of Kubrick's suggestions outlines four allusive passages referring to Lolita and Quilty: "wet shoes, something strange at motel"; "car on hill, which K. would like with all details" (referring to the episode when, as Humbert tries to pursue his pursuer, Lolita starts the car down the hill thus making Humbert run back); "L's conversation with 'stranger' at service station"; and "post office with letter from Mona . . ." (referring to Humbert's perusing at the post office in Wace of a letter from Mona containing an "element of mysterious nastiness"—"qu'il t'y mène"—an allusion to Quilty).[146]

In his "rough outline of our rough outline" of 13 July 1960, Kubrick still struggles with an idea of Quilty's elusiveness: he wants

Humbert to meet Quilty casually at Beardsley ("a scene . . . strange, somewhat arch in a humorous way") so that the audience would have no clue as to what Quilty actually wants but would nonetheless perceive something "dangerous and dark."[147] However, in the actual film, Kubrick chose to rely on the concrete screen persona (or shall we say personae?) of Sellers, rather than the abstract Quilty of Nabokov's creation, and never looked back.

Prompted and pushed by Kubrick, however, Nabokov's screenplay makes Quilty much more visible than he is in the book. In the novel, Quilty, "the ultimate unlover, the brutal and wily user, the American faker,"[148] as opposed to Humbert— "a European connoisseur," is still more powerful because he knows what Humbert does not (and what we do not). His identity (and venality) is enveloped in mystery or, as Corliss puts it: "Nothing is clear about Clare Quilty, except that he is clearly guilty";[149] he is a "criminal mastermind frequently spoken of but rarely seen."[150]

The figure of Quilty, whose actual appearances in the novel, except for the messy scene of his destruction, are few and strikingly farcical, is a classical figure of a doppelgänger, an inverted Humbert figure, the black king playing against the white king on a chessboard (the allusions to a chess game and the capturing of the queen are numerous throughout the book), almost a relative. Humbert, in fact, refers to him as his brother.[151] Quilty is also referred to as Humbert's European cousin Gustave who, in his turn, echoes Gustave Flaubert[152] and Gaston, Humbert's gay chess partner. Quilty is perceived as a shadow, as condensed grayness ("he and the grayness were gone"),[153] as an opaque presence, as a monkeying buffoon—"this semi-automated, subhuman trickster who had sodomized my darling."[154] In his turn, he is constantly pointed to as being somehow disfigured as buffoons are: he is described standing "in the camouflage of sun and shade, *disfigured* by them and *masked* by his own nakedness";[155] or as an incongruous crab, a "horrible Boschian cripple" who, scuttling up the slope, "waved his wrists and elbows in would-be comical imitation of rudimentary wings."[156] The felicitous "masked by his own nakedness" produces an almost eerie effect of actual disappearance of the body, void behind the mask, ultimate anonymity. Quilty's gaze haunts

Humbert while Humbert cannot see him, and when he does he misidentifies him.

Quilty's affinity with Humbert is constantly underlined: "The clues he left did not establish his identity but they reflected his personality, or at least a certain homogenous and striking personality; his genre, his type of humor—at its best at least —the tone of his brain, had affinities with my own."[157] His ape-likeness and perversion are on par with those of Humbert.

There is indeed always more than one Humbert—Humbert Humbert (H. H., Humburg, Humbird, etc.)—Humbert with his double self. Appel noted that "Humbert's self-loathing is often visualized in the metamorphic man-into-monster images of the popular cinema."[158] Dr. Jekyll and Mr. Hyde are more than once evoked in the text and the reference is more or less trivial. The more hidden and less trivial one—given the chess game landscape, as well as Lolita's moves towards becoming a "queen," and other details—points to the author of *Through the Looking Glass*, with his quiet perversion that, unlike in Humbert's case, never quite prevailed over his Victorian self. (Carroll later in life referred to Alice as "an entirely fascinating seven-year-old maiden."[159]) Humbert implements the hesitant possibilities and shatters the queen instead of protecting her, becoming a negative double of Carroll's white knight.

Humbert and Quilty are doubles of a peculiar sort. Paradoxically, they are not doubles in a strictly physical sense: Humbert's masculine and still fragile good looks contrast with Quilty's almost grotesque ugliness, his baldness, his stocky bow-legged figure. If he is Humbert's reflection, he is a reflection in a concave or convex mirror. As Humbert admits, "he mimed and mocked" him.[160] In another novel by Nabokov, *Despair*, the dissimilarity of the doubles is explored to its logical end: the story of a perfectly schemed murder is uncannily undermined by a tragic absurdity, a small detail, that in fact the doubles just do not look alike! One of the most interesting descriptions of Quilty in the text—standing in the shade and watching Lolita play with a dog—is a pure projection of Humbert's vision of himself and of another "dog-scene" on his first night in the Enchanted Hunters Hotel with Lolita:

> There he stood . . . his damp black hair or what was left of it, glued
> to his round head, his little mustache a humid smear, the wool on
> his chest spread like a symmetrical trophy, his naval pulsating,
> his hirsute thighs dripping with bright droplets, his tight wet
> black bathing trunks bloated and bursting with vigor where his
> great fat bullybag was pulled up and back like a padded shield
> over his reversed beasthood.[161]

Given "the melancholy truth" of Quilty's impotence, the above could
be read as an extremely ironic description if not for the revealing
epithets like "symmetrical" and "reversed" pointing back to the
beholder. Quilty, in fact, can be viewed here as obscene translation
of Humbert. Nabokov's language games are well-calculated and,
inverting Humbert's phrase, we can truly count on him "for a fancy
prose style."[162] In an important passage about Quilty's dangerous
game with Humbert ("with infinite skill, he swayed and staggered,
and regained an impossible balance. . ."[163]), Nabokov almost gives
himself away: he comes very close to disclosing his *autoritas*, his
authorial power as both the narrator and creator. Appel points
out in his commentary on the passage: "The verbal figurations
throughout *Lolita* demonstrate how Nabokov appears everywhere
in the texture but never in the text."[164]

The play with distance and proximity, doubling and
dissimilarity in Nabokov's aesthetics serves to construe the figure
of haunting. The utterly paranoid nature of haunting resides in the
building up of a lucid logical sequence based on incipiently absurd
premises. Nabokov grants Quilty unlimited power over Humbert,
just as Dostoevsky grants Ivan Karamazov's "petty demon" the
same kind of power over his flow of consciousness. As Appel shows
in his fascinating commentary on *Lolita*, Quilty just cannot know
certain things about Humbert when he traps, and puns, and snares
him, and still he knows them because Nabokov wants him to know,
"because Quilty and H. H. can be said to 'exist' only insofar as they
have been created by the same man."[165] Beyond the issue of authorial
speech, the question that might be asked is: whose narrative is this?
Both Humbert and Quilty are "enchanted hunters" and this is also
mirrored in multiple and dazzling ways: the narrative of "hunting
enchanters" is, of course, written by Quilty, but, in fact, it is part of

Humbert's narrative, which, in its turn, is—eventually—Nabokov's. In fact, Quilty is nothing but a sign, nothing but names, and with him we enter into the sphere of sheer paronomasia. In the context of Nabokov's fascination with paronomasia, which comes from a long modernist tradition, Simon Karlinsky pointed out:

> Interest . . . in discovering the hitherto unperceived relationships between the semantic and phonetic aspects of speech, pursued not for the purpose of playing with words but for discovering and revealing hidden new meanings, was basic to the prose of [Aleksei] Remizov, [Andrei] Bely and other Russian Symbolists.[166]

Quilty's appropriation of Humbert's and others' identities via the metonymic dissemination of names makes himself invisible, leads to the disappearance of the body that nevertheless leaves traces of its spectral presence on a landscape. Diabolically foreseeing Humbert's investigations, he sprays names like bullets, transforming the landscape into a perverse battlefield of sorts: from N. Petit, Larousse, Ill. (a French allusion and the name of a well-known dictionary) to Lucas Picador (a Carmen allusion), to a rather funereal and mockingly ghostly allusion to Lolita's deceased father Harold Haze (ironic proliferation of fatherly figures?), etc. As is convincingly shown in the commentary to *Lolita*, Humbert in his turn receives a certain frustrated gratification from the "cryptogrammic paper chase,"[167] "cryptogrammic" being an allusion both to a cryptogram and to "cryptogramic" (that is, to Quilty's impotence, at least according to some obscure dictionary definitions).

The moment when Nabokov, who is punning, playing, and toying with both of his disturbed personages, partially reveals the metaphorical essence of the doppelgänger is the passing French allusion in Mona's letter to Lolita. Humbert overlooks it and perceives only an "element of mysterious nastiness."[168] Providing some details about the play at Beardsley, Mona writes: "Remember? *Ne manque pas de dire à ton amant, Chimène, comme le lac est beau car il faut qu'il t'y mène. . . .*"[169] "Qu'il t'y mène" is not only a rather transparent allusion to Quilty. "The one who is leading you"— where? The double is but a metaphor of the *dérive* always leading you back to yourself.

However, the screenplay Quilty, instead of being elusive, becomes, as Boyd aptly put it, "blatantly intrusive."[170] His identity is inevitably made obvious. The paper chase, being a linguistic game par excellence and thus having "zero iconicity," as it were, cannot be transferred to the screen and is eliminated altogether, supplanted by Quilty's actual appearances and phone calls. Nothing pairs him up with Humbert except for what is established as a fact: their sharing of the same perversion and their role in the plot as rivals for Lolita's affection. Nor, admittedly, is Quilty's identity kept secret in Kubrick's film, which resorts to grotesque and carnivalesque exuberance of Sellers's multiple incarnations that, given his record of previous performances of multiple identities, remain fairly transparent even to the most credulous of viewers. However, Kubrick's "final product" relies on different means of representation (his emphasis is on actors, not plots), and he therefore perhaps succeeds where the screenplay fails, but at the expense of fidelity to the letter of the screenplay in order to remain faithful to the originary intent of the novel (more on this in the second part of this chapter).

On the whole, the shift from the novel to the screenplay to film acts as rhetorical reformulation, as moving away from an analogical/mimetic relationship, with its connotations of visual "truth" or resemblance, to what Derrida would call the "anagrammatical," with its connotations of "figural traces," of the text to be written "again" ("ana-"), or "anew."[171] In the course of writing and rewriting, the text of the novel undergoes a Heideggerian *Umschreibung* of sorts[172]—the passage from the literal to the figurative—opening up the rhetorical implications in the process, since it is the general mode of allegory. As remote as Nabokov might seem from Martin Heidegger, if we envision Nabokov's "reformulation" of *Lolita* as such originary translation, we might come to appreciate why Heidegger saw intralingual translation as being's "most intimate involvement with language."[173] The language at work becomes a co-extension of the original formulation on the path to truth. It is therefore significant that the quote from Marcel Proust's *Le temps retrouvé*, which Nabokov chose for his lectures on literature, is about the path to truth as mediation between the contingency of time and timelessness by means of art: "Truth will only begin when the writer takes two different objects, establishes their relationship, and encloses them in the necessary rings of his style (art), or even when, like life itself, comparing similar qualities in two sensations, he makes their essential nature stand out clearly by joining them in a metaphor in order to remove them from the contingencies (the accidents) of time, and links them together by means of timeless words."[174]

## The Metonymical and the Metaphorical Cinematic Translation: Stanley Kubrick's and Adrian Lyne's *Lolitas*

In this section, I will consider the two "intersemiotic" translations of *Lolita*—the screen versions by Kubrick and Lyne—through the critical lens of metonymy and metaphor, as this might help illuminate the issue of fidelity and freedom, which is central to translation theory. Kubrick's *Lolita*, I will argue, is essentially metonymical in nature, while Lyne's relies predominantly on metaphor. Consequently, the two films end up being faithful to very different things in the source text ("the original"), Nabokov's *Lolita*. Since these terms have shifting boundaries, an overview and some working definitions might be in order.

There have been different views as to how metonymy stands in relation to metaphor, both in cognitive linguistics and in art. The dichotomy was drawn by the Russian Formalists; Boris Eikhenbaum, in his study "Anna Akhmatova," explained that while metaphor works on the level of the idea, metonymy is a displacement, a lateral semantic shift on the same literal plane. In the 1950s, Roman Jakobson further extended the impetus to dissociate the two by arguing that the different types of mental mechanisms underlying the workings of metaphor and metonymy might account for different types of aphasic disturbances. This, according to Jakobson, is linked to the distinction in linguistics between the paradigmatic and syntagmatic organization of speech. The two tropes, he held, could be used to describe virtually anything: literary movements, styles in cinematography and painting, and the operations of the human consciousness (Freud's "identification and symbolism" as metaphors versus "displacement" and "condensation" as metonymy). Consequently, Jakobson created what Jill Matus called a "rhetoric of rivalry," in which different scholars have tried to champion one side at the expense of the other.[175] Thus, in post-Freudian psychoanalysis, Jacques Lacan dealt with discourse as a continuous metonymy, which is displaced from the real.

In 1977, David Lodge applied Jakobson's dichotomy specifically to the study of literature and described the metaphorical process as "substitution based on a certain kind of similarity."[176] Selection of vehicle and tenor (the substitute and the substituted) create a tension of reference and play. In the metonymical process, Lodge explained, "deletion is to combination as substitution is to selection . . . . Metonymy and synecdoche, in short, are produced by deleting one or more items from a natural combination, but not the items it would be most natural to omit: this illogicality is equivalent to the coexistence of similarity and dissimilarity in metaphor."[177] While Jakobson noted in general terms the predominance of the metaphoric process in Symbolism and Romanticism, and of metonymy in Realism ("synecdochic details," as he put it),[178] Lodge broadly applied the dichotomy to different literary genres and schools. Modernist and Formalist aesthetics, he wrote, make the reader ponder the workings of consciousness "by a process of inference and association," with art becoming "an autonomous activity, a superior kind of game."[179] Postmodernism instead blurs the situation where one of the modes would be more prominent, making metaphor and metonymy appear in "radically new ways."[180] Incidentally, he sees Nabokov as "a transitional figure between modernism and postmodernism" because he mixes the modes while preserving a "certain balance, or symmetry."[181]

There have been multiple attempts (Albert Henry, Hugh Bredin, Paul de Man, to name just a few) to revise the Jakobsonian juxtaposition either by rethinking metaphor as a combination of metonymies (Henry) or by relegating the two modes to different domains—that of reality and that of purely conceptual operation (Michel Le Guern). De Man's emphasis is on the referential but essentially accidental nature of metonymy, while metaphor, in his view, pulls toward unification of essences:

> Metaphor overlooks the fictional, textual element in the nature
> of the entity it connotes. It assumes a world in which intra- and
> extra-textual events, literal and figural forms of language, can
> be distinguished, a world in which the literal and the figural are
> properties that can be isolated and, consequently, exchanged and
> substituted for each other.[182]

The importance of cinematic metaphor has been widely discussed.
Sergei Eisenstein claimed to have discovered montage as a mo-
de of metaphor.[183] Eikhenbaum discussed cinematic tropes in
"Problematics of Cinema Stylistics."[184] Dudley Andrew dedicates
two chapters to cinematic metaphor in his *Concepts in Film Theory*.[185]
The Jakobsonian division between metaphor and metonymy —
rather than classical rhetoric, which interrelates them — as well as the
Freudian/Lacanian employment of metaphors for describing psychic
processes, are the driving forces behind Metz's *Psychoanalysis and
Cinema: The Imaginary Signifier*. Cinema, like writing, faces problems
of narration; film organizes itself as narrative, and at the earlier stage
of cine-semiology, Pier Paolo Pasolini, Umberto Eco, and Metz were
primarily concerned with film as language and the "grammar" of
this "language." When Metz tried to isolate syntagmatic figures
of the narrative cinema (his Grand Syntagmatique, as typology, is
essentially similar to that of rhetoric), he was still at the "euphoric
scientific phase of the semiotic project,"[186] but in the 1980s his
argument shifted to metaphor/metonymy. However, Roland Barthes
prefers "to evade Jakobson's opposition between metaphor and
metonymy, for if metonymy by its origins is a figure of contiguity,
it nevertheless functions finally as a substitute of the signifier — that
is, as a metaphor."[187]

A similar stance is expressed by Trevor Whittock in his *Metaphor
and Film*, a book extremely critical of Metz (and Freud). He considers
metonymy "so endemic to film that it normally loses any figurative
implications."[188] Consequently, a trope based on film image itself
and involving metonymy is just another subspecies of metaphor.
Whittock argues that "normally the presence of whatever is within
the shot is taken literally: Those things are there, we feel, because
they are contiguous as they would be in real life. But the filmmaker
can give some of the objects or events depicted within the shot

a metaphorical function, without in any way detracting from the probability of their appearance there."[189] He further suggests that the process of filming itself ("selecting camera angles, focusing, and framing") involves "selections and rejections," and thus ties film "inextricably . . . to metonymy of a sort."[190] Whittock refers to Lodge's definition of metonymy and synecdoche as tropes that "entail condensation through deletion."[191] The items that are deleted seem to be selected with "illogicality" (i.e. not those that would seem most dispensable) and this "illogicality," according to Whittock, makes a cinematic metonymy a true trope: "the item selected is seen to possess an apt suggestiveness that goes beyond mere reference to the object it replaces."[192]

This lengthy disquisition on the shifting boundaries of these terms, however, makes one thing abundantly clear: whether metonymy is a subspecies of metaphor or is, indeed, an independent trope, it would be impossible to isolate them completely in the cinematic narrative. Since creating a cinematic image is always transforming an object rather than "copying" it, metaphor, as Whittock rightly assumes, is "encapsulated within the very film image itself."[193] After all, the Greek *metaphora* (as the Latin *translatio*) has the stem meaning "carrying across" (and, also, in rhetoric, transference to another sense).[194] Film adaptation/translation, in a broad sense, is a metaphorical procedure. Therefore, our focus will be on the marked prevalence of metaphor or metonymy as the organizational principle of the cinematic narrative that points to more than a personal style of a concrete filmmaker. In *La métaphore vive*, Paul Ricoeur pointed to the hermeneutic aspect of metaphor (the solution of the enigma, "the logic of discovery"). Though he is concerned with written discourse, not the film narrative, in the case of film the same would apply: a film whose discursive practices heavily lean on metaphor will cry for interpretation; a cinematic narrative whose organizational principle is metonymic would be essentially avoiding interpretation.

"She was a breach baby: she arrived foot first," wrote Corliss of Kubrick's 1962 *Lolita*.[195] Indeed, as the opening credits appear to the emotional theme music of Nelson Riddle and before the word "Lolita" emerges on the screen, we see a girl's left foot drop from the top right corner of the frame. A man's left hand appears from the left; with infinite care and tenderness it supports the girl's foot lightly, while his right hand carefully but awkwardly starts painting each toenail, inserting cotton wads between the toes. "This is the movie metonymy," notes Corliss, "of a sort familiar in Saul Bass credit sequences of the 50s and 60s (the jagged arm for *The Man with the Golden Arm*, the undulating cat for a prostitute in *A Walk on the Wild Side*). These clever titles, by the British firm Chambers & Partners, posit a seesaw equilibrium between man and child, or father and daughter. . . . he is the slave, painting her toes; she is the slave, acceding to his whim—that the rest of the film (especially the scene in which Mason paints Lo[lita]'s toenails) gives the lie to."[196]

Kubrick's film starts with Humbert driving through the fog ("US made UK," as Nabokov wrote in his poem "Pale Film") to Quilty's castle. Traces of the previous night's debauchery are everywhere: garbage on the floor, dirty plates, full ashtrays, and empty bottles on a ping-pong table. Humbert, with a gun in his pocket, walks past a vaguely "Gainsborough-ish" portrait of a young woman placed on its side against the wall. Everything in the ground floor looks as if things have not been unpacked. There are crates and boxes; there is a lonely harp, curiously out of place, like an ironically raised eyebrow. The furniture, like some untidy Christo project, is draped in sheets, as is the object of his quest. "Quilty. Quilty!" Humbert calls out. At the sound of his voice a bottle falls off the top of a draped chair in the background. Quilty/Sellers rises from the chair, wraps the sheet around his body like a toga and says: "Spartacus. You come to free the slaves or some'n?" (a jocular metonymical allusion to Kubrick's previous film). A burlesque of a tussle follows: the superb ping-pong game totally improvised by the genius of Sellers, (even Nabokov himself conceded that along with a shot of scotch in the bathtub, it was a great invention), showcasing Sellers's chameleonic talent, until a wonderfully choreographed play-length sequence (ten minutes) ends with Quilty's death behind the aforementioned portrait of a young woman, pierced by bullets (how did it get to the top of the stairs, if it had been on the ground floor at the beginning?).

It is noteworthy that Kubrick, at least on the superficial level, sticks to Nabokov's screenplay's strategy: he starts the film with the narrative's central event without any expository information. Nabokov's screenplay circumvents the gory details and Kubrick follows suit: the action is mostly linguistic and Quilty fights Humbert with words—his own weapon and plaything, and means for absolution and immortality.

To determine further exactly what is and what is not "translated" by Kubrick, both from Nabokov's novel and his screenplay, Barthes's theory of narrative functions provides a useful tool. Barthes, in "Introduction to the Structural Analysis of Narratives," noted: "A narrative is never made up of anything other than functions: in differing degrees, everything in it signifies."[197] Barthes talks of two groups of functions: "distributional" functions, such as events and actions proper, and those integrational functions he calls "indices."[198] In the narrative grid, distributional functions are horizontal and linear, and they refer to the "functionality of *doing*," whereas indices are vertical and non-linear and refer rather to the "functionality of *being*"—representations of atmosphere and place, psychological underpinnings of characters, etc.[199] Barthes further subdivides those functions and later, in *S/Z*, expands the structure of classical narratives to five narrative codes. Even though Barthes is not specifically concerned with film adaptation, one can infer that the cardinal moments of the narrative (in *Coming to Terms: The Rhetoric of Narrative in Fiction and Film*, Seymour Chatman calls them "kernels")[200] can be transferred to another medium. McFarlane even claims that their alteration (like making up a happy ending where there was none) can cause "critical outrage and popular disaffection."[201] One may add that had Kubrick, pressured by the Legion of Decency, made Humbert and Lolita secretly married all along (a suggestion that apparently made Nabokov give up on the idea of the film in 1959),[202] the outrage would have been tremendous. Among integrational functions, only those that Barthes terms "informants"—"pure data with immediate signification"[203]—can be transferred; "indices proper," like atmosphere or character, cannot be transferred in their entirety.

What are the cardinal hinge-points that did not get transferred? And why? If Kubrick "translated" not the letter but the spirit of the text to the screen, where or how does he compensate for the loss, as any good translation does? Without doubt, at least two hinge-points of the narrative are not transferred: Humbert's history of pedophilia and its centrality to the story, and Lolita's death.

The only regret Kubrick expressed about his *Lolita* was that it should have been more erotic (since the book obscured Humbert's love by focusing on lust instead). He said in an interview: "I would fault myself in one area of the film. . . . Because of all the pressure over the Production Code and the catholic Legion of Decency at the time, I wasn't able to give any weight at all to the erotic aspect of Humbert's relationship with Lolita; and because his sexual obsession was only barely hinted at, it was assumed too quickly that Humbert was in love. Whereas in the novel this comes as a discovery at the end."[204] The complexity of Nabokov's text is, among other things, absolution of a monster by love (or art).

John Trevelyan, the Secretary of the British Board of Film Censors, was the person who could veto the finished film, or any part of it. On the other hand, as Corliss notes, "instead . . . of the Hollywood production code, the Legion of Decency, and any number of local censorship agencies in the US, Kubrick had one man to please and appease."[205] Trevelyan agreed to see the script and, having discovered that much of the adjustments had already been made (elimination of explicit sex scenes, age of the girl), insisted, according to Alexander Walker, on only one major item.[206] Humbert's clinical history of nymphomania, illustrated by a series of nymphets and explained in a lecture delivered in a women's club, had to go. James Mason's Humbert was denied not only a clinical history, but a personal history as well (Annabel, Valeria). Rather than appearing as "madness complicated by genius"[207] — a disturbing aesthetic theory based on a case history — Humbert's infatuation started to look much less threatening when transformed into a "more general, genteel neurosis,"[208] almost a mid-life crisis.

Indeed, Sue Lyon was too old for the part of Lolita from the beginning. She was fourteen when she was cast, fifteen when the movie was filmed. Though she was considered too underage to attend the Hollywood premiere, Lyon in her famous bikini and "Lolita sunglasses" scene looks like a fully formed seventeen-year-old. Or, as Pierre Giuliani wrote, from a perfectly European's perspective: "trop grande, trop agée, trop blonde, trop vulgaire, trop collégienne, trop yankee, trop cruche, trop pepsi ou trop coca . . . qu'importe" ("too big, too grown up, too blond, too vulgar, too like a college student, too American, too stupid, too pepsi or too cola. . .what does it matter?").[209]

The bizarre problem is that there is nothing in Humbert's infatuation with Lolita that could be characterized as perversion. It is known that Groucho Marx announced that he put off reading *Lolita* for six years—until she was eighteen. He was safe, however, watching the movie. Nabokov complained: "words made whispers, twelve made teen" in his "Pale Film." Whatever Kubrick's film is about, child abuse is resolutely not one of its themes.

Though Humbert's diary entry in the film provides one of the very few hints of his obsession with nymphets, the emphasis is shifted to the combination of childishness and vulgarity in Lolita, which strikes the refined connoisseur Humbert. Lolita can indeed convey this thoughtless vulgarity: she is a cruel and treacherous creature (and, made up for the school play production, she truly looks like a young witch); but curled up in Humbert's lap and comforted by him, she is too grown-up to be a victim and too heartless to command our sympathy. She throws tantrums but she is in control and unafraid.

The temporal shift in the film from 1947, in which the book's action is set, provides yet another detail in the relative "normalization" of the Humbert-Lolita relationship. A twelve-and-a half year-old in 1947 was a child, not a pre-teen, and sexual obsession with such a child was enough to have Nabokov's book banned in France for two years. By the time Kubrick's film was made, teen culture and rock music had changed the world, and a rebellious and sexually aware teenager with an older guy in pursuit became much less scandalous. The theme of child abuse had to wait another thirty years until the 1990s.

The restrictions on any explicit sex in the film due to censorship (the film's eight kisses, all in all, now seem innocent) might actually have been a blessing: less is more. Given the relatively recent censoring of Kubrick's last film, *Eyes Wide Shut*, one has an idea of what was left out. As Corliss wrote: "Today it all appears childish.

But the strategy also indicates that sex is a kid's game: all innuendo, excited giggling, raised eyebrows, and getting things wrong."[210] When Lolita suggests that Humbert has not kissed her yet, their car farcically zooms away. Charlotte whispers in Quilty's ear in the school ball scene, provoking his amused and incredulous giggling: "Did I do that?" Lolita whispers into Humbert's ear in the seduction scene ("All righty then," is her only clearly heard remark followed by a discrete fade out). Jerry Stovin and Diana Decker, as John and Jean Farlow, suggest to "sorta swap partners," so when Charlotte informs Humbert she has a surprise, Humbert makes an amused guess that the Farlows have been arrested.

Shelley Winters's Charlotte is all kitsch and burlesque. Her tight leopard skin outfits, her affectation and name-dropping, her pathetic sincerity are a wonderful counterpoint both to Humbert's *finesse* and Lolita's cynicism. As Corliss writes, "Charlotte's sins of style will absolve Humbert, in the viewer's mind, of guilt for her death."[211] She would have seemed severely miscast and grossly overplaying if she were to be considered alongside the Humbert and Lolita of the novel or screenplay, that is, if her acting were not so perfectly balanced with Kubrick's characters—Mason's Humbert and Lyon's Lolita.

James Mason's Humbert, unequivocally, is "the only innocent person in the piece" (as James B. Harris, the producer, put it),[212] an abused father and lover, with hooded eyes and agonized expression. Cast after Lawrence Olivier and David Niven had turned down Kubrick's and Harris's approaches, he was a perfect fit, in casting terms, to Humbert, as well as a perfect counterbalance to Winters's performance of Charlotte's overbearing affectation. In the cha-cha-cha scene, in which Charlotte aggressively corners him, as throughout the film in general, Mason acts as a pained, hurt, polite but reluctant participant. There is also a delightful moment (the result of Oswald Morris's excellent cinematography) when, courted aggressively by Charlotte as a prospective tenant—or husband—he literally wanders out of the frame.

Since Humbert's obsession with little girls and acting it out is not central to the film, Kubrick's first long sequence (the murder), out of the film's thirty-five, makes the viewer aware of the key event to which all the other sequences serve as explication. At the same time, it is aimed at Humbert's exclusion from the control over the narrative: his narrational voice is introduced only at the beginning of the next sequence. In the first long sequence, Quilty is disguised in the background and, when he finally emerges from his easy chair, he engages Humbert in games (ping pong and his reading of Humbert's poem with a buffoonish "twang"). So one is tempted to interpret the rest of the movie as a long flashback, especially when Humbert's voiceover is introduced. Mario Falsetto, in *Stanley Kubrick: A Narrative and Stylistic Analysis*, however, is justified in asking: "But whose flashback?"[213] The film's "present," as he points out, is not easy to locate. Even though the credit "Four years earlier" appears, with six instances of voice-over to follow throughout the film, the end credit tells the viewer of Humbert's death in jail. If the film is one long flashback, as in a diary, and the narrator is Humbert, his narrational voice is in a curious contradiction with the visual.

Humbert's voice-over cannot be interpreted as that of the omniscient narrator, since much of the visual information is withheld from him while it remains accessible to the viewer. One of many examples is a picture of Quilty on the wall, shown in a close-up, while Humbert is sobbing on the girl's bed right underneath. The same effect is achieved with Kubrick's favorite stylistic device, used to some extent in all of his films: organizing the spatial field of the frame so that action is taking place simultaneously in the foreground and the background. Falsetto argues that "the use of foreground/background is a stylistic means of including Quilty in the viewer's spatial field and excluding him from Humbert's."[214] Thus, in the memorable hotel scene, Quilty and Vivian are exchanging meaningful glances and pretending to be reading a paper in the foreground while Humbert is talking to the receptionist in the background, unaware of being watched. It is doubtful that Sellers's masquerade as a police officer or Dr. Zempf in the film, or traces of his character's presence (the mysterious car in pursuit, the sunglasses forgotten near Lolita's hospital bed) constitute an "enigma" for the viewer, but, in a kind of Sophoclean irony, Mason's Humbert certainly is the one with no clue.

Humbert's first instance of voice-over, an impassionate piece of information on his arrival in America and his intention to settle in "Ramsdale, New Hampshire," which immediately follows the gruesome murder scene, is untainted by his knowledge of his own fate. The second is a journal entry ("What drives me insane in the two-fold nature of this nymphet, of every nymphet perhaps. This mixture in my Lolita of tender, dreamy childishness and a kind of eerie vulgarity . . .". The third instance, the longest in the film, is Humbert's mental contemplation of "the perfect murder" of Charlotte, as he loads the gun and then follows Charlotte to the bathroom. It directly addresses the viewer: "But what do ya'know folks. . . ." The fourth instance, after the dramatic events of Charlotte's death, accompanies a travel sequence and has an eerily cheerful tone: "You must now forget Ramsdale, and poor Charlotte, and poor Lolita, and poor Humbert, and accompany us to Beardsley College where my lectureship in French poetry is in its second semester. . . ." The final instance of Humbert's voice—as Lolita and Humbert flee Beardsley after screaming rows and suspicions of neighbors—also sounds overtly enthusiastic: "The brakes were realigned, the water pipes unclogged, the valves ground. We had promised Beardsley School that we would be back as soon as my Hollywood engagement came to an end . . . ." These instances of voiceover are Kubrick's departure from Nabokov's screenplay, but they provide an overall structure to what is now Kubrick's narrative.

As Falsetto notes: "The vocal inflection of Humbert's voice-over changes little throughout the film. It remains generally neutral, if cultured and literary commentary, unaware of the somber events unfolding in the visuals."[215] The disjunction between Humbert's self-delusive narration, straining to maintain normality and control, and his lack of knowledge about himself and fate, his anger and despair in the visuals is specific to Kubrick's version of the tragic (*The Shining* also comes to mind). It borders on farce and Mason is acutely attuned to his role. It would have been incomplete, or just plainly *pathétique*, if not for at least two grotesquely comical instances: "that rapturous swig of Scotch in the bathtub"[216] after Charlotte's death, and the demonically entertaining reading of Charlotte's letter. This is when he both is and is not in control: irony about oneself and one's own misery is self-knowledge, but it is futile, as it offers no control over fate. Irony, as a trope (two meanings for the same phrase) is central to both Kubrick's film and Nabokov's novel. As de Man, drawing on Baudelaire's "De l'essence du rire" ("Essence of Laughter"), points out, *dédoublement*, "the characteristic that sets apart a reflective activity, such as that of the philosopher, from the activity of the ordinary self caught in everyday concerns," is essential for an understanding of irony.[217] The ironic, twofold self is, according to de Man, constituted by language and puts "the innocence or authenticity of our sense of being into question."[218] This "dialectic of identity and difference"[219] is also at work in the construction of doubling (both in the film and the novel), and is inherent to the very process of translation. The "doubleness" involved in irony has to do with the intentions of the speaker/writer, opening up possibilities for multiple, often subversive interpretations, just as in translation, authorial intent opens up multiple hermeneutic possibilities. After all, translation "entails having a punning mind," as Walter Redfern noted in "Traduction, Puns, Clichés, Plagiat."[220]

Kubrick truly succeeds in his translation of *Lolita*'s often ironic intertextuality onto the screen by redeploying the means or vehicles for literary allusions. While the context for a text is all preceding texts, the intertextual context for a film and its actors is previous films and previous roles. Thus one is not just watching Humbert as a character but also James Mason with a train of his previous roles. His roles in British films, before his Hollywood debut in Max Ophüls's *Caught* (1949), established him as a charming villain; his American roles built on this European charm, menacing and tragic at the same time. And just as a literary allusion is not necessarily accessible to every reader, the delightful detail of Mason's role as Flaubert in *Madame Bovary* (1949)—as a novel, an important text for the latticework of literary allusions in *Lolita*—might escape the viewer's attention but adds an additional dimension to *Lolita*'s cinematic version. And of course, Mason's Brutus (*Julius Caesar*, 1953) might be read as an ironic retort to Kubrick's *Spartacus*. Similarly, the viewer of *Lolita* in 1962 would have seen through the ploys of Sellers's Quilty not only because they were exuberantly obvious, but also because the viewer would have recalled Sellers impersonating various characters on the TV shows of the 1950s or cross-dressing as Grand Duchess Gloriana XII in *Mouse That Roared* (1959). Inevitably, the contemporary viewer would be enriching the context of Sellers's appearances as Quilty with his subsequent roles as a goofy Inspector Jacques Clouseau or Group Captain Mandrake and Dr. Strangelove.

A huge achievement of Kubrick's film is in the subtle way the ghostly presence of another, overall narrator, invisible to the viewer and still orchestrating the whole thing, is revealed. It is spectral, precise, merciless, and relentlessly ironic. In de Man's words, this narrator, whom he calls "the author," "asserts the ironic necessity of not becoming dupe of his own irony" and thus would not allow a comforting fiction of a happy recovery.[221] One is reminded of Nabokov's admission: "My characters cringe when I come near them with a whip."[222] One needs the second, third, umpteenth reading of *Lolita* to start noticing yet another instance of the spectral presence of this puppeteer. One might consider, for example, the delightfully cruel irony of Humbert's piercing memories of how the helplessness of baby animals was equally heartbreaking for him and his first, idealized love, Annabel.

Kubrick, as an *auteur*, is as controlling, obsessive and merciless to his characters (be it in *Lolita* or *A Clockwork Orange*) as Nabokov promised to be in his screenplay. Frederic Raphael, Kubrick's last screenwriter on *Eyes Wide Shut*, evokes his own experience of a troubled collaboration with this "cinematic Kasparov."[223] He comments appropriately: "Chess is a game of bloodless sadism and polite execution."[224] The relationship between the two *auteurs*, Kubrick and Nabokov, can be seen also in terms of this "chess game" — a battle for control over the narrative.

The major tension of *Lolita* the novel is between its metonymical plot, metonymy as a drive of narrative — contiguity and succession — and its reading as a metaphor of displacement (or, in a more specific sense, of exile). Metonymy leads you through the expanse of space but metaphor always brings you back to what you are, links you back to the notion of identity. The former is Lolita and Humbert's cross-country ramble with the overwhelming multiplicity of details listed under the Flaubertian *nous connûmes*, the description of the itinerary, the restlessness, the impossibility of staying in place once your place in space or in a generation has been lost;[225] the latter is the paranoid notion of being pursued even if you seem to have escaped, of being haunted—that is, of being continuously brought back, the structure of haunting being essentially that of the ghost of origin, identity.

The space in which the two fugitives, Lolita and Humbert, travel is indeed space that disturbingly has no place or is always displaced. As Lucy Maddox aptly noted, "Humbert pursues his erotic fantasies across a landscape that is at once a constant source of amazement to him and a perfect complement to his obsession,"[226] the most frequent element of this depraved landscape being "the Functional Motel."[227] The space of the book is filled with names, but names that are thoroughly anonymous: "*Nous connûmes* (this is royal fun) the would-be enticements of their repetitious names—all those Sunset Motels, U-Beam Cottages, Hillcrest Courts, Pine View Courts, Mountain View Courts, Skyline Courts, Park Plaza Courts, Green Acres, Mac's Courts."[228]

As a screenwriter, Nabokov had a lot of trouble with the motel scenes. Nabokov's inventiveness in the screenplay was aimed at both preserving the roadside landscape and "local fauna"[229] that he recreated for the novel and explicated it in the course of "translation," hence all those explicitly named "Baskerville Cottages" and "Kozy Kabins Lodge" of the screenplay.[230] Kubrick's "curiously limp car scenes"[231] cannot be explained only by the fact that *Lolita* was filmed in England. Kubrick did have a US-based cinematographer who, in Morris's words, had "brought back miles of stuff for the driving scenes."[232] Kubrick omitted practically all the visuals, except for the most generic roadside footage, and turned various motels into an equally generic motel room. He also dropped the sequence of "Various Rooms" at the Enchanted Hunters Hotel, ten brief shots "to construct a series of situations contrasting with the atmosphere in Room 342."[233] Nabokov was very proud of this sequence in the script but later dismissed it as too stage-bound.

Appel explains this aspect of Kubrick's film by "the director's decision to use some of Nabokov's dialogue but little else," as well as his striving, as a new kind of a filmmaker, "after a supposedly higher form" than the tradition of *film noir*.[234] The same reasons may account for the purging of the film of any traces of popular culture: corny songs, including the theme song that Nabokov hoped Dmitri could perform, and the movie culture. Corliss, on the other hand, sees this purging as a further step towards "ameliorating" Humbert's perversion and thus avoiding censorship: "Hum[bert] and Lo[lita] were now speeding down Anyroad, USA, or UK, and if the viewer inferred from this that they were Anyfolks, all the better."[235]

The anonymity and metonymic repetitiveness of motel names in the novel make them doubles in their own right, even before Quilty populates the landscape with the snare names like "Mirandola, NY" or "Quelquepart Island." The American landscape itself provided Nabokov with all those haunting Troys, Athens, Stamfords, Odessas, which are reminders of Europe and still are mere doubles. The double (or the demon) theme is that "focal strangeness," to borrow Pound's term, around which Nabokov concocts the text like a complicated web. The pursuer in *Lolita* the novel is always a double, be it one's past, oneself, or the other. The double is a metaphorical key to the metonymical plot, a haunting figure linking one back to the notion of identity. To explore a metaphysical problem via the form of fugitive narrative was quite an ingenious solution.

Fugitive narrative as it is explored and exploited in cinematography provided Nabokov with a sort of modern rhetoric that was instrumental for the unfolding of the narrative in the novel. It is important that Quilty is a filmmaker. As he himself tells Humbert, he "made private movies out of *Justine* and other eighteenth-century sex-capades" and is "the author of fifty-two successful scenarios."[236] He promises Lolita to make her a Hollywood starlet, but what he really offers is a "pornographic alternate."[237] Humbert's vision, in which Lolita is preserved as in a "cinematographic still"[238] — parallel to the photograph from the time past, all that remains of Annabel—is "a contrasting movie" to "the lurid reality of Quilty's cinematic plans, which ironically underscores the corruptness of at least one scenarist."[239] Appel notes, "The two contrasting movies 'double' one another as do Humbert and Quilty,"[240] or, one might add, as do Nabokov and Kubrick. Nabokov privileges photographic images because they have a quality of arrested memory and are self-contained, "a frozen segment of remembered time."[241] Photographic images are not "real." They are in the realm of sheer temporality. It is interesting that de Man links the allegorical model of literature with temporality, while Walter Benjamin relates photography to allegory.

As de Man writes in his discussion of symbol and allegory (metaphor/metonymy, or resemblance–analogy/contiguity), "the meaning constituted by the allegorical sign can . . . consist only of *repetition* (in the Kierkegaardian sense of the term) of a previous sign with which it can never coincide, since it is of the essence of this previous sign to be pure anteriority."[242] "The prevalence of allegory," de Man points out, "always corresponds to the unveiling of an authentically temporal destiny. This unveiling takes place in a subject that has sought refuge against the impact of time in a natural world to which, in truth, it bears no resemblance."[243] In other words, subject in allegory no longer can coincide with object, while "in the world of symbol it would be possible for the image to coincide with the substance."[244] The crucial figure of a double (Quilty) reveals "the existence of temporality that is definitely not organic, in that it relates to its source only in terms of distance and difference and allows for no end, for no totality."[245] The predicament of temporality links de Man's allegorical mode to the very process of translation, which, just as de Man's allegory, implies "an unreachable anteriority"—the impossibility of a mimetic mode of complete analogical correspondences.[246]

One might recall that Humbert's obsession with nymphets in the novel itself is defined in allegorical terms in the first place: "It will be marked that I substitute time terms for spatial ones. In fact, I would have the reader see 'nine' and 'fourteen' as the boundaries—the mirrory beaches and rosy rocks—of an enchanted island haunted by those nymphets of mine and surrounded by a vast, misty sea . . . that intangible island of entranced time where Lolita plays with her likes."[247] Other, regular, non-nymphic children "are incomparably more dependent on the spatial world of synchronous phenomena."[248]

It is interesting to observe the dialectic of the metonymic and the metaphoric in the ways Nabokov employs the mode of a fairy tale. Appel notes in his commentary to *Lolita* that "Nabokov has called Lolita a 'fairy tale,' and his nymph a 'fairy princess.'"[249] Appel uncovers a web of references to Hansel and Gretel, Cinderella, Bluebeard, the Little Mermaid, etc, as well as comments on extensive fairy tale parallels in the fantasy world of Nabokov's major novels, from *Invitation to a Beheading*, to *Pale Fire*, to *Ada*.[250] Examples from the novel are endless: Grimm Road leads to Quilty's "medieval castle"; Humbert sees himself alternately as "a fairy tale vampire"[251] or "a fairy-tale nurse";[252] the story of Humbert's infatuation with nymphets starts with Annabel, "the initial fateful elf in my life"[253] and ends in Elphinstone and the "Erlkönig" situation of Lolita's disappearance. It is more significant, perhaps, that, in the most general terms, the plot of *Lolita*, as of many other famous novels—Nabokov liked to point this out in his lectures on world literature—develops along the lines of archetypical fairy tales. To use Appel's words, "the themes of deception, enchantment, and metamorphosis are akin to the fairy tale," while "the recurrence of places and motifs and the presence of three principal characters recall the formalistic design and symmetry of those archetypal tales."[254]

In his lectures, Nabokov often reiterated his idea that all novels are fairy tales and a great novelist is a combination of a storyteller, a teacher, and a magician, a trio in which the magician prevails.[255] However, Nabokov's is a peculiar fairy tale, which reverses the fairy-tale denouement (living happily ever after, which, incidentally, Humbert offers to Lolita and she rejects). The contiguity and repetition of that fairy tale unravel around a center of opacity, a secret metaphor, which defies identification. It is a peculiar periphery of vision, which is nonetheless central to the narrative, much like the field of silence at the center of the loud taxonomy of colors in Pierre Bonnard's late paintings: the symmetry of multi-colored tiles and a silent nude (dead?) woman in a tub in the middle. The metonymical-allegorical structure of *Lolita* is, at least in part, responsible for the novel's resilient resistance to any kind of symbolic interpretation, and for the frustration of the symbolic as a result of "the desire to coincide," to use once again de Man's term.[256] Nabokov had tentatively tried the "symbolical" model in another, much earlier short novel, *The Eye*. The subject in it coincides with the object, the observer with the observed, and towards the end the novel completely and rather disappointingly exhausts its symbolic content. The double in *The Eye* turns out to be the subject, the same deranged voyeur spying on himself, and quite seriously suspected by some of his fellow émigrés of being a "double agent" (itself a *double* entendre). The moment the double and the subject finally coincide is pointedly described as the merging of the character and the reflection in the side mirror of the display window at a flower shop. *Lolita*, however, leaves the tension unresolved, and Quilty and Humbert never merge into one.

The metaphorical mechanism of the metonymical narrative of the novel, set in motion by the figure of a double, is resolved by Humbert's realization that his main crime was the murder of Lolita's childhood. The logic of death is the strongest symbolic moment of the novel: Mrs. Richard F. Schiller (Lolita) dies in childbirth on Christmas Day 1952, giving birth to a stillborn girl, in a remote settlement called Gray Star. Humbert would not know that, as he writes of Lolita's unborn child as a boy—a hope for redemption and absolution. However, the circular narrative itself lends Lolita immortality in words and art. Kubrick's Lolita, on the other hand, does not die, but she does not break our heart either; in fact, she does not evoke pity. Kubrick's Mrs. Richard Schiller is perfectly capable of giving birth to an "accidental" boy by her "accidental" husband, but she is denied immortality.

Nevertheless, Kubrick produced a striking translation of the overall metonymical narrative of the novel into a different, cinematic medium. The film, as has been already said, starts with the murder of Quilty. So there is no suspense when, after what can be argued was one long flashback, Humbert, at the end of the film, enters Quilty's mansion in a *déjà vu* scene. He shouts out again: "Quilty. Quilty!" Once more there is a draped chair (the viewer now knows that Quilty is in it), but a bottle on top of the draped figure is missing this time. Humbert apparently has wandered into a parallel universe, where everything that we have already seen might not have happened. One is reminded of *Ada* and its protagonist Van (not incidentally engaged in the philosophical investigation of the nature of time):

Van sealed the letter, found his Thunderbolt pistol in the place he had visualized, introduced one cartridge into the magazine, and translated it into its chamber. Then, standing before a closet mirror, he put the automatic to his head, at the point of the pterion, and pressed the comfortably concaved trigger. Nothing happened—or perhaps everything happened, and his destiny simply forked at that instant, as it probably does sometimes at night, especially in a strange bed, at stages of great happiness and great desolation, when we happen to die in our sleep, but continue our normal existence, with no perceptible break in the faked serialization, on the following, neatly prepared morning, with a spurious past discreetly but firmly attached behind. Anyway, what he held in his right hand was no longer a pistol but a pocket comb which he passed through his hair at the temples.[257]

Nabokov's narrative, as well as Kubrick's film, is a metonymical universe abounding not only in doppelgängers but also in parallel realities—a breeding pool of possibilities, a Borgesian "jardin de caminos que se bifurcan" ("the garden of forking paths"). Viewed from the point of view of Benjamin's "after-life" of a literary work and especially its Derridean re-interpretation, Kubrick's cinematic translation of *Lolita* is extremely successful despite all its limitations. The capacity of a text to live on depends on its continual reinterpretation, unlimited by one fixed meaning. The metaphorical/metonymical dialectic in Kubrick's film and Nabokov's text—a Derridean double bind of the text being paradoxically both translatable and untranslatable, both achieving and redeploying a meaning—works towards similar ends: the impossibility of organic totality or of any non-ironic, morally grounded, and semantically fixed conclusion.

Lyne's *Lolita*, from a screenplay by Stephen Schiff, arrived in a storm of controversy almost forty years after Kubrick's film. Carolo Pictures bought the film rights in 1990 from the Nabokov estate; the project was "blessed" by Dmitri Nabokov, who never liked Kubrick's version in the first place. However, four screenwriters later, the film went into production only in 1995. Speculations were rife that the "R" rating required for major distribution might not be obtained and that the film would go directly to cable. The reasons for the difficulties of the new *Lolita* are perfect examples of how cinematic translation (adaptation) is directly influenced by what Iurii Tynianov and the Formalists would call "extra-linguistic" reality. The movie studios rejected the new *Lolita* because it was "too expensive, it had little star power and its potentially offensive sex-with-a-child subject matter made the two-hour-and-seventeen-minute film commercially risky."[258] The underlying truth, however, was that many distributors had been scared away from being associated with a pedophile movie at the time of the JonBenét Ramsey murder in the US and the pedophile murder scandal in Belgium. There were other considerations as well. Lyne's previous films had been big commercial crowd pleasers (*Flashdance, Fatal Attraction, Indecent Proposal*), while with *Lolita*, he could not expect more than an art-house audience. "Nobody expected Mr. Fatal Attraction to turn out an art film; maybe that's why the budget was allowed to mushroom (to more than $50 million), as production took place all over the United States," observed Caryn James, whose comments on Lyne's *Lolita* in a review entitled "A Movie America Can't See" were among the most enthusiastic.[259] The film could not be sold on its sex-appeal and did not "come with the artistic cachet that leads to Academy Award nominations."[260] Many distributors claimed they just did not like the film enough to take risks for it. In sum, as one of the business people of Hollywood wryly said, "If you're going to offend the parents of America, you might as well do it with a film you love."[261]

The irony, of course, was that Lyne's *Lolita* was shown freely in Europe. In Paris, for example, as Anthony Lane wrote at the time in *The New Yorker*, "'Lolita' can be viewed any day by anybody. Well, almost anybody: 'Int. — 12 Ans,' say the movie listings, in unfortunate shorthand. The phrase sounds dirtier than anything onscreen, but it simply means that children under twelve are forbidden to see the movie."[262] Eventually, Lyne's *Lolita* was released by the Samuel Goldwyn Company, an independent distributor, in New York and Los Angeles in September 1998, and then in selected theaters around the United States. The reviews, with the exception of the *Los Angeles Times*, were generally much more positive than the distributors had expected, but whether and how this new cinematic translation truly contributed to the "after-life" of the original (to use Benjamin's term) is an altogether different question.

The new *Lolita* is a story about child abuse, in which the viewer is left with no doubt about who is right and who is not. The paradox is that Lyne's version claims to be more faithful to the original. It supposedly enjoyed somewhat greater freedoms of representation than those available to Kubrick, when he had to contemplate the possibility of a marriage between Humbert and Lolita because of the proprieties of the time. To be fair to Lyne, these freedoms were still necessarily limited: whether he contemplated including actual sex scenes in his film or not, the 1996 Child Pornography Prevention Act limited his options. A body double had to be used in all scenes suggesting sexual behavior by a minor and all such scenes had to be discussed with a lawyer. Also, Dominique Swain's mother served as her on-set chaperone: "a deliciously Charlotte-like deal."[263] Uncensored "fidelity to the letter" of the original in Schiff's screenplay, which lovingly restored some of the "cinematic devices" of Nabokov's novel, should have led to greater fidelity in the novel's cinematic representation. Such fidelity supposedly depends on resemblance to the original and thus on the figure of analogy (rhetorically, repetition with a difference). Peter Brunette and David Wills point out in their Derridean take on film theory:

> Analogy introduces difference while retaining a close resemblance to that which it represents. Thus there are good and bad analogies according to whether the resemblance is preserved or difference asserts itself as rupture. What at first was necessary then becomes an imitation threatening to replace or distort its model. Cinema . . . is caught in such a paradox. A discourse such as realism, which rests on the image's analogical relation to reality, leads straight to questions of close or distant analogy, and close or distant quickly becomes a matter of good or bad.[264]

The double-bind of Lyne's film is precisely that the supposed analogical resemblance (and thus greater fidelity) to the original text of the novel becomes confounded with what in such an analogical model would be the originary truth of the "real," "the identification of the subject with the world."[265] Inevitably, morality keeps coming in through the back door. One symptomatic review of the film finds

Nabokov's original to be "cold, self-adoring and mean-spiritedly misogynistic."[266] Accusing Nabokov of being shielded by layers of irony from the underlying truth of his hatred for adult womanhood, the review simplifies the problematics of the novel to Humbert being "sick, sick, sick" and the author having too much contempt for Freud to "allow any subtextual intrusions into [the author's] stylistically sealed cosmos."[267] In an exaggerated way, the review does delineate a new landscape, in which child abuse is worse than murder. Therefore, one of the implied conclusions would be that infidelity to so "suspect" an original would be nothing short of virtue. Symptomatically, despite lifting whole passages from Nabokov's novel, the film remains unfaithful to something essential in its "spirit," and this is clearly perceived as praiseworthy by Andrew Sarris. Thus he points out that, compared to the earlier film (and that "nasty" original!), "the new *Lolita* generates more emotion than was ever contemplated in the predominantly comic conception of the Kubrick version." Within the same context, he also notes that Ennio Morricone's "warmer and more poignant score" is infinitely preferable to Riddle's "cooler and more sardonic accompaniment."[268]

In a more subtle way (and in friendlier reviews), fidelity comes to be understood in its narrow sense and thus, for example, the subtlety of language is equated—by the rule of equivalence in cinematic terms—to the subtlety of the actor's voice. James writes: "Language is essential to *Lolita*, and Mr. Irons captures Humbert's voice perfectly."[269] Jeremy Irons is indeed an excellent actor, who was capable of taking on a role so thoroughly defined by Mason. He and Mason, as Lane notes, "boast two of the most beautiful voices in the history of cinema." Comparing them to Claude Rains and George Sanders, he further says that all of them, "exiled Englishmen," leave one with "the abiding suspicion that there is something dangerous in the deracinated."[270] Irons seems to keep Mason at the periphery of his vision, but otherwise it appears that all of the leading actors in Lyne's film are intentionally preoccupied with a radically new translation of their characters that departs drastically from their counterparts in Kubrick's film. Irons looks younger and thinner than Mason, and every bit any contemporary girl's dream, but his pained, remorse-imbued performance leaves no room for irony, which is such an essential part of Humbert's personality in the novel. When one recalls Humbert's sarcastic grin as he reads Charlotte's love letter in Kubrick's film, a curious realization hits home: Irons never smiles. Charlotte (Melanie Griffith) is screechingly non-exuberant. Quilty (Frank Langella) is unplayfully morbid and dangerous. Finally, Swain, a far better actress than Lyon, is all exaggerated teenage petulance, braids and braces, and acting out, not a poised and coolly ironic coiffed blonde. The rewriting of the characters might make them more "believable" (a characteristic evoked by many reviewers), but one cannot fail to notice that this "believability" implies an assumed referent outside Nabokov's text: believable because teenage girls *are* like this in "reality"; believable because a self-reflexive child-molester *would be* pained by pangs of conscience, etc. In other words, it seems to imply that unambiguous meaning is firmly anchored within the system of representation offered to us.

There are fairly straightforward ways for Lyne's film to claim its faithfulness to the novel, such as, for example, moving the action back to 1947 (with all appropriate period paraphernalia and music) and extending Humbert's flashback to the times when his obsession with nymphets began. This flashback to Humbert's childhood is appropriately gauzy and pretty (Ben Silverstone and Emma Griffiths-Malin play the fourteen-year-old Humbert and Annabel). The photography by Howard Atherton is wistfully nostalgic and dreamy. Nothing helps, however, and the film sags into a melancholic period piece because the period details are easier to translate than the ever-shifting meanings of the novel. Such limited understanding of fidelity in the cinematic translation accounts for taking Nabokov's words literally but putting them exclusively into conscience-stricken voice-overs by Humbert (Jeremy Irons). The lack of ambiguity in the film's message might also be responsible for the dreary literalism of some metaphors, such as, for example, "whore/child": Lolita is first seen by Humbert lying on the grass in a wet, seductively clinging dress, with a sprinkler rotating slowly behind her behind; then she smiles—only to show her braces. Another instance of such literalism is the gory bubble of blood on the lips of the dying Quilty. It belongs to a different film, perhaps of a horror-flick variety. "Word-for-word" fidelity in demonstrating "a big pink bubble with juvenile connotations" growing "to the size of a toy balloon"[271] does not achieve its goal because it cannot playfully extend itself to incorporate the next paragraph's "every shed drop of his bubbleblood" or the two flies on what remains of Quilty, "beside themselves with a dawning sense of unbelievable luck."[272] Citationality and wordplay undermine representation "until the referent can no longer be found," which in the novel calls the very "reality" of the murder scene irrevocably into question.[273] An argument that the destruction of a human being or the sexual corruption of minors are not pretty sights "in reality" would be missing the point, for such an argument assumes a mimetic mode of translation: the intelligible precedes the visible, and the visible is but an imitation of the intelligible.

Perhaps most telling is the overall metaphorical framework of Lyne's *Lolita*. Humbert apologizes in the end for everything he has done to Lolita in destroying her childhood. The film starts on the road: Humbert, after having murdered Quilty, drives dangerously, and one hears the famous lines: "Lolita, light of my life, fire of loins. My sin, my soul." The film ends with the actual (and quite graphic) scene of Quilty's messy destruction and Humbert yet again driving, dangerously swerving, followed by the police. He gets out of the car, walks through the field and watches the town below from the hill. The town is filled with voices and laughter of children at play but, as the voiceover announces, the real anomaly is the absence of Lolita's voice from this chorus: the conclusion on the evils of child abuse is made. However, the very last frame is once again Lolita's sleepy head hitting the pillow on the night she spends with Humbert in the Enchanted Hunters Hotel, before anything happened. The metaphorical return is to the pivotal moment in the protagonists' fates, when everything, if replayed, could have gone differently. Nevertheless, unlike the uncannily different *déjà vu* in Kubrick's *Lolita*, this return is not open-ended; life does not afford an endless bifurcation of time, and the message is that of regret, repentance, and controlled horror at the irrevocability of the past.

Kubrick's film, with all its defects—Lolita's ridiculous, frilly nightgown and the slapstick struggle of an old black servant with a collapsible bed notwithstanding—is infinitely more interesting than Lyne's and, in a strange way, more faithful to the metonymical spirit of Nabokov's text with its defiance of final interpretation and resilience to symbolic identification. The epithet "bizarre," applied to Kubrick's version by some of the reviewers of Lyne's film, might be its best compliment, for the film adequately translates by cinematic means the inherent "bizarreness" of the original *Lolita*. What could be more bizarre, after all, than making a romantic protagonist a creepy child molester?[274] Irony and doubleness are bound to disappear from a text that claims moral clarity. Lyne's film, writes Lane in his generally positive review, "is not risky enough: it turns down the bright, rampant polyphony of Nabokov's creation until we are left with a tone of reedy regret." He adds: "The film is seldom funny; the novel is seldom anything but."[275] At the end of his review, Lane wonders what Nabokov, "hunter of lost youth and scourge of nostalgia," would have thought of it all.[276] One does not know what Nabokov would have made of it, but there are indications that his Dr. Ray would have rejoiced at a review calling the new film "a tragic morality tale."[277]

The process of actually turning the script into the film, Kubrick's reinterpretation of Nabokov's screenplay, is akin to Heideggerian *Umdeutung* ("reframing," "reinterpretation"). This form of translation, according to Heidegger, constitutes the transition to a different domain of experience; the difference in this case is not rhetorical but hermeneutic. Heidegger claims that a poet is only the hermeneut, the translator of language, not the user. Both Kubrick and Lyne engage in reinterpretation, but Kubrick's "reinterpretation" intuits the metonymical nature of Nabokov's text and on a different level reproduces that nature. It is, in this sense, more true (in Heidegger, translation always has to do with truth) to the original than the "truer," more textually reverent version of Lyne.

# NOTES

1   A part of this chapter was published as an article as Julia Trubikhina, "Struggle for the Narrative: Nabokov's and Kubrik's Collaboration on the *Lolita* Screenplay," Nabokov issue of *Ulbandus*, The Slavic Review of Columbia University N 10 (2006-2007): 149-172.

2   Alfred Appel, *Nabokov's Dark Cinema* (New York: Oxford University Press, 1974).

3   Vladimir Nabokov, *Lolita: A Screenplay* (New York: McGrow-Hill Book Company, 1974), xiii, xii.

4   Cited in Richard Corliss, *Lolita* (London: British Film Institute Publishing, 1994), 10.

5   *Lolita: A Screenplay*, ix-x.

6   Keith Cohen, *Film and Fiction: The Dynamics of Exchange* (New Haven: Yale University Press, 1979), 62-63.

7   "Doris Billingsley to Vladimir Nabokov," 22 July 1958, letter of *The Nabokov-Kubrick/Harris Correspondence*, The Berg Collection, New York Public Library, Folders 1-9: Folder 1. Further references to this archive will be cited by the names of the correspondents, dates, and folder numbers.

8   Corliss, *Lolita*, 18-19.

9   Berg Collection, "Stanley Kubrick to Vladimir Nabokov," telegram, 8 December 1959, Folder 1.

10  Ibid., "Véra Nabokov to Stanley Kubrick," 31 December 1959, Folder 2.

11  Ibid.

12  Ibid., "Véra Nabokov to Stanley Kubrick," 12 March 1960, Folder 2.

13  Ibid., "Véra Nabokov to Stanley Kubrick," 19 August 1960, Folder 3.

14  Ibid., "Stanley Kubrick to Vladimir Nabokov," 2 September 1960, Folder 3.

15  Ibid., "Vladimir Nabokov to Stanley Kubrick," 14 December 1960, Folder 4.

16  Ibid., "Vladimir Nabokov to Stanley Kubrick," 23 February 1961, Folder 4.

17  Ibid., "James B. Harris to Véra Nabokov," 21 December 1960, Folder 4.

18  Ibid., "Stanley Kubrick to Vladimir Nabokov," 28 February 1961, Folder 4.

19  Ibid., "Vladimir Nabokov to Stanley Kubrick," 19 April 1961, Folder 4.

20  Ibid., "Véra Nabokov to James B. Harris," 14 December 1960, Folder 4.

21  Ibid., "Véra Nabokov to James B. Harris," 11 March 1961, Folder 4.

22  Ibid., "Véra Nabokov to Stanley Kubrick," 17 October 1961, Folder 4.

23  Ibid., "Vladimir Nabokov to Stanley Kubrick," 17 December 1961, Folder 6.

24  Ibid., "Stanley Kubrick to Vladimir Nabokov," 11 January 1962, Folder 6.

25  Ibid., "Véra Nabokov to Stanley Kubrick," 15 February 1962, Folder 6.

26  Ibid., "Stanley Kubrick to Vladimir Nabokov," telegram, 2 May 1962, Folder 6.

27  Ibid., "Vladimir Nabokov to Stanley Kubrick," Express Letter, 3 October 1962, Folder 7.

28  Ibid., "Stanley Kubrick to Vladimir Nabokov," 5 October 1962, Folder 7.

29  Ibid., "Vladimir Nabokov to Stanley Kubrick," 20 October 1962, Folder 7.
30  Ibid., "Stanley Kubrick to Vladimir Nabokov," 5 February, 1963, Folder 8.
31  Ibid., "Vladimir Nabokov to Stanley Kubrick," 28 February 1963, Folder 9.
32  Ibid., "Stanley Kubrick to Vladimir Nabokov," 3 April 1963, Folder 9.
33  Ibid.
34  Ibid., "Vladimir Nabokov to Stanley Kubrick," 9 November 1972, Folder 9.
35  Christian Metz, *The Imaginary Signifier* (Bloomington: Indiana University Press, 1977), 12.
36  Glenn Horowitz (ed.), *Véra's Butterflies: First Editions by Vladimir Nabokov Inscribed To His Wife*, by Sarah Funke et al. (New York: Glenn Horowitz Bookseller, Inc., 1999), 186.
37  Cited in ibid., 186-187.
38  *Lolita: A Screenplay*, xxiii.
39  Cited in Horowitz (ed.), *Véra's Butterflies*, 193.
40  Ibid.
41  *Lolita: A Screenplay*, x.
42  Ibid., xii-xiii.
43  Brian McFarlane, *Novels to Film: An Introduction to the Theory of Adaptation* (New York: Oxford University Press, 1996), 5-6.
44  See also David Bordwell, *The Classical Hollywood Cinema* (London: Routledge, 1985).
45  Morris Beja, *Film and Literature* (New York: Longman, 1979).
46  Cited in McFarlane, *Novels to Film*, 7.
47  See Christopher Orr, "The Discourse on Adaptation," *Wide Angle* 6/2 (1984): 72.
48  McFarlane, *Novels to Film*, 9.
49  Michael Klein and Gillian Parker (eds.), *The English Novel and the Movies* (New York: Frederick Ungar Publishing, 1981), 9.
50  Ibid., 10.
51  Beja, *Film and Literature*, 80.
52  Dudley Andrew, *The Major Film Theories* (New York: Oxford University Press, 1976), 10.
53  Geoffrey Wagner, *The Novel and the Cinema* (Rutherford, NJ: Fairleigh Dickinson University Press, 1975), 222.
54  Pattrick Cattrysse, "Film (Adaptation) as Translation: Some Methodological Proposals," *Target* 4.1 (1992): 61-62.
55  Ibid., 64.
56  Ibid., 67.
57  McFarlane, *Novels to Film*, 9.
58  Alan Spiegel, *Fiction and the Camera Eye: Visual Consciousness in Film and Modern Novel* (Charlottesville: University Press of Virginia, 1976), xiii.
59  Cohen, *Film and Fiction*, 5.
60  McFarlane, *Novels to Film*, 5.

61    Metz focused primarily on Aristotle's diegesis and its application in narrative cinema; Genette brought it in as "histoire." See Gérard Genette, "Time and Narrative in *A la recherche du temps perdu*," in *Aspects of Narrative*, ed. J. Hillis Miller (New York: Columbia University Press, 1971), 93-118.

62    Robert Burgoyne, Sandy Flitterman-Lewis, and Robert Stam, *New Vocabularies in Film Semiotics: Structuralism, Post-Structuralism and Beyond* (New York: Routledge, 1992), 38.

63    McFarlane, *Novels to Film*, 6.

64    Ibid.

65    Cohen, *Film and Fiction*, 8.

66    Irving "Swifty" Lazar, a "legendary showbiz agent" (see Corliss, *Lolita*, 63). The latter date, 1971, is the time when Nabokov was settling all the remaining formalities with Kubrick while preparing to publish his screenplay.

67    Horowitz (ed.), *Véra's Butterflies*, 199-211.

68    Ibid., 192.

69    Ibid., 194.

70    Humbert (*rhythmically*): "Pills, pills, beautiful pills. 'Your daughter' (*chuckles*) My sleeping beauty! Mr. Dodgson, please, tell me a bedtime story." See *Lolita: A Screenplay*, 202.

71    Boyd, *Vladimir Nabokov: The American Years*, 409. The long version is also at Vladimir Nabokov Archives at Montreux.

72    Ibid.

73    Cited in Corliss, *Lolita*, 19.

74    *Lolita: A Screenplay*, x.

75    Ibid., xxii.

76    Ibid., xxiii.

77    Ibid.

78    McFarlane, *Novels to Film*, 18.

79    Ibid.

80    Boyd, *Vladimir Nabokov: The American Years*, 414.

81    *Lolita: A Screenplay*, 34.

82    Ibid., 201.

83    Ibid., 159.

84    Ibid., 158.

85    Ibid., 83.

86    Boyd, *Vladimir Nabokov: The American Years*, 413.

87    McFarlane, *Novels to Film*, 17-18.

88    *Lolita: A Screenplay*, 1.

89    McFarlane, *Novels to Film*, 18.

90    Ibid.

91    Cited in Corliss, *Lolita*, 10.

92    Ibid., 56.

93    Ibid.

94  *Lolita: A Screenplay*, x.

95  See *Lolita: A Screenplay*, xii. As early as his first sound film, *Blackmail* (1929), Hitchcock appears as a passenger reading a newspaper in the metro; in *Suspicion* (1941), he is a man dropping a letter in the mailbox; in *Shadow of a Doubt* (1943), he is a man who plays bridge on the train; in *Notorious* (1946), he is a guest who drinks a glass of champagne in a gulp at Ingrid Bergman's party, etc. Hitchcock's favorite cameo role, according to him, was his appearance in *Lifeboat* (1944) as a "before and after" photograph in a diet advertisement. In Hitchcock's later films, his cameo roles become wicked self-parodies and comments on his own aging and mortality. Thus in *Frenzy* (1972), a puppet of a corpse with a face of Hitchcock floats slowly in the Thames; and in *Family Plot* (1976), his last film, Hitchcock is seen only as a dark silhouette through the glass door of the births and deaths registry.

96  Ibid., 5.

97  Ibid., 6.

98  Vladimir Nabokov, *The Annotated Lolita*, ed. Alfred Appel, Jr. (New York: McGraw-Hill Book Company, 1970), 12. All further quotes from the English *Lolita* are from this edition, marked "Nabokov" for the novel's text and "Appel" for the Notes.

99  *Lolita: A Screenplay*, 4.

100  Ibid., 73.

101  Ibid.

102  *The Annotated Lolita*, 37.

103  *Lolita: A Screenplay*, 26.

104  *The Annotated Lolita*, 38.

105  *Lolita: A Screenplay*, 32.

106  Ibid.

107  Ibid., 87-88.

108  Peter Brunette and David Wills, *Screen/Play: Derrida and Film Theory* (Princeton: Princeton University Press, 1989), 84.

109  *Lolita: A Screenplay*, 66.

110  Ibid., 6.

111  Berg Collection, "Vladimir Nabokov to Stanley Kubrick," 25 April 1960, Folder 2.

112  Ibid., "Vladimir Nabokov to Stanley Kubrick," 23 March 1960, Folder 2.

113  Ibid., "Vladimir Nabokov to Stanley Kubrick" 25 June 1960, Folder 3.

114  Boyd, *Vladimir Nabokov: The American Years*, 411.

115  *Lolita: A Screenplay*, 187.

116  Berg Collection, "Vladimir Nabokov to Stanley Kubrick" (with three-page typed suggestions by Kubrick for Act 3 with Nabokov's corrections), 9 July 1960, Folder 3.

117  *Lolita: A Screenplay*, 16.

118  Nabokov, *The Annotated Lolita*, 19.

119 Corliss, *Lolita*, 40.
120 Ibid.
121 Nabokov, *The Annotated Lolita*, 311.
122 Further on this, see David Bordwell, *Narration in the Fiction Film* (London: Methuen, 1985).
123 Metz, *The Imaginary Signifier*, 4.
124 McFarlane, *Novels to Film*, 20.
125 Ibid.
126 Ibid., 27.
127 Appel, "Notes," *The Annotated Lolita*, 332.
128 Nabokov, *The Annotated Lolita*, 34.
129 *Lolita: A Screenplay*, 46.
130 Ibid., 64.
131 Appel, "Notes," *The Annotated Lolita*, 331.
132 *Lolita: A Screenplay*, 64, 67.
133 Ibid., 72.
134 Ibid., 70.
135 Ibid., 102.
136 Ibid., 83.
137 Ibid., 139.
138 Ibid., 157.
139 Berg Collection, "Vladimir Nabokov to Stanley Kubrick," 9 July 1960, Folder 3.
140 Ibid., "Stanley Kubrick to Vladimir Nabokov," 13 July 1960, Folder 3.
141 Ibid.
142 Ibid.
143 Ibid.
144 *Lolita: A Screenplay*, 146.
145 Ibid., 107.
146 Nabokov, *The Annotated Lolita*, 225.
147 Berg Collection, "Stanley Kubrick to Vladimir Nabokov," 13 July 1960, Folder 3.
148 Corliss, *Lolita*, 43.
149 Ibid., 46.
150 Ibid.
151 Nabokov, *The Annotated Lolita*, 251.
152 See Lucy Maddox, *Nabokov's Novels in English* (Athens, GA: University of Georgia Press, 1983), 83.
153 Nabokov, *The Annotated Lolita*, 237.
154 Ibid., 297.
155 Ibid., emphasis added.
156 Ibid., 237.
157 Ibid., 251.

158 Appel, *Nabokov's Dark Cinema*, 142.
159 Cited in Jenny Woolf, *The Mystery of Lewis Carroll* (New York: St. Martin Press, 2010), 171.
160 Nabokov, *The Annotated Lolita*, 251.
161 Ibid., 239.
162 Ibid., 11.
163 Ibid., 251.
164 Appel, "Notes," *The Annotated Lolita*, 414.
165 Ibid., 418.
166 Simon Karlinsky, Introduction to *The Nabokov-Wilson Letters*, 21.
167 Nabokov, *The Annotated Lolita*, 252.
168 Ibid., 225.
169 Ibid.
170 Boyd, *Vladimir Nabokov: The American Years*, 413.
171 Peter Brunette and David Wills, *Screen/Play*, 88.
172 Martin Heidegger, *Parmenides. Gesamtausgabe*, vol. 54 (Frankfurt am Main: Vittorio Klostermann, 1975), 17-18. It is analyzed in Parvis Emad, "Thinking More Deeply into the Question of Translation," 323-340. In contrast to the conventional approach to translation (the interlingual), Heidegger sees translation as first occurring within our own language: speaking with ourselves or with others we are translating. It is what he calls reformulation, replacing one expression with another one (choosing different words or a more appropriate word-context [ibid., 327]). This change indicates that thinking is already moved, crossed over into "another truth, another clarity, or even another matter calling for questioning" (see *Parmenides*, 18. Cited in Parvis Emad, "Thinking More Deeply into the Question of Translation," 327). As opposed to interlingual translation whose validity is undermined by the issues of fidelity, Heidegger's *Umschreibung* is the intralingual translation, which shows the proximity to and connection with words (thinking is with words; understanding poetry is this originary translation). Thus reformulation for Heidegger constitutes the "doubling" of language, but not the mere doubling, because the language is coextensive with itself. It directs to the root unfolding of language, a concept which is very important to Heidegger (ibid., 330), with his stance on the priority of language and preoccupation with the mutual unfolding of language and being. Heidegger's vision of language's "way-making"(*be-wegen*) indicates the movement of thinking "along a path in language opening onto the 'truth of being'" (ibid.). It reveals a level of "linguistic activity" that lies deeper than what usually happens in speaking and writing within a multiplicity of meanings. We tend to think of this multiplicity as always readily available as we speak, but actually it is not: it is not that we occasionally mean different things by the same word, but that "as we speak the language, we are addressed and claimed by the being of beings in different ways, depending upon the root unfolding of being" (ibid., 332).

173  Ibid.

174  Vladimir Nabokov, *Lectures on Literature*, ed. Fredson Bowers, introduction by John Updike (San Diego, CA: Harvest Harcourt, 1982), 211.

175  Jill Matus, "Proxy and Proximity: Metonymic Signing," *University of Toronto Quarterly: A Canadian Journal of Humanities* 58.2 (Winter 1988-1989): 313.

176  David Lodge, *The Modes of Modern Writing: Metaphor, Metonymy, and the Typology of Modern Literature* (London: Arnold, 1977), 75.

177  Ibid., 76.

178  Jakobson, "Two Aspects of Language and Two Types of Aphasic Disturbances,"111.

179  Lodge, *The Modes of Modern Writing*, 45-48.

180  Ibid., 228.

181  Ibid., 240, 242.

182  Paul de Man, *Allegories of Reading* (New Haven and London: Yale University Press, 1979), 152-152.

183  Sergei Eisenstein, *Film Form*, trans. and ed. Jay Leyda (New York: Harcourt, Brace & World, 1949), 241.

184  See Herbert Eagle, *Russian Formalist Film Theory* (Ann Arbor: University of Michigan, Michigan Slavic Materials: 1981), 55-80.

185  Dudley Andrew, *Concepts in Film Theory* (Oxford: Oxford University Press, 1984).

186  See Burgoyne, Flitterman-Lewis, and Stam, *New Vocabularies in Film Semiotics*, 41.

187  Roland Barthes, *Image-Music-Text: Essays Selected and Translated by Stephen Heath* (Glasgow: Fontana/Collins, 1977), 50.

188  Trevor Whittock, *Metaphor and Film* (Cambridge: Cambridge University Press, 1990), 35.

189  Ibid., 42.

190  Ibid., 60.

191  Ibid., 59. See also Lodge, *The Modes of Modern Writing*, 76.

192  Whittock, *Metaphor and Film*, 60.

193  Ibid., 29.

194  Willis Barnstone, for example, refers to a sign in modern Greek on vehicles in the port of Piraeus, *Metafora*, meaning simply *transportation*. See Willis Barnstone, *The Poetics of Translation: History, Theory, Practice* (New Haven: Yale University Press, 1993), 15.

195  Corliss, *Lolita*, 66.

196  Ibid., 66-68.

197  Roland Barthes, "Introduction to the Structural Analysis of Narratives," in *Image-Music-Text*, 89.

198  Ibid., 91.

199  McFarlane, *Novels to Film*, 12.

200  Seymour Chatman, *Coming to Terms: The Rhetoric of Narrative in Fiction and Film* (Ithaca: Cornell University Press, 1990), 53.

201 McFarlane, *Novels to Film*, 14.
202 More on this see in Appel, *Nabokov's Dark Cinema*, 231.
203 Barthes, "Introduction to the Structural Analysis of Narratives," 96.
204 Cited in Appel, *Nabokov's Dark Cinema*, 228-229. See also Gene Phillips, "Kubrick," *Film Comment* VII.4 (Winter 1971-1972): 32.
205 Corliss, *Lolita*, 60.
206 See Alexander Walker, *The Celluloid Sacrifice: Aspects of Sex in the Movies* (New York: Hawthorne Books, 1967). Also cited in Corliss, *Lolita*, 60.
207 Corliss, *Lolita*, 78.
208 Ibid.
209 Pierre Giuliani, *Stanley Kubrick*, Collection dirigée par Francois Bordat (Paris: Editions Rivages, 1990), 130.
210 Corliss, *Lolita*, 72.
211 Ibid., 40.
212 Ibid., 32.
213 Mario Falsetto, *Stanley Kubrick: A Narrative and Stylistic Analysis* (Westport, CT and London: Greenwood Press, 1994), 89.
214 Ibid., 34.
215 Ibid., 92.
216 *Lolita: A Screenplay*, xiii.
217 Paul de Man, "The Rhetoric of Temporality," in *Critical Theory Since 1965*, ed. Hazard Adams and Leroy Searle (Tallahassee: Florida State University Press, 1992), 212.
218 Ibid., 214.
219 Ibid., 210.
220 See Walter Redfern, "Traduction, Puns, Clichés, Plagiat," in *Traductio: Essays on Punning and Translation*, ed. Dirk Delabastita (Manchester: St. Jerome Publishing, 1997), 264.
221 Paul de Man, "The Rhetoric of Temporality," 216.
222 *Lolita: A Screenplay*, xii.
223 Frederic Raphael, "A Kubrick Odyssey: The Director's Last Screenwriter Recounts his Labyrinthine Adventure on 'Eyes Wide Shut,'" *The New Yorker* (14 June 1999): 41.
224 Ibid.
225 In this regard see Ellen Pifer, *Nabokov and the Novel* (Cambridge, MA: Harvard University Press, 1980).
226 Maddox, *Nabokov's Novels in English*, 80.
227 Nabokov, *The Annotated Lolita*, 147.
228 Ibid., 148.
229 Corliss, *Lolita*, 78.
230 *Lolita: A Screenplay*, 117.
231 Appel, *Nabokov's Dark Cinema*, 244.
232 Cited in Corliss, *Lolita*, 78.

233 *Lolita: A Screenplay*, 111.

234 Appel, *Nabokov's Dark Cinema*, 234, 245.

235 Corliss, *Lolita*, 78.

236 *The Annotated Lolita*, 300.

237 Appel, *Nabokov's Dark Cinema*, 116.

238 Nabokov, *The Annotated Lolita*, 46.

239 Appel, *Nabokov's Dark Cinema*, 118.

240 Ibid.

241 See Carl R. Proffer, *Keys to Lolita* (Bloomington: Indiana University Press, 1968), 109.

242 Paul de Man, "The Rhetoric of Temporality," 209-210.

243 Ibid., 209.

244 Ibid.

245 Ibid., 218.

246 Ibid.

247 Nabokov, *The Annotated Lolita*, 18-19.

248 Ibid., 19.

249 Appel, "Notes," *The Annotated Lolita*, 340.

250 Ibid., 346-347.

251 Nabokov, *The Annotated Lolita*, 141.

252 Ibid., 41.

253 Ibid., 20.

254 Appel, "Notes," *The Annotated Lolita*, 346.

255 Nabokov also expresses this idea in his "On Good Readers and Good Writers."

256 Paul de Man, "The Rhetoric of Temporality," 205.

257 Vladimir Nabokov, *Ada, or Ardor: A Family Chronicle* (New York: Vintage International, 1990), 445.

258 Bernard Weinraub, "'Lolita' Defying Expectations," *The New York Times*, 5 August 1998.

259 Caryn James, "A Movie America Can't See," *The New York Times*, 15 March 1998.

260 Ibid.

261 Ibid.

262 Anthony Lane, "Lo And Behold: Why Can't America See the New 'Lolita'?" *The New Yorker* (23 February and 2 March 1998): 182.

263 Ibid., 184.

264 Brunette and Wills, *Screen/Play*, 72.

265 Ibid., 71.

266 Andrew Sarris, "New *Lolita* Better Than Kubrick's. But Nabokov Just Gets Nastier," *The New York Observer*, 10 August 1998.

267 Ibid.

268 Ibid.

269 Caryn James, "A Movie America Can't See."

270  Anthony Lane, "Lo And Behold," 183.
271  Nabokov, *The Annotated Lolita*, 306.
272  Ibid.
273  Brunette and Wills, *Screen/Play*, 92
274  See Lane, "Lo And Behold," 183.
275  Ibid., 184.
276  Ibid.
277  Caryn James, "Revisiting a Dangerous Obsession," *The New York Times*, 31 July 1998.

Conclusion

## Vladimir Nabokov
## within the Russian and Western Traditions
## of Translation [1]

In this conclusion, I would like to provide an overview that situates Nabokov vis-à-vis the Russian and Western traditions of translation, and to bring together in this context the central issues of Nabokov's ambivalent relationship to translation. These issues include his origin—his own "secret stem," leading back to Russian Romanticism—as well as translation as a vehicle for expressing Nabokov's own strongly held ideas about art. While Nabokov's practice of translation undergoes significant changes in the course of his career, his adherence to the idea of some "true," "metaphysical" language—ever elusive and ever present—remains surprisingly constant.

In the Foreword to his four-volume translation of *Eugene Onegin*, Nabokov defined three modes of literary translation: paraphrastic, lexical, and literal. Paraphrase is understood as "a free version of the original with omissions and additions prompted by the exigencies of form, the conventions attributed to the consumer, and the translator's ignorance."[2] Nabokov described this type of translator in "The Art of Translation" as "the professional writer relaxing in the company of a foreign confrère."[3] His own English versions of Aleksandr Pushkin, Mikhail Lermontov, and Fyodor Tiutchev, undertaken in *Three Russian Poets*[4] and highly praised by Edmund Wilson, as well as Nabokov's translations of Pushkin's "Little Tragedies" (the subject of his correspondence with Wilson in 1940-1941), would fit this category, as would Vasilii Zhukovskii's nineteenth-century translations of Friedrich Schiller and Thomas Gray. This was Nabokov's point of departure—the Russian tradition of translation. The other extreme, the lexical translation, serves to render the basic meaning of words and their order, and is something a machine "under the direction of an intelligent bilinguist" can do. "The well-meaning hack"[5] is a less than flattering description of such a translator. Finally, there is literal translation, on which Nabokov insists. It is the only "honest translation,"[6] which entails "rendering as closely as the associative and syntactical capacities of another language allow, the exact contextual meaning of the original." The literal translator is "the scholar who is eager to make the world appreciate the works of an obscure genius as much as he does himself."[7] Linking Nabokov's preoccupation with "honesty" to the metaphysical question of truth, Clarence Brown noted: "As his definition of translation is a compromise between two extremes, so his translation itself is a compromise between two languages. It is frankly unsatisfactory—neither one thing nor the other—but it is the best that under the circumstances and under the sway of Nabokov's inexorable principles is possible. The best that is possible means for him the best that is *true*. . . ."[8]

This in-between position is what makes Nabokov's idiosyncratic translation and much of his fiction so lucidly mad. The loss of his native language, along with the necessity to establish his literary reputation anew in his English-speaking environment, made his life-long engagement with Pushkin more important than ever. As Jane Grayson wrote, "it was the example of Pushkin's cultural eclecticism which helped him maintain his point of balance."[9] Pushkin, as the quintessential Russian poet, drew indiscriminately from foreign cultures and, by way of an inexplicable metamorphosis, succeeded in turning these appropriated sources into something original and decisively "native." Nabokov's contribution to Pushkin studies is now recognized first and foremost for his investigation of Pushkin's multi-cultural eclecticism. Nabokov adopted similar "cross-cultural reference, intertextuality, [and] multilingual play" as his own artistic method.[10]

Pushkin's cultural eclecticism had its roots in eighteenth-century Russian cultural developments. It was one of the reasons why Pushkin's true—perhaps only—cultural hero was Peter the Great, who had forcefully transposed European culture onto the resisting Russian soil. Borrowing and appropriating from elsewhere was recognized by Peter as discipleship in nation-building. In his case, the result was a national empire; in Pushkin's, a national literature. The attempt of eighteenth-century Russian classicism to "translate" the whole of European culture into Russian culture, while the very literary language itself was a work-in-progress, was broad in scope: from actual texts, to architecture, to fashion. By way of Pushkin, this strategy of unapologetic borrowing and appropriation became Nabokov's artistic makeup—a fully embraced multiculturalism. An interesting parallel here is that Nabokov's English itself was an ongoing work-in-progress. In this sense, Iurii Lotman's idea of cultural translation as a translation of a code or a structure,[11] rather than verbal communication of information, is very true in the case of Nabokov.

However, the Russian classicist tradition of translation also bore the mark of utilitarianism inherent in that age. Petrine reforms required first and foremost the translation of "useful" texts — educational, scientific, and military. It was a state project, carried out under the surveillance and enormous exhortation of the tsar himself. An unconfirmed story of an eighteenth-century translator who, having failed to translate a French book on horticulture, committed suicide, is therefore very characteristic of the project. Mikhail Lomonosov's, Antiokh Kantemir's, and Vasilii Trediakovskii's works on literary translation, developed at the end of the eighteenth century by Nikolai Karamzin's circle, were spurred by a practical need for a new, adequate Russian literary language. Fidelity was understood by a classicist translator in its narrow, practical sense: only that which in the original was close to the ideal, as seen by the translator, deserved accuracy. Thus Aleksandr Sumarokov in 1748 translated *Hamlet* as a conflict between feeling and duty. Most European literature came to Russia through translations from the French, and occasionally from the German — which renders the very idea of authorship problematic. As Nabokov wrote in "The Servile Path": "In consequence, Shakespeare is really [Pierre-Prime-Félicien Le Tourneur] Letourneur, [George Gordon] Byron and [Thomas] Moore are [Amédée] Pichot, [Walter] Scott is [Auguste-Jean-Baptiste] Defauconpret, [Laurence] Sterne is [Joseph Pierre] Frénais, and so on."[12] A good example, albeit already anachronistic, would be the translation in 1830 by Aleksandr G. Rotchev, absurdly entitled "Macbeth. Tragedy of Shakespeare. From the Works of Schiller." In a similar vein, the enthusiasm of neo-classical French criticism for Alexander Pope, for example, and the Russian worship of the French, especially Voltaire, contributed to the Pope vogue in Russia even before he was translated. By the same token, because Voltaire, Denis Diderot, and Jean-Jacques Rousseau had praised Salomon Gessner's *Idyllen* (which were imitations of Thompson) while remaining unaware of John Milton and Shakespeare, it was therefore Thompson — not Milton or Shakespeare — who would spur fifty years of imitations in Russia and prompt Karamzin to call "The Seasons" "zerkalo natury" ("the mirror of nature") in his *Letters of a Russian Traveller*.[13] Filtered through French and German renderings, Thompson did not so much inspire original Russian nature poetry, but rather introduced a new sentimental and melancholic worship of nature that had no specific national characteristics—nature in the abstract. Edward Young's "sepulchral philosophy" (by way of the French translation by Le Tourneur and of German translations by Friedrich Gottlieb Klopstock and Heinrich von Kleist, both big influences on Karamzin) brought into vogue the poetics of melancholy. Thomas Gray's graveyard poetry further promoted the sentimentalist/Romantic sensibility and appeared in multiple Russian renditions, most of them coming into being by way of a third language. Only by the time Romanticism completely prevailed over classicism would translations via a third language become exceptions.

The disparaging view of the function and role of translation in the new Russian sentimentalist/early Romantic aesthetics is expressed very explicitly (and derisively) in *Novyi Stern (A New Sterne)*, an 1805 comedy by prince Aleksandr Shakhovskoi. Its hero, Count Pronskii, becomes so obsessed with Sterne's sentimentalism that, instead of going into the military service, he embarks on a journey in the Russian countryside during which he writes a journal à la Sterne and scares the Russian peasantry with his apostrophes to nature and Sterne. He bemoans the death of a "Lady," who turns out to be his English dog, and falls for a peasant girl who giggles and thinks he is speaking in German. When Pronskii's servant asks where this sentimental mania comes from, a friend of Pronskii's father, sent to rescue the stray youth from this predicament, responds: "It was formed in England, rehashed in France, exaggerated in Germany, and came to us in a sorry fate."[14]

However, apart from teaching the Russians exaggerated affectation, sentimentalist and Romantic translation also served a much more serious purpose. It slowly worked as deferred action, as Freudian *Nachträglichkeit*, to generate a new origin. In his 1912 "Remembering, Repeating and Working Through," Freud formulated *Nachträglichkeit* thus: "There is one special class of experiences of the utmost importance for which no memory can as a rule be discovered. These [are] experiences which occurred in very early childhood and which were not understood at the time but which were subsequently [*nachträglich*] understood and interpreted."[15]

Within psychoanalysis, this has to do with the establishment of meaning, with restoring the link between cause and effect, broken not because of the failure of causality, but because the patient cannot recall. The patient is outside the event, and the mental functioning of the individual is defined not only in terms of causality, but also by the dichotomy between the inside and the outside—a gap to be bridged by the analyst.[16] "The question of origin is posed within the field of desire," writes Andrew Benjamin in *Translation and the Nature of Philosophy*.[17] If one considers Russian literary translation in this light, the desire for an origin "necessitates a narrative that includes and completes."[18] In the "subsequent action" of translation, reworking places foreign literary experiences *within* native literary subjectivity. The nineteenth-century Romantic tradition that nurtured the Russian school of translation suggested the existence of an absolute, if unattainable, "ideal" translation. In his theoretical translation principles, Zhukovskii, the founding father of Russian Romanticism, was close to the classicist and Karamzinist positions insofar as the "existence" of the ideal translation was concerned. The difference was in the understanding of the nature of the ideal: in classicism it was objective and mimetic; in Romanticism it was subjective and unattainable. The methods changed along with the transformation in this understanding. The important and revolutionary innovations in poetic language (for instance, the creation of the Russian hexameter and octave, experiments with rhyme and blank verse in the works of Nikolai Gnedich, Stepan Shevyrev, Pyotr Kireevskii, Pavel Katenin, and Konstantin Batiushkov) were brought about in the process of translation. Pushkin's translations of André Chénier, Catullus, Anacreon, and Horace were not just translations per se but also experiments in genre, understood as a "larger context"[19] beyond the "smaller context" of the original works. Such experimentation allowed Pushkin, in his translation of the French alexandrine of Chénier, to alternate between hexameter and iambic meters, or to introduce rhymes in Anacreon; in other words, to acquaint the nineteenth-century reader with a broad variety of unaccustomed strophic and metric arrangements.

Novalis, in one of his fragments, identified three types of translation: grammatical, free [*verändernd*], and mythical.[20] Grammatical translations require only minimal discursive abilities and have no artistic value. Free translation is understood as a true Romantic translation. Such a translator "muß der Dichter des Dichters sein, und des Dichters eigener Idee zugleich reden lassen" ("must be the poet of the poet and be able to render at the same time the poet's own ideas [and the ideas of the translator]").[21] Free translation is therefore re-creative and co-creative; the relationship to the original is as that of a genius of mankind to each individual man. (Pushkin actually called translation "re-creation.") The general and the whole express itself through the individual and the particular. Similar ideas of the Romantic aesthetic of the part and a whole are postulated in Hegel's *Aesthetics*.

The ultimate form of translation for Novalis is the "mythical" translation that recreates not the work itself but its ideal. It is perhaps significant that Zhukovskii's programmatic poem had the title "Ineffable" (1819) and subtitle "A Fragment." Its central rhetorical question is: "Is there power to express the Ineffable?" ("Nevyrazimoe podvlastno l vyrazheniu?") The ending of the poem claims that "only silence speaks with clarity" ("I lish molchanie poniatno govorit")—a motif that is later passed on to Tiutchev's famous "Silentium!"[22] Only the metaphysical language (i.e. the absence of language!) adequately expresses the soul. Zhukovskii's French contemporary, Alphonse de Lamartine, in his poem "Dieu" (published in 1820) similarly juxtaposes the language of "sons articulés" ("articulate sounds") and the other language: "l'autre, éternel, sublime, universel, immense/ Est le langage inné de toute intelligence." ("The other [is] eternal, vast, immense, /the innate language of intelligence")[23] In the 1820s, Romanticism in France forms into an independent literary movement and, through such literary journals as *La Muse Française*, spreads its influence and shapes new literary tastes in Europe and Russia.

Novalis does not provide examples of "mythical" translations; their *helle Spuren* ("light traces"), according to him, are found only in some critical descriptions of works of art. This allows us to identify the origins of the status of superiority that both Benjamin and Nabokov attributed to translation as criticism/"scholiastic passion" as well as the origins of their engagement with the discourse of "truth." Benjamin wrote: "If there is such a thing as a language of truth, the tensionless and even silent depository of the ultimate truth which all thought strives for, then the language of truth is—the true language. And this very language . . . is concealed in concentrated fashion in translation. . . . For there is a philosophical genius that is characterized by a yearning for that language which manifests itself in translation."[24] Nabokov's narrator in *The Real Life of Sebastian Knight*, who himself is engaged in a "translation" project, trying to re-create his brother and his brother's life, says: "I sometimes feel when I turn the pages of Sebastian's masterpiece that the 'absolute solution' is there, somewhere, concealed in some passage I have read too hastily, or that it is intertwined with other words whose familiar guise deceived me."[25] While any investigation of facts is necessarily only a "version" of the truth, what manifests itself in Sebastian's writing taunts the narrator with a possibility of uncovering his brother's true identity.

Nabokov's understanding of fidelity in translation is that of the closest possible approximation to the "absolute solution"—to the original's intent rather than that of reproducing the original's harmony. Fidelity for Benjamin is also more powerful than mere communication of sense: "a translation, instead of resembling the meaning of the original, must lovingly and in detail incorporate the original mode of signification, thus making both the original and the translation recognizable as fragments of a greater language, just as fragments are part of a vessel."[26]

While Nabokov's adherence to the profoundly Romantic idea of a true "metaphysical" language stayed surprisingly constant, his practice—or his understanding of the nature of the necessary compromise I have mentioned in Chapter 2—did change over the years. Nabokov's translations of *Three Russian Poets*, published in 1944, follow the Romantic tradition insofar as a free translation is viewed as a viable re-creation by means of another language. However, Nabokov's Romantic approach is closer to that of Pushkin than Zhukovskii, and this approach would be essential for Nabokov's further development, both as a translator and as a writer. The roots of Pushkin's Romanticism lay in the French Enlightenment and the neo-classical tradition of the seventeenth century, not in the German tradition of Goethe and Schiller. From the Enlightenment Pushkin inherited his affirmation of rational intellect. Like Pushkin—and unlike Zhukovskii or Lamartine—Nabokov has no doubts that language is capable of expressing absolutely everything he wants or needs to express (Pushkin called his poetic speech "my obedient words"). Such Romantic juxtapositions as expressible-material and ineffable-spiritual, dead and alive, particular-individual and general-absolute, exterior world and inner life, are not central to Pushkin's poetic world. In Nabokov's translations of Lermontov and Tiutchev, in whose poetry such juxtapositions are present, they are transformed by Nabokov for his own purposes. For example, in translating Tiutchev's famous poem "Silentium!," itself based on the juxtaposition of silence as truth and "uttered thought" as a lie, Nabokov conveys the last eight lines as follows:

> Dimmed is the fountainhead when stirred:
> drink at the source and speak no word.
> Live in your inner self alone
> within your soul a world has grown,
> the magic of veiled thoughts that might
> be blinded by the outer light,
> drowned in the noise of day, unheard . . .
> take in their song and speak no word.[27]

The translation is very close to the original in content ("respect for the content, if not the form of the original" was postulated by the mature Romantic movement in opposition to the tendencies to "improve" or "ennoble" the original, rampant in sentimentalism and early Romanticism).[28] This closeness in content makes the only instance of seemingly slight change potentially significant: in Nabokov's interpretation, the inner world might be disturbed by the "outer light" and "noise of the day," not as in Tiutchev—literally—"deafened by the outer noise" and "dissipated by the rays of the Day." What gets suppressed in Nabokov's translation, whether consciously or unconsciously, is one of the most important of Tiutchev's Romantic juxtapositions—that of the Night and Day (and, by extension, that of chaos and cosmos). A poet in Nabokov's interpretation becomes someone self-sufficient, secure in his inner world, who does not need the world at large. Such a poet can "draw the curtains," literally and metaphorically, on the world outside. Tiutchev's original, one of the twenty-four poems published by Pushkin in his literary journal *The Contemporary* in 1836 as "Poems sent from Germany," much more forcefully relates this inner world to the element of the Night, the primordial chaos of the unconscious. It would be much more problematic to "draw the curtains" on one's unconscious. The adjacent poems of the 1836 selection speak even more explicitly of the "world of the night soul," listening to the "terrifying songs of ancient chaos."

Since Nabokov's translations of *Three Russian Poets* follow the Romantic mode and are of course rhymed, one might argue that the change just accommodated the rhyme pattern. Nabokov's Romantic translations generally expose the "rather mechanic nature of rhyming."[29] Prince Pyotr Viazemskii, Pushkin and Zhukovskii's friend and contemporary, who was one of the earliest Russian proponents of literalism in translation, once observed of free Romantic translations that these "reincarnations of souls from foreign languages into Russian" were inevitably limited, as they failed to convey the "soil and climate of their native land."[30] As early as 1830 he recommended translating verse in terse prose, since "it is hard to be free in double chains—those of idea and those of expression," and claimed that only such exceptions as Zhukovskii were capable of creating an illusion that they were "walking their own road."[31] Later Nabokov himself would heed Viazemskii's advice.

One might suggest, however, that the nature of Nabokov's understanding of translation at the time of *Three Russian Poets* allowed for precisely those "reincarnations of souls" and the mutual fluidity of the two separate processes—that of translation and that of original creation. Thus Nabokov, who like Pushkin was not as focused on the juxtaposition of the impotent consciousness and the primordial unconscious as was Tiutchev, ends up expressing his own most profoundly held ideas through translation. This becomes evident when one compares the translation of "Silentium!" to Nabokov's own poem of the same year, "Slava" ("Fame"), which I discussed in more detail in Chapter 2. The poem affirms the self-contained sufficiency of the writer's inner world; the night, now explicitly mentioned, becomes a coded text, but the key to the code, the means to transcending self, is found in the self alone—Tiutchev with a Nabokovian twist. As often happens in Nabokov, the "sign words" in this poem—special "markers" whose appearance summons particular references—also point back to Tiutchev. Nabokov's reference in "Slava" to the immersion in "svoe *kliuchevoe*" (italics added; translated into English by Nabokov as "my wellspring"), the journey that takes the writer along the path to a metaphysical mystery of self transcendence, derives from Tiutchev's "kliuchi" ("fountainhead," in Nabokov's translation of "Silentium!"), from which one ought to drink silently in order to be truthful to the metaphysical absolute.[32]

When Nabokov's views on translation undergo a change, his anti-utilitarian literalness still remains profoundly Romantic insofar as its rebellion against classicist "purposefulness" is concerned, just as is Walter Benjamin's radical "no poem is intended for the reader, no picture for the beholder, no symphony for the listener."[33] Much as it was for Benjamin, the mere transmission of information is for Nabokov a "hallmark" of a bad translation. Benjamin's Judaic tendency toward conceptualizing translation as a cabalistic text is echoed by Nabokov's "acrimoniousness toward heretical corruption of a sacred text."[34] Antoine Berman, in his "Critique, commentaire et traduction," brings up the Talmudic tradition, which strives to preserve the text from that "violation interprétative" which, as he quotes Tamara Kamenzaian, "l'aurait plongée [la Tora] dans l'oubli" ("would have plunged it [Tora] into oblivion").[35] In "The Task of the Translator," Benjamin writes that all the great texts contain their translation between the lines, and that "this is true to the highest degree of sacred writings."[36] Nabokov's later hostility to the "inventions" and "self-inventions" of free translators is paradoxically very much like what Harold Bloom, drawing on Giambattista Vico, called "the prohibition of the divination" on which the Jewish religion was founded.[37]

The notion of Romantic irony, crucial for Benjamin, was also instrumental for Nabokov in his fiction and translation (in equal measure) because of its role in foregrounding ironic play, referentiality, and intertextuality. Romantic irony, as the alternation or indeed simultaneous coexistence of opposing meanings — faith and skepticism, reality and illusion, the absolute and the relative — are realized in Nabokov's oeuvre both through the radical playfulness of his art and the metaphysical uncertainty at the core of it. Irony in Nabokov's work takes on different forms: the subversive irony of quoting (I referred to this in my analysis of Nabokov's poem "On Translating *Eugene Onegin*"),[38] which allows for a disjunction of meaning between what is stated and what is intended; the tragic irony of Fate's relentless power and patterns; Sophoclean irony, which makes Nabokov's characters haplessly ignorant of the web prepared for them by the omniscient author (an "anthropomorphic deity"); and finally, punning and verbal play, in which context gives validity to both meanings at once. Although all of these mechanisms are used in both Nabokov's "original" works and translations, Nabokov's idiosyncratic punning has a special significance in translation. He often engages not only in intralingual word play, but also in interlingual play. By doing this, he draws attention "to the utterance as a piece of organized language" and "bring[s] about functional syncretism (i.e. the combination of several functions intersecting in one and the same carrier)."[39]

By the end of the nineteenth century in Russia, Romantic free translation had come to be understood as the leading mode. Imitation, a sub-genre widespread at the beginning of the nineteenth century, had practically disappeared, and "grammatical" translation (to use Novalis' term) had become obsolete. Symbolist translation, an inheritor of the Romantic free translation that had evolved by the end of the nineteenth century, is especially repulsive to Nabokov. In many instances he ridicules Konstantin Balmont, who imposed his own melodious "sweetness" on all translated poets alike—from Shota Rustaveli to Pedro Calderon de la Barca. In Nabokov's letters to Wilson, as well as in "The Art of Translation," he evokes a grotesque episode: Sergei Rachmaninov had asked him to translate into English a Russian poem that he wanted to set to music. After a closer inspection it turned out to be Balmont's translation of Poe's "Bells." Nabokov amusingly entertains the possibility that one day someone will "come across my English version of that Russian version" and the poem "will go on being balmontized until, perhaps, the 'Bells' become silence."[40]

In many ways Russian modernism reconsidered the rules set by the Romantic/Symbolist tradition. Nikolai Gumilev's famous "commandments for a translator" provide a good example. According to these commandments, a good translator has to faithfully render: "1) the number of lines, 2) meter, 3) alternation of rhymes, 4) character of enjambment, 5) character of rhyme, 6) vocabulary, 7) type of comparison, 8) individual devices, 9) changes in tonality."[41] Valerii Briusov, though a Symbolist himself, eventually broke with Symbolist translation and experimented with literalness. Nabokov tends to constitute his approach as unique, but it must be noted that Briusov's literal translation of Virgil's *Aeneid* in many ways anticipated Nabokov's literalness.[42] As a result, Briusov's rendering of the structure of Latin sentences in Russian seems in every way as odd and eccentric as Nabokov's rendering of Pushkin's Russian sentences in English.

Russian Formalism also developed as a reaction against Symbolist scholarship. In major works such as Boris Eikhenbaum's *Theory of the Formal Method* and Iurii Tynianov and Roman Jakobson's "Problems in the Study of Literature and Language," the Formalists expanded the boundaries of literary scholarship to include the extraliterary and introduced a structuralist, systemic approach to literature and language. While Nabokov obviously does not share the emphasis of some of the Formalists (such as Eikhenbaum) on the context of social evolution, he would agree with Tynianov's hierarchical literary system—an approach that placed the relation of a literary text to the norm (convention, social order) at the lowest level of the system. Nabokov's relationship with Formalism was more complex than he cared to admit. "Art as device" was at the heart of the Formalist controversy over what language is directed toward—the "real" world or the sign itself? Vladislav Khodasevich, in his 1937 article "On Sirin," was first to point out Nabokov's kinship to Formalism: "Under thorough scrutiny Sirin proves for the most part to be an artist of form, of the writer's device . . . . Sirin does not hide them [devices] because one of his major tasks is just that—to show how the devices live and work."[43] Khodasevich also described Nabokov's device as close to the Formalists' *ostranenie* (estrangement, defamiliarization): art as deception, composed of simulacra of the "real world," but with their nature being diametrically different from that of the "real."[44] However, a much more profound kinship is evident in the Formalists' understanding of the poetic text as a system of near total correspondence. The work of art is a meta-system, governed by structural laws, in which all formal elements function in relation to all other intratextual and intertextual elements. Nabokov's exercising of a "system of total tyranny" over the organizational elements of his texts, be these "original" works or translations, makes the text's structure a secret "link and bobolink," which, paraphrasing his own definition from *The Gift*, could explain "everything." In this sense, Nabokov's metaphysics is a metaphysics of a consistent structuralist: his "secret" (the gift) lies in knowing the hidden structure of the world of a work of art in its totality, thus making the author decisively parallel to God (who, supposedly, knows the workings of the hidden mechanism of the "real" world in its totality).[45] Despite Nabokov's disagreements with Jakobson, in some ways he comes close to Jakobson's idea of the poetry of grammar that he regarded as untranslatable.[46] In his 1960 essay, "Poetry of Grammar and Grammar of Poetry," Jakobson treats the poetic text as "proto-text" for "the most formalized use of language," in which "the suggestive possibilities of language are exploited fully."[47] Jakobson painstakingly analyzes the grammatical structures of Pushkin's poem "I Loved You," a poem which, lacking translatable tropes or "interesting" images, relies almost entirely on grammatical play (the distribution of personal pronouns, the specific use of adverbs, the near absence of prepositions, etc.). Jakobson's conclusion is that even a virtuoso translator "could not help but reduce to nil" the artistic strength of Pushkin's "grammatical" quatrains.[48]

Nabokov's rejection of the post-revolutionary developments in translation, and especially his rejection of the Soviet school, is largely due to personal reasons, but it also has to do with his aesthetic aversion to totalitarian mentality. (In light of Nabokov's formalist totality, I detect a certain irony here.) I mentioned earlier Nabokov's scorn for Soviet commentators as expressed in his Commentary to *Eugene Onegin*. The Soviet school of translation rejected the formalist approach (among other things it gave up the rules of equalinearity and equametrical arrangement), subjected translation to the law of consumer-oriented "functional equivalency" (close to that of Eugene Nida), and regressed back to the nineteenth-century Romantic notion of fidelity. For obvious reasons, untranslatability was not an issue for the Soviet school. André Lefevre explains the dominance of the "normative" practice of translation by the rigid categories of "right" and "wrong," instilled for centuries in Europe and the Americas by institutions such as "the church, the state and its educational system."[49] Obviously, the state and its educational institutions in the Soviet Union dominated the thinking about translation. As Lefevre notes, cultures that "derive their ultimate authority from a text—be it the Bible, the Qur'an, or *The Communist Manifesto*," are bound to be vigilant about the issues of "norm" and ideology.[50] Nevertheless, translation practice in the Soviet Union retained Romantic and modernist achievements along with the culturally established high status of literary translation. This was due, at least in part, to the forced "self-exile" into the field of translation of many of the finest Russian writers and poets because of harsh censorship and the impossibility of publishing their original work.

On the other hand, it is not difficult to see that Nabokov's translation theory is also at odds with the Poundian influence that largely informed Western and especially Anglo-American theory and practice in the twentieth century. Translation played an important role in Ezra Pound's own evolution as a poet. The achievement of Pound's translations lay not in comparative poetics but in rethinking the nature of an English poem: he was, in T. S. Eliot's words, "an inventor of Chinese poetry for our time" rather than a mere translator. Drawing on multiple mistranslations of Pound's—a notorious conflation of two poems in one title and a large number of errors—Hugh Kenner argues that many were deliberate. Pound would dismiss vast commentaries, which could explain obscure meanings, and instead would summon up the tradition through allusions, for the sake of making the poems in English "uncluttered and self-sufficient."[51] He would counterpose a "focal strangeness"[52] to the stance that "correct" is always synonymous with "traditional." A text, a word, means what has been continuously understood by it, and systematized understanding has always been based on a long tradition of interpretation. The far-reaching consequences of Pound's understanding, as well as of his "mistranslations," eventually came to signify the new practice of poetical translation in general. Pound would be content to "leave it on record that the Chinese had come to him by way of Japan, as 'Jupiter' comes from 'Zeus' by way of Rome."[53] Nabokov's "servile path" of fidelity in translation stands in sharp contrast to Pound's defiant license in appropriating the classics for the sake of the terseness of his own poetic word.

Having traced Benjamin's and Nabokov's theoretical origins to their Romantic roots, one cannot fail to notice the vertiginous gap their approach opens up between theory and practice. Benjamin posits translation in metonymic contiguity to the original, "just as a tangent touches a circle lightly" only to pursue "its own course according to the laws of fidelity in the freedom of linguistic flux" in perpetual renewal of language.[54] The metaphor/metonymy tension also informs Nabokov's fiction, endlessly deferring an ultimate interpretation. It is this tension that makes it so hard to situate Nabokov's translation within the Russian and Western traditions. This becomes especially clear in comparing Nabokov's translation theory to the poststructuralist and deconstructionist theories of language of Paul de Man, Michel Foucault, and Jacques Derrida. Their double vision of translation—translation that kills the original and still constantly rewrites it (thus problematizing authorship), that both manifests and conceals, deferring meaning in the play of intertextuality—could easily be Nabokov's vision as well. However this vision always confronts Nabokov's Romantic and insatiable desire for absolute identification, for the "absolute solution." Having consciously assumed the "servile path" of "the translator's invisibility" (to use Lawrence Venuti's term), Nabokov nonetheless thrust himself into the limelight with his *Eugene Onegin*, forcing everyone to discuss his amazing translation. Finally, Nabokov's understanding of fidelity to the original resulted in "foreignizing translation in opposition to the Anglo-American tradition of domestication," and in his denial of the notion of "abusive fidelity" that would adjust a foreign text to the dominant cultural discourse of the target language.[55] All this situated Nabokov in the perennial exile status of "non-citizenship": between the Russian and English languages, Russian and Western traditions, and theory and practice.

## NOTES

1    Parts of this conclusion, along with parts of the introduction, were previously published as: Julia Trubikhina, "Romantic Unreformed: Vladimir Nabokov's Literalness Within Russian and Western Translation Theories," *The ATA Chronicle* vol. xxix, 7 (July 2000): 43-49.

2    See *Eugene Onegin*, 1964, vii.

3    Nabokov, "The Art of Translation," 267.

4    See Vladimir Nabokov, *Three Russian Poets: Selections from Pushkin, Lermontov and Tyutchev* (Norfolk, CT: New Directions, 1944).

5    Nabokov, "The Art of Translation," 267.

6    *The Nabokov-Wilson Letters*, 234.

7    Nabokov, "The Art of Translation," 267.

8    Brown, "Nabokov's Pushkin and Nabokov's Nabokov," 198.

9    Grayson, "Introduction," *Nabokov's World*, 9.

10    Ibid., 10.

11    For further discussion of this, see Iurii Lotman, "Lektsii po strukturalnoi poetike," *Lotman i tartusko-moskovskaia semioticheskaia shkola* (Moscow: Gnozis, 1994), 11-265.

12    Vladimir Nabokov, "The Servile Path," in *On Translation*, ed. Reuben A. Brower (Cambridge, MA: Harvard University Press, 1959), 98.

13    See Nikolai Karamzin, *Pisma russkogo puteshestvennika*, in *Izbrannye sochineniia v dvukh tomakh*, Vol. 1 (Moscow-Leningrad: Khudozhestvennaia literatura, 1964), 572.

14  Cited in Ernest J. Simmons, *English Literature and Culture in Russia (1553-1840)* (New York: Octagon Books, Inc., 1964), 200.

15  Cited in Benjamin, *Translation and the Nature of Philosophy*, 146.

16  Ibid., 115.

17  Ibid.,110.

18  Ibid.

19  For the detailed discussion of this, see Efim Etkind, *Russkie poety-perevodchiki ot Trediakovskogo do Pushkina* (Leningrad: Nauka, 1973), 209.

20  Ibid., 75-77. Also see Aleksandr Dmitriev (ed.), *Literaturnye manifesty zapadno-evropeiskikh romantikov* (Moscow: Izdatelstvo Moskovskogo universiteta, 1980), 105.

21  Ibid. Translation is mine. Sarah Austin paraphrases this idea of Novalis: "He must be the poet of the poet, and thus be able to make him speak at once after his own original conception, and after that which exists in his (translator's) mind." See Sarah Austin [ed.], *Characteristics of Goethe*, Vol. 1 (1833; Reprint, London: Forgotten Books, 2013), 30.

22  Vasilii Zhukovskii, "Nevyrazimoe," in *Sochineniia v stikhakh i proze* (St.Peters-burg: Izdanie knigoprodavtsa I. Glazunova, 1901), 241.

23  Alphonse de Lamartine, "Vingt-Huitième Méditation: Dieu," in *Ouevres de Lamartine de l'Académie Française* (Bruxelles: Société Belge de librairie, 1840), 52. Translation is mine. See also Alphonse de Lamartine, *Poetical Meditations*, trans. Gervase Hittle (New York: Edwin Mellen Press Ltd., 1993), 174.

24  Benjamin, "The Task of the Translator," 77.

25  Vladimir Nabokov, *The Real Life of Sebastian Knight* (Norfolk, CT: New Directions, 1959), 180.

26  Benjamin, "The Task of the Translator," 78.

27  *Three Russian Poets*, 34.

28  See Maurice Friedberg, *Literary Translation in Russia: A Cultural History* (University Park: Pennsylvania State University Press, 1997), 43.

29  See André Lefevre, *Translating Literature: Practice and Theory in a Comparative Literary Context* (New York: The Modern Language Association of America, 1992), 72.

30  See Iurii Levin and Andrei Fedorov (eds.), *Russkie pisateli o perevode: XVIII-XX vv* (Leningrad: Sovetskii pisatel, 1960), 131-132.

31  Ibid., 133.

32  It is significant that the "sign word" *kliuchi*, associated with Tiutchev, also occurs in another, much earlier poem by Nabokov, "On the death of Aleksandr Blok," in which each of the poets from his much later *Three Russian Poets*—Pushkin, Lermontov, and Tiutchev—is defined by his own "marker." Pushkin is a "rainbow over the entire earth"; Lermontov—"the Milky Way over mountains"; and Tiutchev is a "*kliuch*, struiashchiisia vo mgle" ("wellspring flowing in the dark"). See Vladimir Nabokov, *Stikhotvoreniia i poemy* (Moscow: Folio, 1997), 179.

33 Benjamin, "The Task of the Translator," 69.

34 In the apt formulation of John O. Lyons's early article on Nabokov, "*Pale Fire* and the Fine Art of Annotation," in *Nabokov: The Man and His Work*, ed. L. S. Dembo (Madison: The University of Wisconsin Press, 1967), 161.

35 Antoine Berman, "Critique, commentaire et traduction," *Poésie* N 37, no. 2 (1986): 91.

36 Benjamin, "The Task of the Translator," 82.

37 Harold Bloom, "Poetry, Revisionism, Repression," in *Critical Theory Since 1965*, ed. Hazard Adams and Leroy Searle (Tallahassee: Florida State University Press, 1992), 333.

38 See pp. 26-27.

39 Gideon Toury, "What Is It That Renders a Spoonerism (Un)Translatable?" in *Essays on Punning and Translation*, ed. Dirk Delabastita (Manchester and Namur, Belgium: St. Jerome Publishing, 1997), 272.

40 Nabokov, "The Art of Translation," 268.

41 Nikolai Gumilev, "Perevody stikhotvornye," in *Pisma o russkoi poezii* (Moscow: Sovremennik, 1990), 74.

42 For a more detailed discussion of Briusov's translation of *Aeneid*, see Chapter 2 and Mikhail Gasparov's article on Briusov translation of *The Aeneid*, "Briusov i bukvalizm," 29-61.

43 See Vladislav Khodasevich, "On Sirin," 97.

44 Ibid., 98.

45 There are multiple examples of this; the chess metaphor obviously comes to mind. However, I would like to point out how the stratagem of a chess problem is related to a "secret": "The crude might of the queen was transformed with refined power, restrained and directed by a system of sparkling levers; the pawns grew cleverer; the knights stepped forth with a Spanish caracole. Everything had acquired sense and at the same time everything was concealed. Every creator is a plotter; and all the pieces impersonating his ideas on the board were here as conspirators and sorcerers. Only in the final instant was their *secret* spectacularly exposed" (*The Gift*, 172; emphasis is mine). "Khod konia" — "knight's move," an expression with a reference to chess, implies a decisive shift in a struggle, leading to the achievement of the goal (the revelation of the secret). It is often used by Nabokov to denote the shift in mimetic correspondence that I described in the analysis of "On Translating *Eugene Onegin*." Chess parallels are important for the Formalists, too. One of Shklovskii's books is actually entitled *Khod konia* (*The Knight's Move*), 1923.

46 See Roman Jakobson, "Poetry of Grammar and Grammar of Poetry," and "On Linguistic Aspects of Translation," in *Language and Literature*, 121-145 and 428-436 respectively.

47 See the editors' introduction to "Poetry of Grammar and Grammar of Poetry," 117.

48 Jakobson, "Poetry of Grammar and Grammar of Poetry," 132.

49  Lefevre, *Translating Literature*, 6.
50  Ibid., 120.
51  Kenner, *The Pound Era*, 206.
52  Ibid., 208.
53  Ibid., 222.
54  Benjamin, "The Task of the Translator," 80.
55  Lawrence Venuti, *The Translator's Invisibility: A History of Translation* (New York: Routledge, 1995), 23.

# Selected Bibliography

Alexandrov, Vladimir E. *Nabokov's Otherworld*. Princeton: Princeton University Press, 1991.

------, ed. *The Garland Companion to Vladimir Nabokov*. New York: Garland, 1995.

Allegro (Poliksena Solovieva). *Alisa v strane chudes. Tropinka* 2 (January 1909); 5 (March 1909); 7 (April 1909); 15 (July 1909); 17 (September 1909); 19-20 (October 1909).

Andrew, Dudley. *The Major Film Theories*. New York: Oxford University Press, 1976.

------. *Concepts in Film Theory*. Oxford: Oxford University Press, 1984.

Appel, Alfred, Jr. *Nabokov's Dark Cinema*. New York: Oxford University Press, 1974.

Ascher, Maria Louise. "The Exile as Autobiographer: Nabokov's Homecoming." In *Realism and Exile*, edited by Dominica Radulescu, 67-86. Lexington: Lauham, 2002.

*A. S. Pushkin i V. V. Nabokov: Sbornik dokladov mezhdunarodnoi konferentsii 15-18 aprelia 1999 g.* St. Petersburg: Dorn, 1999.

Bannet, Eve Tabor. "The Scene of Translation: After Jakobson, Benjamin, de Man, and Derrida." *New Literary History* 24, no. 3 (Summer 1993): 577-595.

Barabtarlo, Gennady. *Aerial View: Essays on Nabokov's Art and Metaphysics*. American University Studies Ser. XXIV, American Literature, vol. 40. New York: Peter Lang Publishing, 1993.

Barnstone, Willis. *The Poetics of Translation: History, Theory, Practice*. New Haven: Yale University Press, 1993.

Barthes, Roland. *Image-Music-Text: Essays Selected and Translated by Stephen Heath*. Glasgow: Fontana/Collins, 1977.

Bassnett-McGuire, Susan. *Translation Studies*. London and New York: Methuen, 1980.

Beaujour, Elizabeth Klosty. *"Nikolka Persik."* In *The Garland Companion to Vladimir Nabokov*, edited by Vladimir Alexandrov, 556-560. New York: Garland, 1995.

------. *Alien Tongues: Bilingual Russian Writers of the "First" Emigration*. Ithaca: Cornell University Press, 1989.

------. "Bilingualism." In *The Garland Companion to Vladimir Nabokov*, edited by Vladimir Alexandrov, 37-43. New York: Garland, 1995.

------. "Translation and Self-Translation." In *The Garland Companion to Vladimir Nabokov*, edited by Vladimir Alexandrov, 714-24. New York: Garland, 1995

------. "Vladimir Nabokov." In *Alien Tongues: Bilingual Russian Writers of the "First" Emigration*, 89-118. Ithaca: Cornell University Press, 1989.

Beja, Morris. *Film and Literature*. New York: Longman, 1979.

Benjamin, Andrew. *Translation and the Nature of Philosophy: A New Theory of Words*. London and New York: Routledge, 1989.

Benjamin, Walter. "The Task of the Translator." In *Illuminations*, edited by Hannah Arendt, 69-83. New York: Schocken Books, 1978.

Berman, Antoine. "Critique, commentaire et traduction." *Poésie* 37, no. 2 (1986): 88-106.

Besemeres, Mary. "Self-Translation in Vladimir Nabokov's *Pnin*." *Russian Review* 59, no. 3 (2000 July): 390-407.

Bessonova, A., and V. Viktorovich. "Nabokov—interpretator 'Evgeniia Onegina'." In *A. S. Pushkin i V. V. Nabokov: Sbornik dokladov mezhdunarodnoi konferentsii 15-18 aprelia 1999 g*, edited by Vadim Stark, 279-289. St. Petersburg: Dorn, 1999.

Bethea, David. "Brodsky's and Nabokov's Bilingualism(s): Translation, American Poetry and the Muttersprache." *Russian, Croatian and Serbian, Czech and Slovak, Polish Literature* 37 (15 February 1995-1 April 1995): 2-3, 157-184.

Bloom, Harold. "Poetry, Revisionism, Repression." In *Critical Theory Since 1965*, edited by Hazard Adams and Leroy Searle, 331-343. Tallahassee: Florida State University Press, 1992.

Bordwell, David. *Narration in the Fiction Film*. London: Methuen, 1985.

------. *The Classical Hollywood Cinema*. London: Routledge, 1985.

Borinsky, Alicia. "Where Do You Come From? Posing and the Culture of Roots." In *Reading the Shape of the World*, edited by Henry Schwarz and Richard Dienst, 278-287. Boulder, Co: Politics and Culture, 1996.

Boyd, Brian. *Nabokov's Pale Fire: The Magic of Artistic Discovery*. Princeton: Princeton University Press, 1999.

------. *Vladimir Nabokov: The American Years*. Princeton: Princeton University Press, 1992.

------. *Vladimir Nabokov: The Russian Years*. Princeton: Princeton University Press, 1990.

Briusov, Valerii. "Fialki v tigle." In *Izbrannye sochineniia v dvukh tomakh*. Vol. 2. Goslitizdat: 1955, 188ff.

Bronfen, Elizabeth. *Over Her Dead Body: Death, Femininity and the Aesthetic*. New York: Routledge, 1992.

Brown, Clarence. "Nabokov's Pushkin and Nabokov's Nabokov." In *Nabokov: The Man and His Work*, edited by L. S. Dembo, 195-209. Madison: University of Wisconsin Press, 1967.

Brunette, Peter, and David Wills. *Screen/Play: Derrida and Film Theory*. Princeton: Princeton University Press, 1989.

Bukhs, Nora. "Sur la structure du roman de V. Nabokov 'Roi, dame, valet'." *Revue des Etudes Slaves*. Paris, no. 59-4 (1987): 799-810.

Buks, Nora. (Nora Bukhs). *Eshafot v khrustalnom dvortse: O russkikh romanakh Vladimira Nabokova*. Moscow: Novoe literaturnoe obozrenie, 1998.

Burgoyne, Robert, Sandy Flitterman-Lewis, and Robert Stam. *New Vocabularies in Film Semiotics: Structuralism, Post-Structuralism and Beyond*. New York: Routledge, 1992.

Carroll, Lewis. *Alice's Adventures in Wonderland*. Illustrated by J. Tenniel. *Ania v strane chudes*. Perevod V. Nabokova, risunki L. Kerrolla. Vstupitelnaia statia i kommentarii k tekstu N. Demurovoi. Moscow: Raduga, 1992.

[Carroll, Lewis]. *Prikliucheniia Alisy v strane chudes Liuisa Kerrolia*. Perevod A. N. Rozhdestvenskoi s predisloviem i vstupitelnoi statei. Izdanie t-va M. O. Volf. St. Petersburg and Moscow, n. d.

------. *Prikliucheniia Ani v mire chudes*. Sostavleno po L. Karroliu M. Granstrem. St. Petersburg: Izdatelstvo E. A. Granstrem, 1908.

Cattrysse, Pattrick. "Film (Adaptation) as Translation: Some Methodological Proposals." *Target* 4, no. 1 (1992): 53-76.

Cervantes, Miguel de. *The Ingenious Gentleman Don Quixote de la Mancha*. Translated by Peter Motteux. New York: Random House, 1950.

Chatman, Seymour. *Coming to Terms: The Rhetoric of Narrative in Fiction and Film*. Ithaca, NY: Cornell University Press, 1990.

Chekhov, N. V. and A. K. Pokrovskii, *Materialy po istorii russkoi detskoi literatury (1750-1855)*. Vypusk 1. Moscow: Institut metodov vneshkolnoi raboty, 1927.

Chukovskii, Kornei, and Andrei Fedorov. *Iskusstvo perevoda*. Leningrad: Akademiia, 1930.

Chukovskii, Kornei. *Vysokoe iskusstvo: O printsipakh khudozhestvennogo perevoda*. Moscow: Iskusstvo, 1964.

Coates, Jennifer. "Changing Horses: Nabokov and Translation." In *The Practices of Literary Translation: Constraints and Creativity*, edited by Jean Boase-Beier and Michael Holman, 91-108. Manchester: St. Jerome Publishing, 1998.

Cohen, Keith. *Film and Fiction: The Dynamics of Exchange*. New Haven: Yale University Press, 1979.

Cohen, Morton N. *Lewis Carroll: A Biography*. London: Paremac, an imprint of Macmillan Publishers Ltd, 1995.

Connolly, Julian W. "*Ania v strane chudes*." In *The Garland Companion to Vladimir Nabokov*, edited by Vladimir Alexandrov, 18-24. New York: Garland, 1995.

------. *Nabokov's Early Fiction: Patterns of Self and Other*. Cambridge: Cambridge University Press, 1992.

Corliss, Richard. *Lolita*. London: British Film Institute Publishing, 1994.

Courtier, Maurice. "Writing and Erasure, or Nabokov's Other Texts." In *Nabokov's World*, edited by Jane Grayson, Arnold McMillin, and Priscilla Meyer, vol. 1: 173-185. 2 vols. New York: Palgrave, 2002.

Davydov, Sergei. "Nabokov: geroi, avtor, tekst." In *Vladimir Nabokov: Pro et Contra; Materialy i issledovaniia o zhizni i tvorchestve V. V. Nabokova*, edited by B.V. Averin, Vol. 2, 315-327. St. Petersburg: Izdatelstvo Russkogo Khristianskogo Gumanitarnogo instituta, 2001.

De Man, Paul. "Conclusions: Walter Benjamin's 'The Task of the Translator'." In *The Resistance to Theory*, 73-105. Minneapolis: University of Minnesota Press, 1986.

------. "Return to Philology." In *The Resistance to Theory*, 21-26. Minneapolis: University of Minnesota Press, 1986.

------. "The Rhetoric of Temporality." In *Critical Theory Since 1965*, edited by Hazard Adams and Lery Searle, 199-222. Tallahassee: Florida State University Press, 1992.

------. *Allegories of Reading*. New Haven and London: Yale University Press, 1979.

Deleuze, Gilles. "The Schizophrenic and Language: Surface and Depth in Lewis Carroll and Antonin Artaud." In *Textual Strategies: Perspectives in Post-Structuralist Criticism*, 277-295. Ithaca, NY: Cornell University Press, 1979.

------. *What is Philosophy?* Translated by Hugh Tomlinson and Graham Burchell. New York: Columbia University Press, 1994.

Demurova, Nina. "Vladimir Nabokov, Translator of Lewis Carroll's *Alice in Wonderland*." In *Nabokov at Cornell*, edited by Gavriel Shapiro, 182-191. Ithaca and London: Cornell University Press, 2003.

------. "Alice Speaks Russian: The Russian Translations of *Alice's Adventures in Wonderland* and *Through the Looking Glass*." *Harvard Literary Bulletin* 5, no. 4 (Winter 1994-1995): 11-29.

------. "Alisa na drugikh beregakh." In Lewis Carroll, *Alice's Adventures in Wonderland*, J. Tenniel. *Ania v strane chudes*, 7-28. Perevod V. Nabokova, risunki L. Kerrolla. Vstupitelnaia statia i kommentarii k tekstu N. Demurovoi. Moscow: Raduga, 1992.

------. "Golos i skripka. (K perevodu ektsentricheskikh skazok Liuisa Kerrolla)." *Materstvo perevoda* Sb. 7 (1970): 150-185.

Diment, Galya. "*Three Russian Poets*." In *The Garland Companion to Vladimir Nabokov*, edited by Vladimir Alexandrov, 709-713. New York: Garland, 1995.

Dolinin, Alexander. *"Eugene Onegin."* In *The Garland Companion to Vladimir Nabokov*, edited by Vladimir Alexandrov, 117-129. New York: Garland, 1995.

Eikhenbaum, Boris. "Problematics of Cinema Stylistics." In *Russian Formalist Film Theory. Michigan Slavic Materials 19*, 55-80. Ann Arbor: University of Michigan Press, 1981.

Eisenstein, Sergei. *Film Form.* Translated and edited by Jay Leyda. New York: Harcourt, Brace & World, 1949.

Emad, Parvis. "Thinking More Deeply into the Question of Translation." In *Reading Heidegger: Commemorations*, edited by John Sallis, 323-340. Bloomington and Indianapolis: Indiana University Press, 1993.

Eskin, Michael. "'Literal Translation': The Semiotic Significance of Nabokov's Conception of Poetic Translation." *Interdisciplinary Journal for Germanic Linguist and Semiotic Analysis* 2, no. 1 (Spring 1997): 1-32.

Etkind, Efim. *Russkie poety-perevodchiki ot Trediakovskogo do Pushkina.* Leningrad: Nauka, 1973.

------. *Poeziia i perevod.* Moscow and Leningrad: Sovetskii pisatel, 1963.

Falsetto, Mario. *Stanley Kubrick: A Narrative and Stylistic Analysis.* Westport, CT and London: Greenwood Press, 1994.

Freud, Sigmund. *Introductory Lectures on Psychoanalysis.* Translated and edited by James Strachey. New York: W. W. Norton & Company, Inc., 1966.

Friedberg, Maurice. *Literary Translation in Russia: A Cultural History.* University Park: The Pennsylvania State University Press, 1997.

Fundaminskii, M. I. "O pervykh detskikh entsiklopediiakh v Rossii." In *Kniga v Rossii XVII—nachala XIX v. Problemy sozdaniia i rasprostraneniia*, 146-160. Leningrad: Biblioteka Akademii Nauk SSSR, 1989.

Gasparov, Mikhail. "Briusov i bukvalizm. (Po neizdannym materialam i perevodu 'Eneidy')." In *Poetika perevoda: Sbornik statei*, 29-62. Moscow: Raduga, 1988.

Genette, Gérard. "Time and Narrative in *A la recherche du temps perdu*." In *Aspects of Narrative*, edited by J. Hillis Miller, 93-118. New York: Columbia University Press, 1971.

Gentzler, Edwin. *Contemporary Translation Theories.* New York: Routledge, 1993.

Giuliani, Pierre. *Stanley Kubrick.* Collection dirigée par Francois Bordat. Paris: Editions Rivages, 1990.

Goethe, Johann Wolfgang. *Westöstlicher Diwan.* München: Deutcher Tachenbuch Verlag, 1961.

Gogol, Nikolai. *The Complete Tales of Nikolai Gogol.* Edited and revised by Leonard J. Kent, translated by Constance Garnett. Vol. 1. Chicago and London: University of Chicago Press, 1985.

Goldblatt, Harvey. "The Song of Igor's Campaign." In *The Garland Companion to Vladimir Nabokov*, edited by Vladimir Alexandrov, 661-671. New York: Garland, 1995.

Grayson, Jane, Arnold McMillin, and Priscilla Meyer, eds. *Nabokov's World*. 2 vols. New York: Palgrave, 2002. Volume 1: *The Shape of Nabokov's World*; Volume 2: *Reading Nabokov*.

Grayson, Jane. "The French Connection: Nabokov and Alfred de Musset: Ideas and Practices of Translation." *Slavonic and East European Review*. 73. 4 (1995 Oct): 613-658.

------. "The Shape of Nabokov's World." Introduction to *Nabokov's World*, edited by Jane Grayson, Arnold McMillin, and Priscilla Meyer, vol. 1, 1-18. New York: Palgrave, 2002.

------. *Nabokov Translated: A Comparison of Nabokov's Russian and English Prose*. Oxford: Oxford University Press, 1977.

Greene, Diana. "Mid-Nineteenth-Century Domestic Ideology in Russia." In *Women and Russian Culture: Projections and Self-Perceptions*, edited by Rosalind Marsh, 78-97. New York and Oxford: Berghahn Books, 1998.

Gumilev, Nikolai. "Perevody stikhotvornye." In *Pisma o russkoi poezii*, 69-74. Moscow: Sovremennik, 1990.

Guy, Laurence. "*Feu Pâle*, ou l'indicible tourment du bilinguisme et de la traduction littéraire chez Nabokov." In *Double Vision: Studies in Literary Translation*, edited by Jane Taylor, 119-146. Durham, England: University of Durham, 2002.

Hegel, G. W. F. *Philosophy of Nature: Being. Part Two of the Encyclopaedia of the Philosophical Sciences (1830)*. Translated by A. V. Miller, with foreword by J. N. Findlay. Oxford: Clarendon Press, 1970.

Heidegger, Martin. *Parmenides. Gesamtausgabe*. Vol. 54, Frankfurt a. M.: Vittorio Klostermann, 1975 ff.: 17-18.

Holmgren, Beth, ed. "English as Sanctuary: Nabokov and Brodsky's Autobiographical Writings." In *The Russian Memoir: History and Literature*, 167-185. Evanston: Northwestern University Press, 2003.

Horowitz, Glenn, ed. *Véra's Butterflies: First Editions by Vladimir Nabokov Inscribed to his Wife*. By Sarah Funke, with contributions by Brian Boyd, Stephen Jay Gould, et al. New York City: Glenn Horowitz Bookseller, Inc., 1999.

*Imperiia N: Nabokov i nasledniki*. Sbornik statei. Edited by Yurii Leving and Yevgenii Soshkin. Moscow: Novoe literaturnoe obozrenie, 2006.

Ivanov, V. V. "Functions and Categories of Film Language." Translated by Stephen Rudy. *Film Theory and General Semiotics: Poetics in Translation* 8 (1981): 1-35.

Jakobson, Roman. "On Linguistic Aspects of Translation." In *Language in Literature*, edited by Krystyna Pomorska and Stephen Rudy, 428-435. Cambridge, MA: Harvard University Press, 1987.

------. "Poetry of Grammar and Grammar of Poetry." In *Language in Literature*, edited by Krystyna Pomorska and Stephen Rudy, 121-145. Cambridge, MA: Harvard University Press, 1987.

------. "Two Aspects of Language and Two Types of Aphasic Disturbances." In *Language in Literature*, edited by Krystyna Pomorska and Stephen Rudy, 95-114. Cambridge, MA: Harvard University Press, 1987.

James, Caryn. "A Movie America Can't See." *The New York Times*, 15 March 1998.

------. "Revisiting a Dangerous Obsession." *The New York Times*, 31 July 1998.

Johnson, Barton D., and Brian Boyd. "Prologue: The Otherworld." In *Nabokov's World*, edited by Jane Grayson, Arnold McMillin, and Priscilla Meyer, vol. 1, 19-25. New York: Palgrave, 2002.

Johnson, Barton D. "Vladimir Nabokov and Walter de la Mare's 'Otherworld'." In *Nabokov's World*, edited by Jane Grayson, Arnold McMillin, and Priscilla Meyer, vol. 1, 71-87. New York: Palgrave, 2002.

Karlinsky, Simon, ed. *Correspondence Between Vladimir Nabokov and Edmund Wilson, 1940-1971*. New York: Harper & Row, 1979.

------. "*Anya in Wonderland*: Nabokov's Russified Lewis Carroll." *TriQuarterly* 17 (Winter 1970): 310-315.

Kenner, Hugh. *The Pound Era*. Berkeley: University of California Press, 1971.

Kerroll, Liuis. *Ania v strane chudes*. Perevod V. Sirina (V. Nabokov), illiustratsii S. Zalshupina. Berlin: Izdatelstvo "Gamaiun," 1923.

------. *Prikliucheniia Alisy v strane chudes. Skvoz zerkalo i chto tam uvidela Alisa ili Alisa v zazerkale*. Perevod N. M. Demurovoi, stikhi v perevode S. Ia. Marshaka i D. T. Orlovskoi. Sofia: Izdatelstvo literatury na inostrannykh iazykakh, 1967.

------. *Prikliucheniia Alisy v strane chudes. Skvoz zerkalo i chto tam uvidela Alisa ili Alisa v zazerkale*. Perevod N. M. Demurovoi, stikhi v perevode S. Ia. Marshaka, D. T. Orlovskoi i O. A. Sedakovoi. Illustratsii Dzh. Tenniela. Moscow: Nauka, 1990.

Khodasevich, Vladislav. "Okno na Nevskii." In *Sobranie sochinenii v chetyrekh tomakh*, vol. 1, 487-490. Moscow: Soglasie, 1996.

------. "On Sirin." Translated by Michael H. Walker, edited by Simon Karlinsky and Robert P. Hughes. *TriQuarterly* 17 (Winter 1970): 96-101.

Kinyon-Kuchar, Kamila. "Models of Exile: Koestler, Nabokov, Kundera." Doctoral dissertation, University of Chicago, 2000.

Kirianova, V. Iu. "Detskaia entsiklopedicheskaia kniga v dorevoliutsionnoi Rossii." *Sovetskaia pedagogika* 10 (1984): 198-212.

Klein, Michael, and Gillian Parker, eds. *The English Novel and the Movies*. New York: Frederick Ungar Publishing, 1981.

Klekh, Igor. "O pisateliakh—dvuiazychnom i beziazychnom." *Voprosy literatury* 1 (January and February 2001): 172-183.

Kozlova, Svetlana. "Gnoseologiia otrezannoi golovy i utopia istiny v 'Priglashenii na kazn,' 'Ultima Thule' i 'Bend Sinister' V. V. Nabokova." In *V. V. Nabokov: Pro et Contra: materialy i issledovaniia o zhizni i tvorchestve V. V. Nabokova*, vol. 2, 782-809. St. Petersburg: Izdatelstvo Russkogo Khristianskogo Gumanitarnogo instituta, 2001.

Kristeva, Julia. *Revolution in Poetic Language*. New York: Columbia University Press, 1984.

Krylov, Ivan A. *Basni*. Moscow: Detgiz, 1951.

Lacan, Jacques. *The Four Fundamental Concepts of Psycho-Analysis*. New York: Norton, 1981.

Lane, Anthony. "Lo And Behold: Why Can't America See the New 'Lolita'?" *The New Yorker* (23 February and 2 March 1998): 182-184.

Lefevre, André. *Translating Literature: Practice and Theory in a Comparative Literary Context*. New York: The Modern Language Association of America, 1992.

Lermontov, Mikhail. *A Hero of Our Time*. Translated by Vladimir Nabokov in collaboration with Dmitri Nabokov. Ann Arbor: Ardis, 1988.

Lévy-Bertherat, Ann-Deborah. "Le dilemme du bilinguisme: Pnine ou la metamorphose inachevée." *Europe: Revue Litteraire Mensuelle* 73, no. 791 (March 1995): 48-56.

*Literaturnye manifesty zapadno-evropeiskikh romantikov*. Moscow: Izdatelstvo Moskovskogo universiteta, 1980.

Lodge, David. *The Modes of Modern Writing: Metaphor, Metonymy, and the Typology of Modern Literature*. London: Arnold, 1977.

Loreto, Paola. "Kubrick's and Lyne's *Lolitas*, or: What Gets Lost in a Beautiful Betrayal." In *America Today: Highways and Labyrinths*, edited by Gigliola Nocera, 409-420. Siracusa, Italy: 2003.

Lotman, Mikhail Iu. "A ta zvezda nad Pulkovym...: Zametki o poezii i stikhoslozhenii V. Nabokova." In *V. V. Nabokov: Pro et Contra: materialy i issledovaniia o zhizni i tvorchestve V. V. Nabokova*, vol. 2, 213-226. St. Petersburg: Izdatelstvo Russkogo Khristianskogo Gumanitarnogo instituta, 2001.

Lotman, Iurii. "Lektsii po strukturalnoi poetike." In *Lotman i tartusko-moskovskaia semioticheskaia shkola*, 11-265. Moscow: Gnozis, 1994.

------. *Besedy o russkoi kulture: Byt i traditsii russkogo dvorianstva (XVIII-nachalo XIX veka)*. St. Petersburg: Iskusstvo—SPb, 1994.

Lyons, John O. "*Pale Fire* and the Fine Art of Annotation." In *Nabokov: The Man and His Work*, edited by L. S. Dembo, 157-164. Madison: University of Wisconsin Press, 1967.

Malikova, M. "Obraz Pushkina u Nabokova: Neskolko nabliudenii." *A. S. Pushkin and V. V. Nabokov: Sbornik dokladov mezhdunarodnoi konferentsii 15-18 aprelia 1999 g*, 257-258. St. Petersburg: Dorn, 1999.

Martin, Jean-Clet. "The Eye of the Outside." In *Deleuze: A Critical Reader*, edited by Paul Patton, 18-28. Oxford, UK: Blackwell Publishers, 1996.

Matus, Jill. "Proxy and Proximity: Metonymic Signing." *University of Toronto Quarterly: A Canadian Journal of Humanities* 58, no. 2 (Winter 1988-1989): 313ff.

McDermott, John Francis, ed. *The Russian Journal and Other Selections from the Works of Lewis Carroll*. New York: E.P. Dutton & Co, 1935.

McFarlane, Brian. *Novels to Film: An Introduction to the Theory of Adaptation*. New York: Oxford University Press, 1996.

Metz, Christian. *The Imaginary Signifier*. Bloomingdale: Indiana University Press, 1977.

Nabokoff-Sirine, Vladimir. "Pouchkine, ou le vrai et le vraisemblable." *La nouvelle revue française* 48 (1937): 362-378.

Nabokov, Dmitri, and Matthew Bruccoli, eds. *Vladimir Nabokov: Selected Letters 1940-1977*. San Diego, New York, and London: Harcourt, Brace, Jovanovich, 1989.

Nabokov, Vladimir. "Letter to Saturday Review June 19, 1959." In Vladimir Nabokov: Selected Letters 1940-1977, edited by Dmitri Nabokov and Matthew Bruccoli, 292. San Diego, New York, and London: Harcourt, Brace, Jovanovich, 1989.

------, trans. "Translator's Foreword." In Mikhail Lermontov, *A Hero of Our Time*, v-xix. Ann Arbor: Ardis, 1988.

------. "Fame." In *Poems and Problems*, 111-112. New York: McGraw-Hill, 1970.

------. "Letter to Edmund Wilson." In *Correspondence Between Vladimir Nabokov and Edmund Wilson, 1940-1971*, edited by S. Karlinsky, 220. New York: Harper & Row, 1979.

------. "Pushkin, or the Real and the Plausible." Translated by Dmitri Nabokov. *New York Review of Books* (31 March 1988): 38-42.

------. "The Paris Poem." In *Poems and Problems*, 122-123. New York and Toronto: McGraw-Hill, 1970.

------. "Letter to *Encounter*, February 18, 1966." In *Correspondence Between Vladimir Nabokov and Edmund Wilson, 1940-1971*, edited by S. Karlinsky, 385. New York: Harper & Row, 1979.

------. "Letter to Roman Jakobson, April 14, 1957." In *Vladimir Nabokov: Selected Letters 1940-1977*, edited by Dmitri Nabokov and Matthew Bruccoli, 216. San Diego, New York, and London: Harcourt, Brace, Jovanovich, 1989.

------. "On Translating *Eugene Onegin*." *The New Yorker* (8 January 1955): 34. Reprinted in Vladimir Nabokov, *Poems and Problems*, 175. New York and Toronto: McGraw-Hill, 1970.

------. "Prof. Woodbridge in an Essay on Nature Postulates the Reality of the World." *New York Sun,* 10 December 1940.

------. "The Servile Path." In *On Translation,* edited by Reuben A. Brower, 98. Cambridge, MA: Harvard University Press, 1959.

------. The Nabokov-Kubrick/Harris Correspondence. Folders 1-9; *Lolita,* three versions of the screenplay. The Berg Collection, New York Public Library.

------. *Ada.* New York: Vintage International, 1990.

------. *Drugie berega.* Moscow: Khudozhestvennaia literatura, 1988.

------. *Eugene Onegin: A Novel in Verse by Alexander Pushkin.* Translated from Russian, with a commentary, by Vladimir Nabokov. 4 vols. Bollingen Series LXXII, Pantheon Books. New York: Bollingen Foundation, 1964. Revised edition, Princeton: Princeton University Press, 1975.

------. *Glory.* Translated by Dmitri Nabokov in collaboration with the author. New York: Vintage International, 1991.

------. *King, Queen, Knave.* New York: McGraw-Hill, 1968.

------. *Kommentarii k "Evgeniiu Oneginu" Aleksandra Pushkina.* Moscow: NPK "Intelvak," 1999.

------. *Laughter in the Dark.* Revised edition. New York: New Directions, 1960.

------. *Lectures on Literature,* edited by Fredson Bowers. Introduction by John Updike. San Diego, CA: Harvest Harcourt, 1982.

------. *Lectures on Russian Literature,* edited by Fredson Bowers. New York: Harcourt, Brace, Janovich/Bruccoli Clark, 1981.

------. *Lolita: A Screenplay.* New York: McGraw-Hill Book Company, 1974.

------. *Mary.* New York: McGraw-Hill, 1970.

------. *Nikolai Gogol.* New York: New Directions Paperback, 1978.

------. *Pale Fire.* New York: Vintage International, 1989.

------. *Pnin.* New York: Avon, 1969.

------. *Speak, Memory: An Autobiography Revisited.* New York: G. P. Putnam's Sons, 1966.

------. *Stikhotvoreniia i poemy.* Moscow: Folio, 1997.

------. *Strong Opinions.* New York: McGraw-Hill, 1973.

------. *The Annotated Lolita,* edited with preface, introduction and notes by Alfred Appel, Jr. New York and Toronto: McGraw-Hill Book Company, 1970.

------. *The Gift.* New York: Vintage International, 1991.

------. *The Real Life of Sebastian Knight.* Norfolk, CT: New Directions, 1959.

------. *Three Russian Poets: Selections from Pushkin, Lermontov and Tyutchev.* Norfolk, CT: New Directions, 1944.

------. "The Art of Translation." In *Literature and Liberalism: An Anthology of Sixty Years of the "New Republic,"* edited by Edward Zwick, 264-270. Washington: The New Republic Book Comp., Inc.

Nakhimovsky, Alexander., and Slava Paperno, comps. *An English-Russian Dictionary of Nabokov's Lolita*. Ann Arbor: Ardis, 1982.

Nassar, Joseph Michael. "The Russian in Nabokov's English Novels." Doctoral dissertation, State University of New York at Binghamton, 1977.

Nietzsche, Friedrich. *The Birth of Tragedy*. In *The Birth of Tragedy And Other Writings,* edited by Raymond Geuss and Ronald Speirs. Cambridge: Cambridge University Press, 1999.

Orr, Christopher. "The Discourse on Adaptation." *Wide Angle* 6, no. 2 (1984): 72-76.

Page, Norman, ed. *Nabokov: The Critical Heritage*. London, Boston, Melbourne, and Henley: Routledge and Kegan Paul, 1982.

Parker, Fan. *Lewis Carroll in Russia: Translations of Alice in Wonderland 1879-1989*. New York: Russian House Ltd, 1994.

Phillips, Gene. "Kubrick." *Film Comment* VII, no. 4 (Winter 1971-1972): 32.

Píchová, Hana. *The Art of Memory in Exile: Vladimir Nabokov and Milan Kundera*. Carbondale, IL: Southern Illinois University Press, 2002.

Pifer, Ellen. *Nabokov and the Novel*. Cambridge, MA: Harvard University Press, 1980.

------. "Reinventing Nabokov: Lyne and Kubrick Parse *Lolita*." In *Nabokov at Cornell*, edited by Gavriel Shapiro, 68-77. Ithaca: Cornell University Press, 2003.

[Pisarev, Stepan]. *Plutarkha Khersoneiskogo o detovodstve, ili vospitanii detei nastavlenie. Perevedennoe s ellino-grecheskogo iazyka S[tepanom] P[isarevym]*. St. Petersburg, 1771.

Prendergast, Christopher. *The Order of Mimesis: Balzac, Stendahl, Nerval, Flaubert*. Cambridge: Cambridge University Press, 1986.

*Polnyi katalog izdanii tovarishchestva* [M. O. Volf.] *1853-1905: Sistematicheskii katalog noveishikh knig po belletristike i vsem otrasliam znaniia*. St. Petersburg—Moscow: Tovarishchestvo M. O. Volf, 1913.

Proffer, Carl R. *Keys to Lolita*. Bloomington: Indiana University Press, 1968.

Proskurina, Vera. "Nabokov's *Exegi Monumentum*: Immortality in Quotation Marks (Nabokov, Pushkin and Mikhail Gershenzon)." In *Nabokov's World*, edited by Jane Grayson, Arnold McMillin, and Priscilla Meyer, vol. 1, 27-39. New York: Palgrave, 2002.

Raguet-Bouvart, Christine. "Les masques du traducteur chez Vladimir Nabokov." In *Masques et mascarades: Dans la literature nord-américaine*, edited by Christian Lorat et al, 115-127. Talence, France: Maison des Sciences de l'Homme d'Aquitaine, 1997.

------. "Vladimir Nabokov: The Translator's Perplexity in a Maze of Languages." In *Cross-Words: Issues and Debates in Literary and Non-Literary Translating*, edited by Christine Pagnoulle and Ian Mason, 121-138. University of Liège: L3-Liège language and literature, 1995.

Raphael, Frederic. "A Kubrick Odyssey: The Director's Last Screenwriter Recounts his Labyrinthine Adventure on 'Eyes Wide Shut'." *The New Yorker* (14 June 1999): 40-47.

Redfern, Walter. "Traduction, Puns, Clichés, Plagiat." In *Essays on Punning in Translation*, edited by Dirk Delabastita, 261-269. Manchester: St. Jerome Publishing, 1997.

Reichertz, Ronald. *The Making of the "Alice" Books: Lewis Carroll's Uses of Earlier Children's Literature*. Montreal and Kingston, London, and Buffalo: McGill-Queen University Press, 1997.

Rogachevskaia, Ekaterina. "Nabokov v Internete." In *Imperiia N: Nabokov i nasledniki*, edited by Iurii Leving and Evgenii Soshkin, 193-209. Moscow: Novoe literaturnoe obozrenie, 2006.

Rosengrant, Judson. "Nabokov's Autobiography: Problems of Translation." Doctoral dissertation, Stanford University, 1983.

------. "Nabokov, Onegin, and the Theory of Translation." *SEEJ* Spring, 38, no. 1 (1994): 13-32.

Rowe, W. W. *Nabokov's Spectral Dimension*. Ann Arbor: Ardis, 1981.

Rushailo, A. M. "Iubilei Alisy v strane chudes." Liuis Kerroll. *Prikliucheniia Alisy v strane chudes. Skvoz zerkalo i chto tam uvidela Alisa ili Alisa v Zazerkale*, v-vi. Perevod. N. M. Demurovoi, stikhi v perevode S. Ia. Marshaka, D. T. Orlovskoi i O. A. Sedakovoi. Illustratsii Dzh. Tenniela. Moscow: Nauka, 1990.

*Russkie pisateli o perevode*. Leningrad: Sovetskii pisatel, 1960.

Sallis, John, ed. *Reading Heidegger: Commemorations*. Bloomington and Indianapolis: Indiana University Press, 1993.

Sarris, Andrew. "New *Lolita* Better Than Kubrick's: But Nabokov Just Gets Nastier." *The New York Observer*, 10 August 1998.

Sewell, Elizabeth. *The Field of Nonsense*. London: Chatto and Windus, 1952.

Shapiro, Gavriel, ed. *Nabokov at Cornell*. Ithaca, NY: Cornell University Press, 2003.

Simmons, Ernest J. *English Literature and Culture in Russia (1553-1840)*. New York: Octagon Books, Inc., 1964.

Sisson, Jonathan Borden. "Cosmic Synchronization and Other Worlds in the Work of Vladimir Nabokov." Doctoral dissertation, University of Minnnesota, 1979.

*Sonia v tsarstve diva*. Moscow: Tipografiia A. Mamontova i Ko. Montievskii per., d. 3, 1879.

Spiegel, Alan. *Fiction and the Camera Eye: Visual Consciousness in Film and Modern Novel*. Charlottesville: University Press of Virginia, 1976.

Struve, Gleb. *Russkaia literatura v izgnanii*. Paris: YMCA-Press, 1965.

Tammi, Pekka. *Russian Subtexts in Nabokov's Fiction: Four Essays*. Tampere, Finland: Tampere University Press, 1999.

Tarvi, Liuba. "Poetika i bilingvizm: iz opyta sravnitelnogo analiza stikhov V. V. Nabokova." In *Nabokovskii vestnik*, Vypusk 4, 101-113. St. Petersburg: Dorn, 1999.

------. "Pushkin and Nabokov: Iz opyta po klonirovaniiu oneginskoi stroki na angliiskom." In *A. S. Pushkin i V. V. Nabokov: Sbornik dokladov mezhdunarodnoi konferentsii 15-18 aprelia 1999 g.*, 297-313. St. Petersburg: Dorn, 1999.

Todd, William Mills, III. "*A Hero of Our Time.*" In *The Garland Companion to Vladimir Nabokov,* edited by Vladimir Alexandrov, 178-183. New York: Garland, 1995.

Todorov, Tzvetan. *The Fantastic: A Structural Approach to a Literary Genre.* Cleveland and London: The Press of Case Western Reserve University, 1973.

Toury, Gideon. "What Is That Renders a Spoonerism (Un)Translatable?" In *Essays on Punning and Translation*, edited by Dirk Delabastita, 271-291. Manchester, UK and Namur, Belgium: St. Jerome Publishing and Presses Universitaires de Namur, 1997.

Trahan, Elizabeth Welt. "The Strange Case of Vladimir Nabokov as a Translator." In Marylin Gadis Rose et al. *What Price Glory — In Translation?*, 27-37. Whitestone, NY: Griffon House for Council on National Literatures, 1987.

Trousdale, Rachel. "Imaginary Worlds and Cultural Hybridity in Dinesen, Nabokov and Rushdie." *The Humanities and Social Sciences* 63, no. 3 (September 2002), Dissertation Abstracts International.

Trubikhina, Julia. "The Translator's Doubts: Vladimir Nabokov and the Ambiguity of Translation." (PhD diss., New York University, 2005).

------. "Romantic Unreformed: Vladimir Nabokov's Literalness within Russian and Western Translation Theories." *The ATA Chronicle* xxix, no. 7 (July 2000): 43-49.

------. "Struggle for the Narrative: Nabokov's and Kubrik's Collaboration on the *Lolita* Screenplay." The Nabokov issue of *Ulbandus*, The Slavic Review of Columbia University, N10 (2006-2007): 149-172.

------. "Metaphysical 'Affinity of the Unlike': Strategies of Nabokov's Literalism." *Intertexts*, The Special Nabokov Issue. Volume 12/1 (2008): 55-72.

Urnov, Dmitrii M. "Put k russkim chitateliam." Posleslovie k knige Dzh. Vinterikh (John T. Winterich). *Prikliucheniia znamenitykh knig.* Sokrashchennyi perevod s angl. E. Skvaiers, 219-233. Moscow: Kniga, 1985.

*V. V. Nabokov: Pro et Contra: Materialy i issledovaniia o zhizni i tvorchestve V. V. Nabokova.* Seriia "Russkii put." Sostavitel B. V. Averin. St. Petersburg: Izdatelstvo Russkogo Khristianskogo gumanitarnogo instituta, vol. 1, 1997; vol. 2, 2001.

Vengerova, Zinaida. "O tom, kto napisal 'Alisu'." *Tropinka* 22 (November 1909): 813-825.

Venuti, Lawrence. *The Translator's Invisibility: A History of Translation.* New York: Routledge, 1995.

Wagner, Geoffrey. *The Novel and the Cinema.* Rutherford, NJ: Fairleigh Dickinson University Press, 1975.

Walker, Alexander. *The Celluloid Sacrifice: Aspects of Sex in the Movies.* New York: Hawthorne Books, 1967.

Weaver, Warren. *Alice in Many Tongues: The Translations of* Alice in Wonderland. Madison: University of Wisconsin Press, 1964.

Weinraub, Bernard. "'Lolita' Defying Expectations." *The New York Times,* 5 August 1998.

Whittock, Trevor. *Metaphor and Film.* Cambridge: Cambridge University Press, 1990.

Wood, Michael. *The Magician's Doubts: Nabokov and the Risks of Fiction.* Princeton: Princeton University Press, 1995.

Woolf, Virginia. "Lewis Carroll." In *The Moment: Collected Essays.* Vol. 1, 254-255. New York: Harcourt Brace & World, Inc., 1967.

Woolf, Virginia. *Mrs. Dalloway.* New York: Harcourt & Company, 1981. New York: Harper & Row, 1979.

Zhirmunskii, Viktor. *Gete v russkoi literature.* Leningrad: Nauka, 1981.

Zhutovskaia, Nina M. "Vladimir Nabokov—perevodchik 'Evgeniia Onegina.'" *Nabokovskii vestnik,* Vypusk 1 (1998): 108-117.

Zimmer, Dieter. "Mimicry in Nature and Art." In *Nabokov's World,* edited by Jane Grayson, Arnold McMillin, and Priscilla Meyer, vol. 1, 47-57. New York: Palgrave, 2002.

Zinik, Zinovy. "The Double Exile of Vladimir Nabokov." In *Nabokov's World,* edited by Jane Grayson, Arnold McMillin, and Priscilla Meyer, vol. 1, 196-215. New York: Palgrave, 2002.

# Index

CPSIA information can be obtained at www.ICGtesting.com
Printed in the USA
BVOW06*2332300815

415596BV00002B/5/P